Popular Science

WOODWORKING PROJECTS

1987 Yearbook

Published by **Popular Science Books**, New York, NY

Distributed to the trade by **Rodale Press, Inc.**, Emmaus, PA

Published by
Popular Science Books
Times Mirror Magazines, Inc.
380 Madison Avenue
New York, NY 10017

Distributed to the trade by
Rodale Press, Inc.
33 East Minor Street
Emmaus, PA 18049

Designed by Linda Watts, Bookworks, Inc.

ISBN: 0-943822-82-3

Manufactured in the United States of America

Introduction

As you peruse the list of contributors to this year's edition of the *Woodworking Projects Yearbook*, you'll find the name of Harry Cooper of Vine Grove, Kentucky. Harry made the "Hallway Ensemble" and the "Doll Cradle". Next to his name, you'll find a short biography that tells you something about his woodworking. Usually, these brief paragraphs are all the space I have to tell about each contributor. But in Harry's case, I think something more deserves to be said.

Harry Cooper has always worked with wood. He became a professional cabinetmaker when he was released from duty, after World War II, and continued right up until his retirement several years ago. When he retired, he sold all his tools. "I was sick and tired of woodworking," Harry recalls. "I just thought I'd take it easy."

But taking it easy didn't agree with Harry. Before long, he realized he missed the smell of a fresh cut board, the excitement that builds as a project takes shape. "I also realized that, for the first time in my life, I had the time to make just what *I* wanted to make — there was nothing I *had* to do." Harry bought a few small tools and got back to woodworking. He had no grandiose projects in mind; the things he began to build were simple and utilitarian.

He kept plenty busy. Friends would say to him, "You know what I'd like…" and he'd make it. There was always something to make — Harry had lots of friends. Sometimes one friend would see what he'd made for another, and they'd want one too. "I built a potato bin one time," Harry remembers, "and pretty soon everyone wanted a potato bin. I'm lucky I survived the potato bin craze."

Today, Harry is plagued by emphysema and has to use oxygen. "I've breathed so much sawdust," he explains, "my lungs are just gone". But that doesn't keep him from woodworking. His son, Jack, describes how Harry works: "He pounds a nail, sits down and rests a while, then gets up and pounds another nail." Even with the best excuse in the world for taking it easy, Harry continues to build his projects, one nail at a time.

I doubt that any of the other woodworkers who helped to put this book together — Casey Chaffin, Jim McCann, Rude Osolnik, Ethan Perry, Bob Pinter, Tom Stender, and David Wakefield — will mind that I've singled Harry out as I have. Harry's is a story worth telling for this reason: Harry doesn't work wood just to complete a project. He seems to take his joy and satisfaction from the process itself. Woodworking — and working well — is reason enough to be a woodworker.

To put it another way, Harry Cooper not only does some of the best woodworking around; he represents what is best about woodworkers.

* * *

As much as I'd like to end this introduction on that note, I've got one more thing to say. Those of you who have been receiving these books for several years know that it's time for my annual "Editors-are-human-so-doublecheck-the-measurements" speech.

When I first began woodworking, I would get annoyed that there seemed to be so many errors in project plans. Then, when I began to put together plans for publication, I found out just how hard it is to get everything just right. Even when you build a project, there are things that you may overlook when writing it up. To keep errors to a minimum, the measurements in this book are checked at six different stages by woodworkers, proofreaders, and experienced editors. Still, all of the people who do the checking are only human.

Please, before you cut up good wood, check and double-check all the measurements in the Bill of Materials against the dimensions on the plans. It's just good woodworking practice to sit down with a calculator and add up the numbers before you embark on a project. If there is a problem with the measurements, this will save you time and lumber. Even if all the measurements are correct, it will still save you time. Checking the numbers, one by one, helps you to trace the thoughts of the craftsman who originally designed the piece. This in-depth understanding of a project saves you frustration and helps your work to proceed steadily and smoothly.

With all good wishes,

Nick Engler

Nick Engler

Contributors

Casey Chaffin ◆ As far back as Casey can remember, he's always had a project going. He learned his woodworking "the hard way". According to Casey, "I just jumped into projects and stuck with them. I made a lot of mistakes, but through trial and error I taught myself to be a woodworker."

He taught himself pretty well, too. Today, Casey is the Woodworking Academy Instructor for Shopsmith, Inc., in Dayton, Ohio. Every year, he teaches thirty or more three-day classes in general woodworking, plus dozens of seminars on specific methods and techniques. Woodworking students from all over North America and Europe have had the benefit of his experience.

Harry Cooper ◆ Harry is not only a fine woodworker; he's a financial wizard. He began woodworking when he retired several years ago. His first tools were a set of carving knives that cost $8.50. Today, his shop in Vine Grove, Kentucky, is equipped with over $4500.00 hand and power tools — and he's paid for them all by making what he calls "scrap box projects".

Harry started out by whittling name plaques from wood he scavenged. "I carved those signs till I ran out of grape crates," Harry recalls. By then, he had made enough money to buy a few good tools — but he continued to work with wood that other folks were about to throw away. This never hindered his craftsmanship. His creations are small, but classy. Today, he admits that every once in a while he breaks down and buys a board or two of real never-been-nailed-up lumber — but not very often.

Nick Engler ◆ Nick founded the woodworking magazine *HANDS ON!*, and managed that publication for several years. During that time, he helped to publish not only the magazine, but over 100 project plans, several books, how-to manuals, and a syndicated newspaper column for woodworkers.

Today, he is the co-owner of *Bookworks, Inc.*, a firm in West Milton, Ohio, that specializes in the production of how-to books. Nick and the staff at Bookworks put together this edition of the *Woodworking Projects Yearbook* for Popular Science Books.

Jim McCann ◆ Jim has been woodworking ever since he was a little shaver (pun intended). His father taught him the basics when he was a kid, and he got formal training at Eastern Kentucky University.

He joined the staff at *HANDS ON!* in 1979 as a craftsman and designer. During his stay at the magazine, he put together over 100 projects and wrote the "Ask Smitty" column, offering advice and tips to woodworkers. Today, Jim works in the engineering laboratory of Shopsmith, Inc., helping to design power tools for home workshops. He's also inherited his father's tools and has set up shop in Trotwood, Ohio.

Rude Osolnik ◆ Rude taught wood arts at Berea College for 40 years and was the Chairman of the Industrial Arts Department before he retired several years ago. But Rude hasn't stopped teaching just because he retired; now he conducts seminars in lathe turning all over the United States.

Rude remains a prolific woodturner. He sells his turnings through various art galleries across the country. He and his wife operate their own gallery, *Benchmark*, in Berea, Kentucky. Benchmark not only features Rude's turnings, but many other examples of fine woodworking from some of Rude's former students.

Dale Nish lists this former professor in his book, *Master Woodturners*, where he calls Rude "the most versatile turner in America".

Ethan Perry ◆ Ethan graduated from the Philadephia College of Art with a Bachelor of Fine Arts in Woodworking and Furniture Design. He didn't waste any time looking for a job; he went right into business for himself, making custom furniture. Today, he operates his own woodworking studio in Frenchtown, New York.

Ethan's designs tend toward the contemporary. His work is influenced by traditional furniture forms. For example, you can see the Windsor influence in the dining chair in the **Projects** section. He also uses organic and graphic forms. His designs have numerous woodworking shows and galleries throughout the country.

Bob Pinter ◆ Although he's only been woodworking for twelve years, Bob's craftsmanship has already been judged as some of the best in the country. Time and time again, he's captured the blue ribbons at woodworking shows, competing against professional craftsmen with lifetimes of experience.

Bob started woodworking in an apartment, building large furniture projects with hand tools — power tools made too much noise. Today, he has a well-equipped power shop in Tipp City, Ohio, but he continues to do much of his work by hand. "Why should I let the machines have all the fun?" he asks.

Thomas Stender ◆ Walk into Tom Stender's house in Boston, New York, and you'll think you've died and gone to woodworker's heaven. Ever since he began woodworking in earnest, Tom has been slowly filling his home with fine hand-crafted furniture. There's a little bit of everything here — Queen Anne, Chippendale, Shaker, Country, Contemporary, you name it. "When I started building things in the barn," he explains, "I thought I'd let the house be the showroom."

Tom began making custom furniture in 1975. At first, he built modern "Studio" pieces, but quickly found that he liked the classical styles much better. Today, he designs and builds elegant furniture in the same tradition as craftsmen from the eighteenth and early nineteenth centuries. He doesn't do many 'reproductions', however. All his designs are original, built along traditional lines.

David Wakefield ◆ David is a native of Australia, and the son of Oliver Wakefield, a famous English comedian. His family traveled extensively, but David eventually came to rest in Athens, Ohio, where he operates his own woodworking business, *Howling Wolf Woodworks*.

At first, David produced acoustical guitars. But later he expanded his line to include custom furniture and wooden toys. The toys proved to be his most popular designs, and today he produces them almost exclusively. He's just published a book, *Animated Toys*, that contains thirty of his best toy designs. The book is available through Popular Science Books.

And Others... It takes more than a few woodworkers to put together a book of woodworking projects. We'd also like to acknowledge Mary K. Baird, Linda Ball, Adam Blake, Donna Cheshire, Mary Jane Favorite, Alexandra Eldridge, and Hue Park.

And special thanks to Wayne Howe and Shopsmith, Inc. for allowing us to publish some of their materials.

Contents

Projects

Techniques

The Workshop

PROJECTS

Designed and Built by Thomas Stender

Gateleg Table

Two extra legs add to the beauty of this classic Queen Anne reproduction.

abriole legs are among the most graceful and appealing forms in woodworking. It's always a pleasure to find four well-made cabrioles on a piece of fine furniture. But to find six! The pleasure increases proportionately.

This particular piece of fine furniture was crafted by Thomas Stender. Tom is a professional woodworker in Boston, New York, who specializes in building classic American furniture. This six-legged table is a faithful reproduction of a Queen Anne 'gateleg' table, a design that was

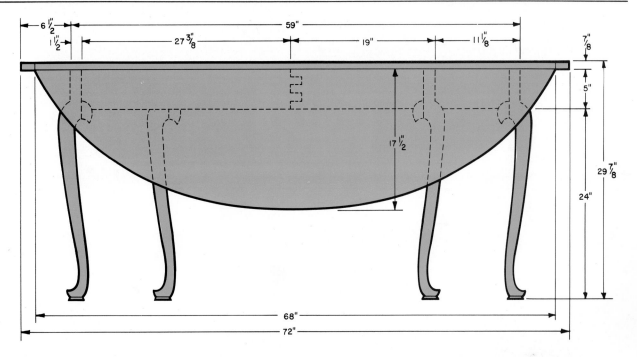

FRONT VIEW

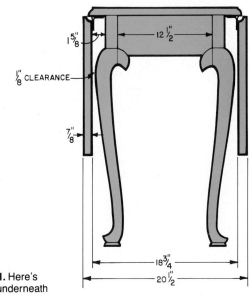

SIDE VIEW

Figure 1. Here's a peek underneath Tom Stender's gateleg table. Notice the knuckle joint and the swinging 'gate'.

popular during the latter half of the eighteenth century. Two of the six legs swing out like gates to support the drop leaves. (See Figure 1.)

The design is not difficult to reproduce, but it does require some patience. The 'knuckle' joint that allows the legs to pivot, and the 'rule' joint where the drop leaves fold must be made with precision. Before you begin this project, make absolutely sure that your tools are sharp and properly aligned. Take some extra care in setting up for each step, and your patience will pay off.

Choosing the Wood

The most popular wood during the Queen Anne period was mahogany. However, this was an exotic wood in colonial America, and only the best-paid cabinetmakers could afford to work with it. More often, they chose to build their furniture from native American hardwoods; in particular, walnut, cherry, and maple. Tom chose to make this particular table from walnut.

In choosing your lumber, look for straight grains and avoid figured wood. Burls and knots can be very attractive, but they may weaken this particular piece. The leg stock especially must be free of defects.

In choosing wood for the top and the leaves, you can put up with *some* figuring. But be wary of using boards that may warp or cup when the weather changes. The leaves are not braced in any way, and they could give you trouble later on, long after you've finished this project. Bring the lumber into your shop and let it sit for several weeks until it gets acclimated to an indoor environment. Then inspect the individual boards for cups and warps. If you find any, set the board aside and use another.

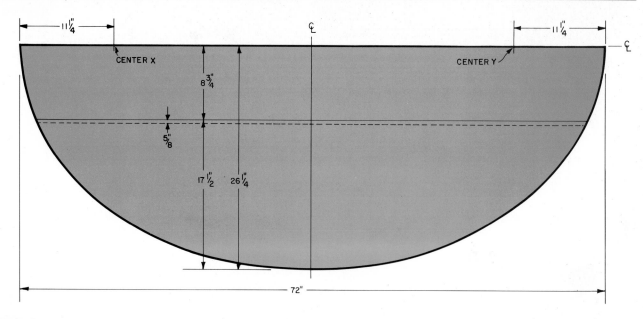

TABLE TOP LAYOUT

Tip ◆ If you can get it, use quarter-sawn or rift-sawn lumber for the top and leaves. This type of lumber is more stable and less prone to cupping than plain-sawn lumber.

Making the Cabriole Legs

If you've made cabriole legs for a previous project, then you understand how to make a compound cut on your bandsaw: Cut the design in one face, tape the waste back to the workpiece, and cut the second face. However, these legs aren't quite that simple. The cabriole legs that Tom used for this table have 'pad' feet and 'ears'. Because of these little touches, the procedure for making the legs is somewhat more involved.

Start by making a template. Enlarge the leg and ear pattern, and trace it on a stiff piece of cardboard or hardboard. Mark a reference line on the leg template where the knee breaks for the post, as shown in the working drawings. You'll need this reference line later on.

Square up the leg stock to 3″ x 3″. Place the template on the leg stock, making sure that the back edge of the leg is flush with the inside corner. This will give you a constant reference every time you reposition the template. Trace the leg pattern on the two *inside* faces of each workpiece, and mark the reference lines on each face with a square. (See Figure 2.) Mount the stock on the lathe and turn the pad and heel of the foot. (See Figure 3.) *Do not* turn up past the heel.

Remove the legs from the lathe, and cut the mortises in the top of the leg. Use a drill press to make a series of holes, then clean up the sides and the corners with a hand chisel.

Figure 2. After you've traced the leg pattern onto the stock, mark the reference line — where the knee meets the post — with a square.

Figure 3. Turn the pad and heel of each leg. *Do not* turn up past the heel.

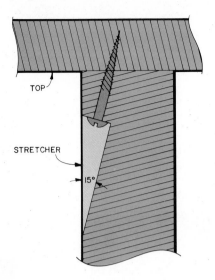

SCREW POCKET DETAIL

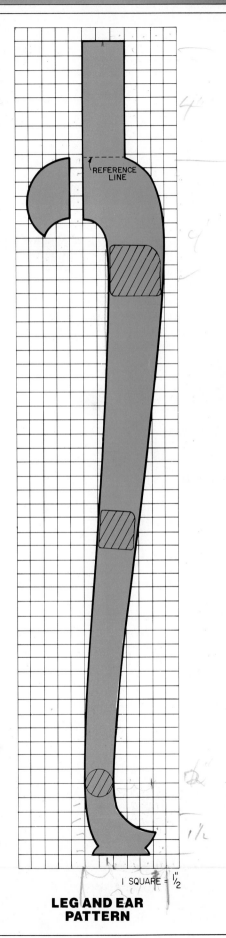

(See Figure 4.) Remember that the 'gate' legs only get one mortise! You need to make the joinery before you go much further because, if you don't, the leg won't lie flat on the worktable. That would make it extremely hard to cut an accurate mortise.

Using a bandsaw, cut the faces of the corner posts down to the reference line. However, *don't* cut the waste from the posts just yet. (See Figure 5.) Glue the ear stock onto the legs, carefully lining the top of the ear up with the reference line.

Figure 4. Cut the joinery in the legs before you bandsaw the shape of the legs. To make a mortise with your drill press, drill a series of holes. Then square up the corners and the faces with a hand chisel.

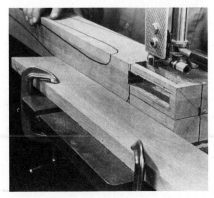

Figure 5. Cut the face of the post down to the reference line. However, do not cut the waste free from the post at this time.

1 SQUARE = 1½"

LEG AND EAR PATTERN

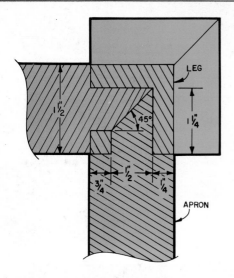

LEG-TO-APRON JOINERY LAYOUT

Remember that the gate legs only have one ear! Then, once again using the reference line, trace the leg pattern onto the end of each ear, as shown in Figure 6. Trace the ear pattern onto the back of the ears.

Adjust the upper blade guide on your bandsaw so that it clears the ear stock, and cut the waste free of the corner posts. One ear should lie flat on the table, while the other should point up. Also cut the knee and the ear, saving all the scrap. (See Figure 7.) Lower the blade guide to clear the leg stock only, and cut the foot, ankle, and leg taper. Once again, save all the scrap. (See Figure 8.)

Tape the scrap back onto the workpiece to make the stock reasonably square again, and turn the stock 90° so that the other ear lies on the table. Repeat the sequence of cuts. When you remove all the stock, you'll have a rough cabriole leg with pad feet and ears. (See Figure 9.) Repeat these steps for all five legs.

> **Tip** ◆ Use double-faced carpet tape to stick the waste back on the workpiece as you get ready to make the second set of cuts. This tape not only holds the waste without covering any of the pattern lines, it fills in the kerf on the bandsaw so that the stock is fairly flat and square.

Figure 6. Glue the ear stock to the legs. Using the reference lines, trace the leg pattern onto the end of each ear. Trace the ear pattern onto the back of each ear.

Figure 7. Adjust the height of the upper blade guide on your bandsaw so that it clears the ear stock, and cut the waste free from the post. Then cut the knee and the ear. Save the scrap.

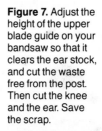

LEG-TO-APRON JOINERY DETAIL

Smooth the sawn surfaces of the legs and round the corners with a spokeshave. (See Figure 10.) Carefully remove the 'rift' on the top of the foot, being careful not to remove too much of the foot. When you've got the legs as smooth as you can get them with a spokeshave, work with rasps, scrapers, and sandpaper until you have the legs looking like you want them.

Making the Knuckle Joints

Cut the aprons, stretchers, and gates to size, and cut tenons in the ends of the pieces where shown in the working drawings. Also, make screw pockets on the inside faces of the end aprons and stretchers. You'll use these screw pockets to join the table top to the completed apron assembly.

The side aprons and gates are joined by 'knuckle' joints. These joints are really wooden hinges that open to 90°. To make a knuckle joint, first scribe a 1½″ circle onto the top edge of each workpiece, so that it just touches the ends and both sides of the wood. (See Figure 11.) Mark the center of the circle, and draw two diagonal lines at 45° to the inner and outer faces of the workpieces through the center of the circle.

KNUCKLE JOINT LAYOUT

Figure 8. Readjust the blade guide and cut the foot, the ankle, and the taper on the leg. Once again, save the scrap.

Figure 9. Tape the scrap back to the work piece, turn the leg 90°, and cut the other face.

Figure 10. Smooth the surface and round the corners of the finished legs with a spokeshave. Carefully shave off the rift on the top of the foot.

Figure 11. Scribe 1½″ circles on the top edges of the gates and aprons, as shown. Mark the center of these circles, then draw two diagonal lines, one at 45° to the inner face of each workpiece and the other at 45° to the outer edge, through the centers of the circles.

Using a bandsaw, cut along these diagonal lines, up to the circle. Then cut along the circle, rounding off the end of the workpiece and creating a 'knuckle'. (See Figure 12.) Once you've made the general shape of the knuckle, cut the 'fingers' on a bandsaw, stopping at the line where the diagonal cut meets the curve on the knuckle. (See Figure 13.) Cut three fingers on the gate pieces and two on the side aprons —five fingers per joint, each 1⁹⁄₃₂″ long and 1″ tall. They should fit together without much friction, but there shouldn't be much slop either. Clean up any millmarks on the fingers with a rasp and sandpaper.

With a hand chisel, 'dig out' the excess material between each finger. Be careful not to carve into the diagonal faces —these faces serve to stop the gate when it pivots to 90°. Just remove the material you need so that the fingers fit together correctly, with the center of each round finger directly above the others. (See Figure 14.)

When you're satisfied that the fingers fit properly, clamp the apron and gate together temporarily. Check that the faces of both pieces are flush with each other and held perfectly straight, as if they were one board. Locate the center of the circle you scribed earlier, and drill a ¼″ hole, 4¾″ deep down through all five fingers. Stop just before the drill emerges from the bottom of the last finger. (See Figure 15.) When you drill this hole, be absolutely certain the apron and gate are square to the drill bit. The bit must bite down through the center of each finger without drifting.

Temporarily put a pivot pin in the knuckle joints and check their action. They should work smoothly, without binding. The gate should open to 90° and stop, without drifting up or down as it opens.

When you're satisfied that all parts fit together and work together correctly, assemble the legs, aprons, gates, and stretchers. Use glue in all joints except, of course, the knuckle joints. Pin the legs to the aprons with dowels from the outside, and screw the stretchers to the aprons.

Making the Rule Joints

Glue up the stock for the top and drop leaves. Since the top is reinforced by the aprons, make sure that the end grain (growth rings) in the top boards all curve in the same direction — *towards* the top surface. That way, if any of the top boards want to cup sometime in the future, their movement will be restrained. *Alternate* the direction of the end grains in

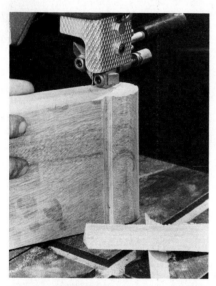

Figure 12. Shape the knuckles on a bandsaw. First cut the diagonal lines up to the circle. Then saw around the circumference of the circle, creating a round knob or 'knuckle' on the ends of the workpiece.

Figure 13. Cut mating fingers in the gates and aprons with a bandsaw — three in each gate, two in each apron. Use a fence to position and guide each cut. Stop the cuts at the line where the diagonal face meets the round knuckle. When you're finished, each finger should be exactly 1⁹⁄₃₂″ long and 1″ tall.

Figure 14. With a carving chisel, dig out the excess material between each finger, so that the fingers mate properly. Be careful not to carve into the diagonal faces.

Figure 15. Drill a stopped ¼″ hole down through the center of all five fingers in each knuckle joint, stopping before you drill completely through the fifth finger.

the leaves, since these aren't braced. The surface of the leaves may become slightly wavy in the future, but they shouldn't cup badly.

Don't cut the shape of the top just yet. That comes much later, almost at the end of this project. Instead, leave the stock slightly oversize and go ahead with the joinery: Cut the rule joints in the top and leaves with a router or shaper. This rule joint consists of a matching thumbnail and cove. Cut the thumbnail in the top, and the cove in the leaves. (See Figure 16.)

Join the top and leaves with drop-leaf hinges. Unlike most hinges, which are installed so that the pin straddles the joint between two boards, drop-leaf hinges are offset slightly to one side. The exact position of the hinge is determined by the radius of the thumbnail and cove. The hinge pin should rest at the center of the arc of the rule joint. (See Figure 17.)

Calculate the proper position for the hinges, and chisel out a mortise for them. Install the hinges and check the action of the rule joints. If you're satisfied, center the top on the apron assembly and attach it with wood screws. Pass the screws up through the aprons and stretchers from underneath, using the screw pockets you made earlier.

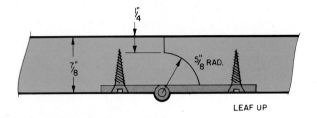

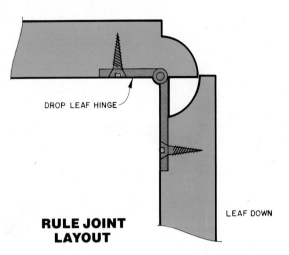

DROP LEAF HINGE

LEAF UP

LEAF DOWN

RULE JOINT LAYOUT

Figure 16. A rule joint consists of a mating bead and cove, with a small 'step' at the top of the joint. This step creates the 'rule' when the joint is closed.

Figure 17. Locate the hinge pin at the center of the arc of the bead.

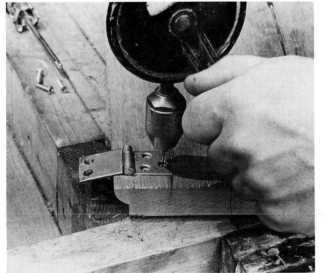

Cutting the Table Top

When the leaves are extended, the top should make an oval 72″ long and 52½″ wide. There are many ways to scribe this oval, but perhaps the old string-and-tacks method is the easiest. Put two tacks in your stock along the major axis of the oval you want to scribe. Locate these tacks 11¼″ in from the edge of the oval, or 24¾″ from the center. Make a loop of string 121½″ long and put it around the tacks. Stretch it taut, then use it as you would a string compass to draw the oval.

Tip ◆ To scribe an accurate oval, be sure to use a type of string that doesn't stretch.

Cut along the line with a sabre saw. Then sand the millmarks from the edge. Be very careful when you sand that you don't cut too deep. You want to preserve the 'fair' curve of the oval. If you cut too deep, the oval will be irregular. To aid in making an accurate oval, saw a little wide of the line, then sand down to it.

Remove the hinges, the screws that hold the top to the apron assembly, and the gate pivots. Finish sand any parts that still need it. Then apply a finish to the table. Be sure to apply a finish to *all* sides of *every* piece.

Tip ◆ Apply just as many coats to the surfaces that won't be seen as those that will. This will help keep any parts from cupping or warping. If the finish is thinner on one side of a board than the other, the wood will absorb moisture faster on the 'thin' side. The thin side will expand more, and the board will cup or warp.

When the finish is complete, reassemble the parts of the table. To preserve the finish and to keep the wood in good shape, rub the table down with a good carnauba wax or lemon oil every few months.

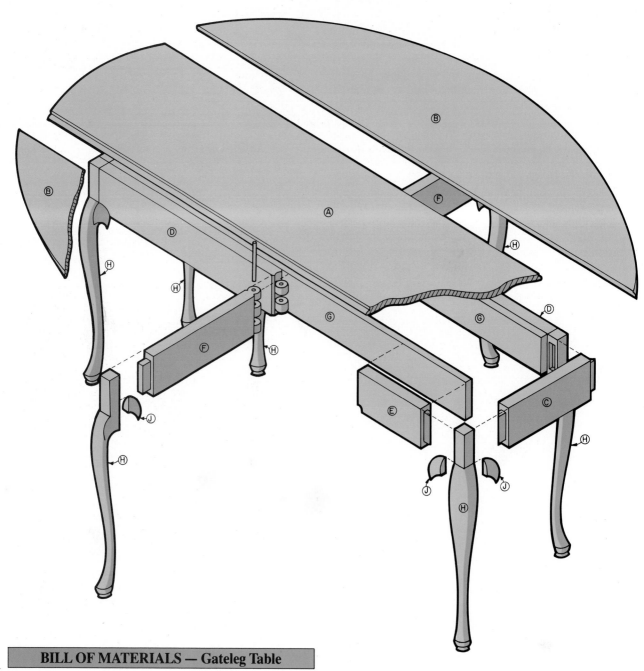

BILL OF MATERIALS — Gateleg Table

Finished Dimensions in Inches

A.	Top	$\frac{7}{8}$ x $18\frac{3}{4}$ x 72
B.	Leaves (2)	$\frac{7}{8}$ x $17\frac{1}{2}$ x 68
C.	End Aprons (2)	$1\frac{1}{2}$ x 5 x $14\frac{3}{4}$
D.	Long Side Aprons (2)	$1\frac{1}{2}$ x 5 x $29\frac{25}{32}$
E.	Short Side Aprons (2)	$1\frac{1}{2}$ x 5 x $10\frac{3}{4}$
F.	Gates (2)	$1\frac{1}{2}$ x 5 x $18\frac{5}{8}$
G.	Stretchers (2)	1 x 5 x 56
H.	Legs (6)	3 x 3 x 29
J.	Ears (10)	$1\frac{1}{2}$ x $1\frac{1}{2}$ x $2\frac{7}{8}$

Hardware

#10 x $1\frac{1}{2}''$ Flathead wood screws (12-16)
$\frac{1}{4}''$ Dia. x $4\frac{3}{4}''$ pins (2)

EXPLODED VIEW

TIPS

GATELEG TABLE

Drawing an Oval

In scribing an oval, the trick is in calculating the position of the tacks and the length of the string. Here's how to do it:

◆ Every oval has two axes — a *major* axis (the long dimension) and a *minor* axis (the short dimension). In Figure A, the major axis is AB, and the minor axis is CD. The center of the oval, where the two axes cross, is Z. Adjust your compass to half the length of the major axis, AZ. Put the point of the compass at C, and scribe arcs to intersect the major axis on either side of Z. Let's call these points of intersection X and Y.

◆ Make a loop of string that is twice as long as the distance AY. Put two tacks in your stock, one at X and the other at Y. Put the loop over both tacks and stretch it taut, making a triangle. Hold a pencil at the point of the triangle, and draw the oval, pulling the string around the tacks. (See Figure B.)

◆ Of course, to do these calculations for something as large as the gateleg table, you'll have to draw the oval to scale, then make your calculations from the scale drawing.

Figure A. Put tacks at points X and Y. Make a loop of string twice as long as AY.

Figure B. Stretch the string taut and use it as you would a compass to draw the oval. Be sure to use non-stretchable string.

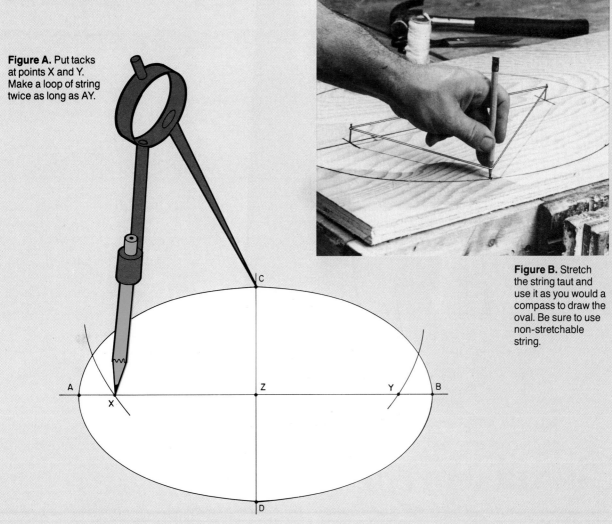

Designed and Built by Nick Engler

Cheval Mirror

Here's a modern variation of a classic design.

I n case you're wondering, the word 'cheval' is French for 'horse'. What does a horse have to do with a dressing mirror? According to woodworking folklore, the horse in this project is a *sawhorse*. A 'cheval mirror' is a mirror supported by sawhorses.

Why do we retain the original French name? Why don't we just call it a 'sawhorse mirror'? I don't have the official answer to that, but I've given it some thought. How would

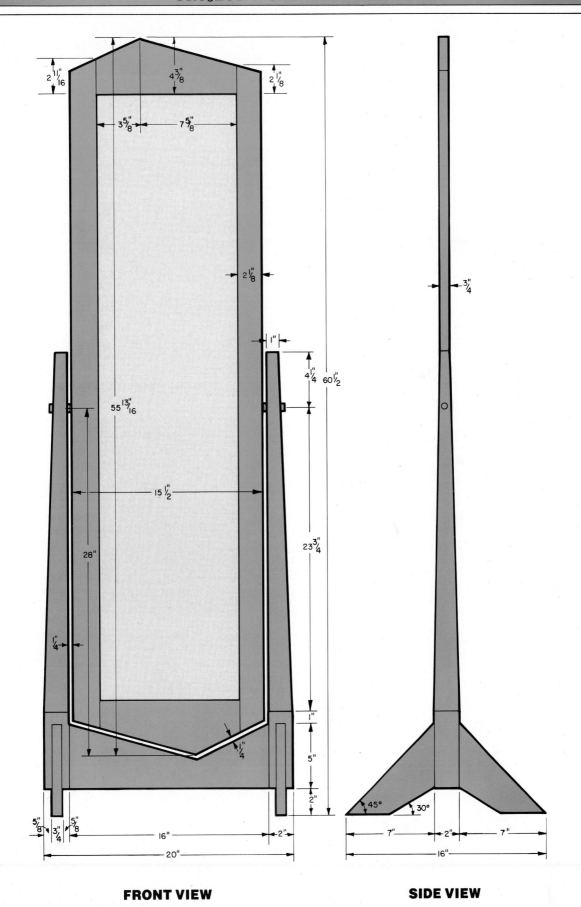

FRONT VIEW

SIDE VIEW

you like to tell your spouse you've just spent $50 on lumber and materials so that you can build a 'sawhorse mirror'? 'Cheval' sounds so much classier.

It's a classy project, too, and not much harder to build than a sawhorse. The stand is just seven pieces, and the mirror is no more complicated than a picture frame. With a little bit of planning, you can put one of these together in an evening or two.

Making the Sawhorse

The stand consists of two uprights, four feet, and a crosspiece. Begin by cutting the joinery in the two uprights. Drill a series of ¾″ holes, 1″ deep near the base of each upright to form a long mortise. (See Figure 1.) Square the edges and the corners of each mortise with a hand chisel. (See Figure 2.) Then rotate the uprights 90° and cut slot mortises with a bandsaw. (See Figure 3.) These mortises should be exactly the same

dimensions as the first mortises, although they'll go all the way through the stock. When you're finished, there should be identical slots in three of the four faces of each upright.

After you've cut the joinery, taper the uprights on the bandsaw. Cut the taper in the outside faces first — the faces *without* a mortise. Then tape the waste stock back onto the uprights, and taper the front and back faces. (See Figure 4.) *Do not* taper the inside faces.

Cut out the feet according to the working drawings, and cut the crosspiece to size. However, *don't* make the cutout for the mirror in the crosspiece. That comes later.

> **Tip** ◆ For maximum strength, the wood grain of each leg should run through the length of the leg.

Dry assemble the legs to the uprights to check the fit. The legs fit in the slot mortises. The other mortises — the

Figure 1. Drill a line of ¾″ holes, 1″ deep near the base of each upright. These holes should be centered on one face of the upright so that they form a long mortise.

Figure 2. Square off the corners and the edges of the mortise with a hand chisel.

Figure 3. Turn the uprights 90°. Using a bandsaw, cut slot mortises through the stock in the base of each upright. These mortises should be the same dimensions as the first mortises you made with a drill and hand chisel.

Figure 4. Taper the uprights by making a compound cut on your bandsaw. Cut the taper in the outside face first, tape the waste back to the uprights, then taper the front and back faces. *Do not* taper the inside faces.

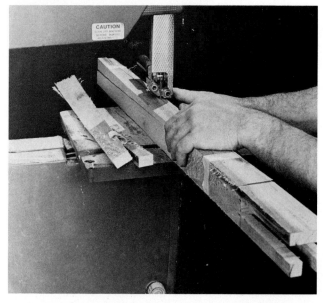

mortises you cut with a drill and hand chisel — are for the crosspiece. If the legs fit too snug, clean up the inside of the mortises with a rasp. If they fit too loose, shim them with veneer — or make new uprights. When you're satisfied that the legs fit, check the fit of the crosspiece in its mortises.

Drill a countersunk hole toward the top of each upright, as shown in the working drawings. These holes are for the mounting bolts.

Finish sand all pieces, and glue the legs to the uprights. Be very careful that the bottom edges of the legs are square to the uprights. If they aren't, the mirror won't stand straight.

Making the Mirror Frame

While the glue is setting up on the legs, make the mirror frame. This frame is designed to accept a 12″ x 48″ mirror. If you buy your mirror at a glass store, you'll find this is a standard size. They won't even have to cut it for you.

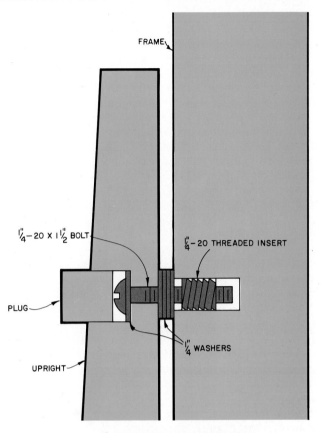

MIRROR PIVOT DETAIL

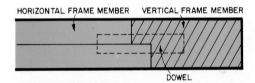

CROSS SECTION

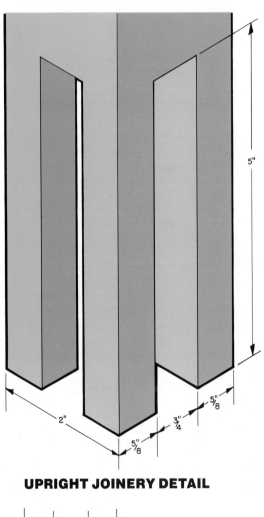

UPRIGHT JOINERY DETAIL

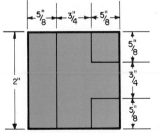

UPRIGHT JOINERY DETAIL/ BOTTOM VIEW

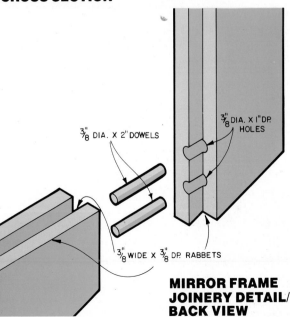

MIRROR FRAME JOINERY DETAIL/ BACK VIEW

15

Cut the frame members to size, but don't cut the angled shapes on the top and bottom parts yet. That comes later, after you've assembled the mirror.

Dowel the frame members together, drilling each dowel hole ⅜″ deeper than need be. For instance, if you use 2″ dowels, drill each hole 1⅜″ deep. Don't glue the frame parts up just yet; you need to cut a few more joints.

Make a ⅜″ wide, ⅜″ deep rabbet along the *back inside* edge of all frame members. Also cut these rabbets in the *front* edge of the *ends* of the top and bottom frame parts. Then dry assemble all the frame parts to check the fit. The rabbets on the ends of the top and bottom frame members should overlap the rabbets on the inside edge of side frame members, and all the dowel holes should still line up. When assembled, there should be a rabbet all around the inside back edge of the frame.

When you're satisfied that all the parts of the frame fit correctly, finish sand the parts and glue up the frame. Let the glue set up, then cut the shapes in the top and bottom of the frame as shown in the working drawings. Sand out any millmarks.

Assembling the Mirror to the Sawhorse

Dry assemble the crosspiece to the uprights and clamp it in place temporarily. Measure from the top of the crosspiece to the center of the bolt holes in the uprights. This measurement should be 24¾″. Next measure 24½″ — ¼″ less than the distance from the crosspiece to the bolt holes — from the bottom corners of the mirror to a point along the outside edge of the side frame members.

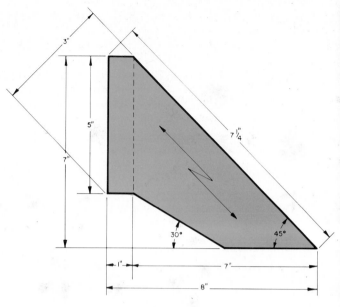

FOOT LAYOUT

Figure 5. Draw lines on the crosspiece, parallel to the outline of the bottom frame and ¼″ below it. Cut this second set of lines with a bandsaw.

Mark these points, then drill the side members for ¼″ threaded inserts. Install the inserts with a screwdriver, then temporarily assemble the mirror frame to the stand with ¼″ bolts. Center the frame so that it's exactly ¼″ away from each upright. Rotate the frame so that the bottom member hits the crosspiece. Mark the outline of the bottom member of the crosspiece and disassemble the mirror.

Draw two more lines on the crosspiece, parallel to the outline of the bottom frame member and ⅛″ below it. (See Figure 5.) Cut these lines with a bandsaw. Sand out the millmarks and reassemble the uprights, crosspiece and mirror frame to check the fit. The frame should pivot freely back and forth over the crosspiece *almost* touching it, but not quite.

When you're satisfied that the mirror frame fits the stand correctly, glue the crosspiece in place and clamp up the stand with the mirror still installed. Let the glue set completely before removing the frame.

Disassemble the frame from the stand. Do any necessary touchup sanding on the subassemblies, and apply a finish. When the finish has set up completely, buff it out and install a mirror in the frame. Back up the mirror with a ¼″ thick piece of plywood or hardboard, and keep the mirror and the backing plate in the frame with turn buttons.

Reassemble the mirror frame to the stand. But this time, install washers on the ¼″ bolts, between the uprights and the frame, to keep these parts about ¼″ apart. Depending on the type of washers you use, it will take 4-5 per side. Also install a washer under the head of each bolt, in the countersunk holes. These washers will allow you to tighten the bolts and adjust the 'action' of the pivots. The tighter the bolts, the harder it will be to pivot the mirror.

Finally, install wooden plugs in the countersunk holes to cover the bolt heads. Don't glue these plugs in place; they should fit snugly in the holes without glue. But you should be able to remove them in case you need to readjust the action.

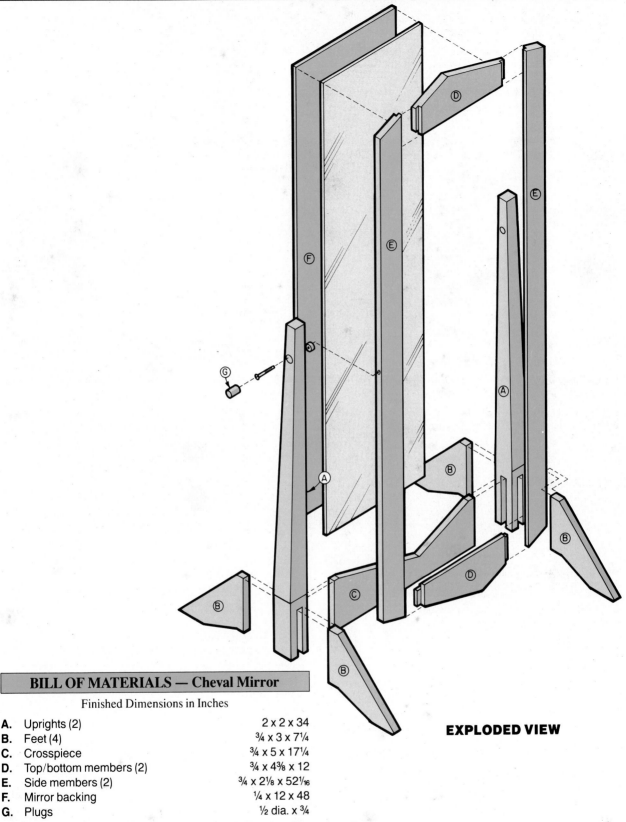

EXPLODED VIEW

BILL OF MATERIALS — Cheval Mirror

Finished Dimensions in Inches

A.	Uprights (2)	2 x 2 x 34
B.	Feet (4)	¾ x 3 x 7¼
C.	Crosspiece	¾ x 5 x 17¼
D.	Top/bottom members (2)	¾ x 4⅜ x 12
E.	Side members (2)	¾ x 2⅛ x 52¹/₁₆
F.	Mirror backing	¼ x 12 x 48
G.	Plugs	½ dia. x ¾

Hardware

¼"-20 Threaded inserts (2)
¼"-20 x 1½" Stove bolts (2)
¼" Flat washers (10-12)
Turn buttons and screws (6)
⅛" x 12" x 48" Mirror

Designed and Built by David Wakefield

Animal Gliders

Take to the skies — riding your favorite animal.

O f all the toys you could build, this is one that will give your child the most pleasure for the longest time. When the designer of this toy, David Wakefield, had a toy store several years ago, he kept a swing hanging on the front porch. "There would always be someone swinging when I got to work in the morning," he said, "and when I went home in the evening, and even if I happened to walk by at night." Children love to ride swings for hours on end.

Use a strong hardwood for all the parts of this swing. Weight is no concern; it is most important that this toy be *rugged*. The animal heads are made from long, thin pieces. The main parts of the swing are somewhat thicker, but some parts do get quite thin after you drill and shape them. All of these parts must absorb abuse, so make them from the hardest woods you can find.

Make the Swing

Let's begin by making the swing portion of this toy — you can decide what sort of a head you'd like to mount to it later.

Mark off three 1¹/₆″ holes on the edge of the vertical support, where shown in the working drawing. The upper hole is for the handle, the middle hole is for the pivot, and the lower hole is for the footrest. The holes are drilled ¹/₁₆″ oversize so that these parts will slip in and out easily. If you want a tighter fit, drill 1″ holes and hand sand the dowels until you get the fit you want. However, don't make the parts fit too snug. This project will be used outside — when it gets wet, the wood may swell up and cause the pivot to bind up.

Drill the holes with a multispur bit. This helps to keep the inside edges of the holes smooth. Put a scrap block under the piece to keep the bit from tearing out the wood when it comes out the other side.

> **Tip ◆** If your drill press doesn't have a long enough 'throw' to drill the hole in one step, drill the hole as deep as you can. Then raise up the drill *and* the workpiece. Put a 1″-2″ thick scrap of wood under the piece, and drill the hole the rest of the way through. (See Figures 1 and 2.)

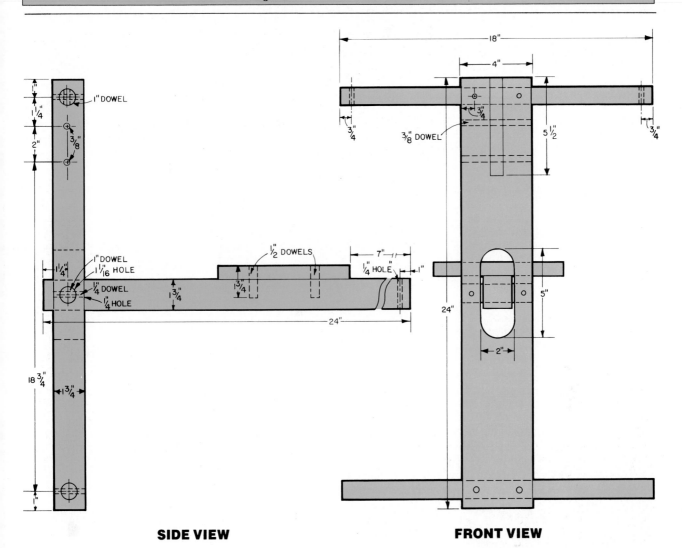

SIDE VIEW   **FRONT VIEW**

Before you change bits, drill the pivot hole in the horizontal support. The pivot dowel should fit loosely in this hole, so as not to interfere with the swinging action. Change bits and drill the ¼″ holes in the other end of the horizontal support, and in the ends of the handle.

Figure 2. Continue drilling until the bit breaks through. If the scrap is thick enough, it will give you the height you need to finish the hole.

Figure 1. If your drill press doesn't have a long enough 'throw' to drill the hole in one step, drill the hole part way and put a scrap under the workpiece.

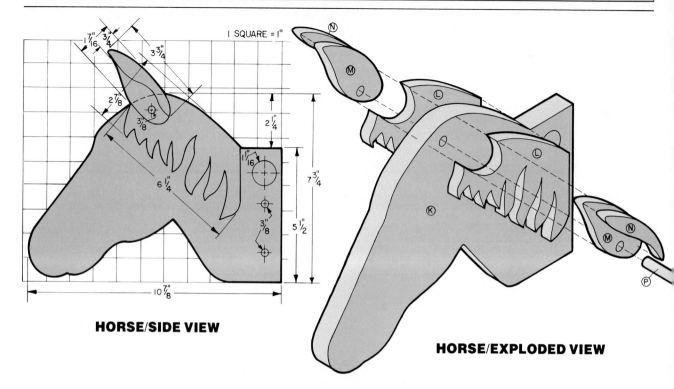

HORSE/SIDE VIEW

I SQUARE = 1"

HORSE/EXPLODED VIEW

Next, cut the mortise in the wide face of the vertical support. To make this mortise, first drill two large holes at both the top and the bottom of the mortise. Then saw out the rest of the waste with a coping saw. (See Figure 3.) You can also use a jigsaw or a sabre saw. Smooth the inside of the mortise and round over the edges with a rasp. (See Figure 4.)

Figure 3. To make the mortise in the vertical support, first drill two holes at the top and bottom of the slot. Then cut out the waste with a coping saw, jigsaw, or sabre saw.

Figure 4. Smooth the inside of the mortise with a rasp.

Sand the faces, ends, and edges of the supports. Cut out the seat, and sand all surfaces. Then glue and clamp the seat to the horizontal support. Be careful to center and align the seat as shown in the working drawings. The back edge of the seat should be 7″ from the rear end of the horizontal support.

Tip ◆ Use waterproof resorcinol glue when assembling the parts of this project. This glue is available in most hardware stores, and it's impervious to weather.

After the glue has dried, drill the holes for the seat dowels. Smear glue around the inside edges of these holes,

I SQUARE = 1"

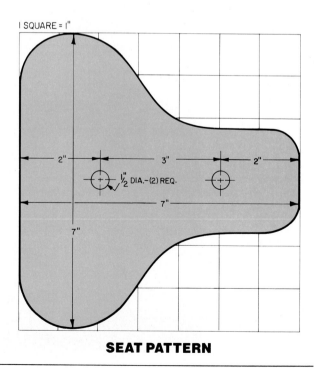

2" 3" 2"

½ DIA.–(2) REQ.

7"

7"

SEAT PATTERN

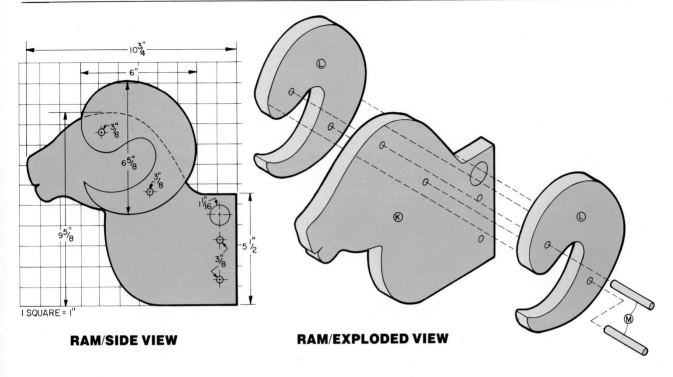

RAM/SIDE VIEW

RAM/EXPLODED VIEW

and tap dowels into them so that just a little of the dowel protrudes above the surface of the seat. When the glue dries on the dowels, sand them flush with the seat.

While you're waiting for the glue to dry on the seat and seat dowels, cut the slot in the upper end of the vertical support. Use a bandsaw to make this slot, cutting it just a little small. Then rasp the inside edges until the stock for the head fits snugly — but not too snugly — in the slot.

Temporarily assemble all the parts of the swing — supports, handle, footrest, and pivot — to make sure that they fit properly. Then disassemble the parts and get ready to make the head.

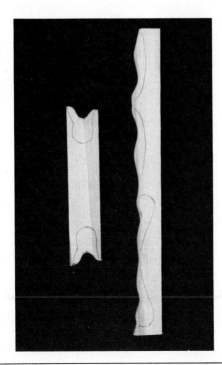

Figure 5. Round over the edges of small parts, like ears, before you cut them completely free of the waste stock.

Making the Head

The first step in making the head is choosing which one you want. There are several choices: Wolf, moose, horse, ram, and elephant. Or you can make up your own.

The construction of these heads is similar. Cut out the parts on the bandsaw or jigsaw, sand the parts smooth, then glue and dowel them together as shown in the working drawings.

Some edges of some parts need to be rounded with a router or rasp. In most cases, it will be easier to do this *before* you assemble the head. However, be careful that you don't round over edges that have to mate flush with other parts. When rounding small parts, like ears, it's safer to machine most of the edges before you cut them free of the waste stock. (See Figure 5.)

Most of the ears and other parts are glued flat on the head. However, a few animals require special cautions:

Horse — The horse's ears are not glued on top of the mane as you might think from looking at the pattern drawing. Instead, the ears are inset in the mane, as shown in the explode and Figure 6. To make the mane stand out, make it from a wood that contrasts with the head and ear stock.

Figure 6. The horse's ears are inset into the mane. So that these parts stand out, make them from different colors of hardwoods.

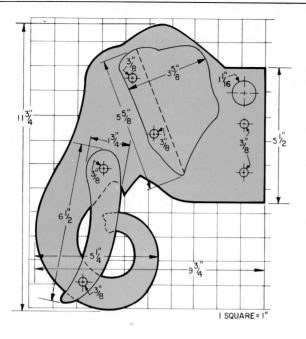

ELEPHANT/SIDE VIEW

1 SQUARE = 1"

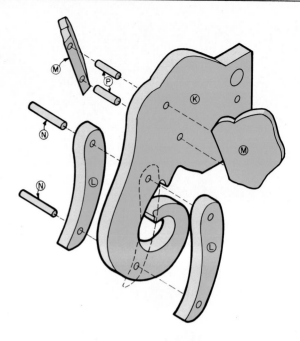

ELEPHANT/EXPLODED VIEW

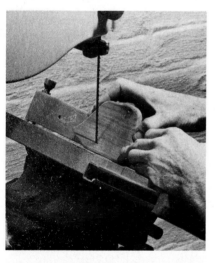

Figure 7. Rip the elephant's ears at 30°. Reverse the second ear so that you feed it into the blade in the opposite direction that you fed the first ear. Save the scraps.

Elephant — The elephant's ears stick out from the head at 30°. To make the ears, first cut two ear shapes on the bandsaw, following the pattern. Label the ears A and B. Set your bandsaw table at 30°, and rip ear A about ⅜″ in back of the leading edge. (See Figure 7.) Rip ear B in the same manner, but *reverse* the ear before you cut it. Feed ear B into the blade flopped from the way you fed ear A. That way, the ears will be mirror images of each other. Sand the sawn edges and glue the beveled edges of the ear to the head. Use the scrap wedges to help clamp the ears while the glue dries. (See Figure 8.) After the glue sets up, reinforce the ears with dowels.

Moose — The moose's antlers are attached to the head with a classic lap joint. Cut a notch 1″ long in the top of the head and 1¾″ long at the bottom of the antlers, where shown in the working drawings. Fit the two parts together, and dowel the antlers to the head.

Final Assembly and Finishing

Now that you've made all the parts of the swing, it's time to put it together.

Insert the handle, pivot, and footrest into the vertical support. These parts will be doweled in place. Rotate them in their holes so that when you drill for the dowels, you will be drilling *across* the annual rings, rather than with them. (See Figure 9.) This will help prevent these parts from splitting later on. Drill the dowel holes, then disassemble the parts.

Glue the head in the slot in the vertical support, and reinforce the joint with dowels. Let the glue dry, and sand the dowels flush. Then glue the handle and the footrest in the support, and dowel them in place. Finally, assemble the

Figure 8. Glue the ears to the head, using the scrap wedges to help clamp the ears in place. Reinforce the ears with dowels after the glue dries.

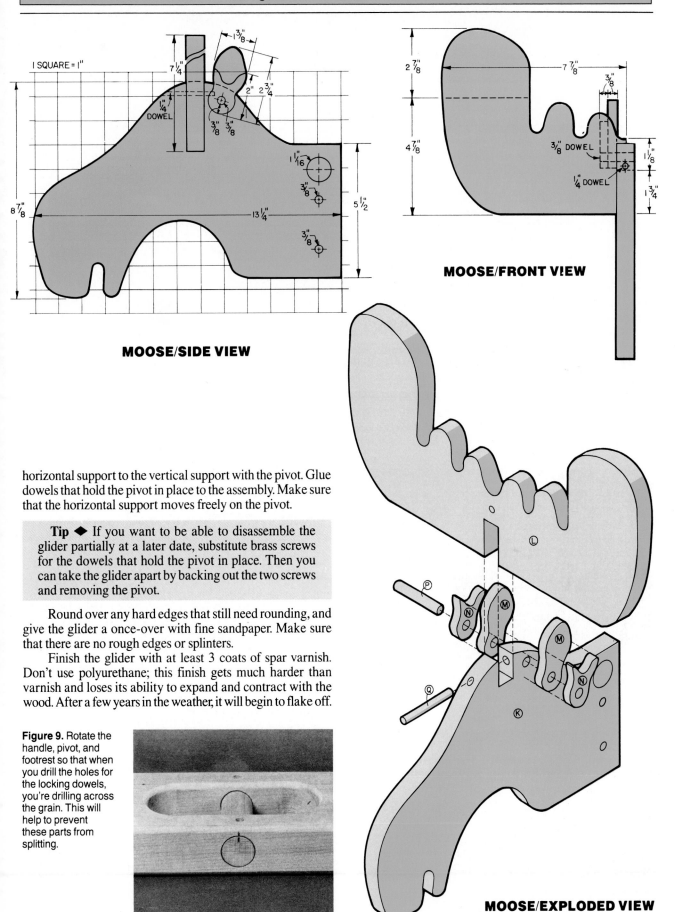

I SQUARE = 1"

MOOSE/SIDE VIEW

MOOSE/FRONT VIEW

horizontal support to the vertical support with the pivot. Glue dowels that hold the pivot in place to the assembly. Make sure that the horizontal support moves freely on the pivot.

Tip ◆ If you want to be able to disassemble the glider partially at a later date, substitute brass screws for the dowels that hold the pivot in place. Then you can take the glider apart by backing out the two screws and removing the pivot.

Round over any hard edges that still need rounding, and give the glider a once-over with fine sandpaper. Make sure that there are no rough edges or splinters.

Finish the glider with at least 3 coats of spar varnish. Don't use polyurethane; this finish gets much harder than varnish and loses its ability to expand and contract with the wood. After a few years in the weather, it will begin to flake off.

Figure 9. Rotate the handle, pivot, and footrest so that when you drill the holes for the locking dowels, you're drilling across the grain. This will help to prevent these parts from splitting.

MOOSE/EXPLODED VIEW

23

Hanging the Swing

To hang the swing, use ¼″ nylon parachute cord. Thread this through the holes in the handle and in the rear of the horizontal support. Lightly burn the ends of the cords with a match to keep them from unraveling, and tie knots in the ends so they don't slip out of their holes.

The glider must be hung from *three* separate points. The ropes should all be parallel to each other when the glider hangs motionless. If the front and back ropes spread apart, they will prevent the glider from swinging. If the ropes come together, the glider will be unstable and it will tend to twist. The two ropes on the handle can be spread apart *slightly*; this will add some stability. But don't let them come together. (See Figures 10 and 11.)

If you are hanging the swing from a tree, simply attach the cords to the branches, using ⅜″ screw eyes. If you are hanging it inside, locate the ceiling joists and sink the eye screws into them. Most joists are located on either 16″ or 24″ centers. The dimensions of the swing are such that it will hang neatly from either type of house framing.

Don't just tie the cords to the eyes; use heavy-duty S-hooks. This will keep the cords from wearing as the child swings, and it will also make it easy for you to take the glider down and put it back up again.

David Wakefield is a professional toymaker and the proprietor of 'Howling Wolf Woodworks' of Millfield, Ohio. He's just published a book on "How to Make Animated Toys", which includes thirty of his ingenious designs.

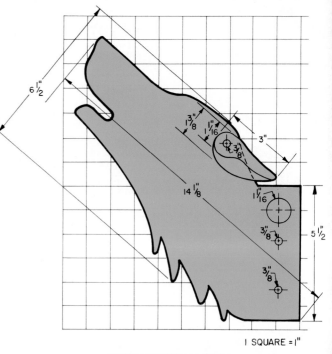

I SQUARE = 1″

WOLF/SIDE VIEW

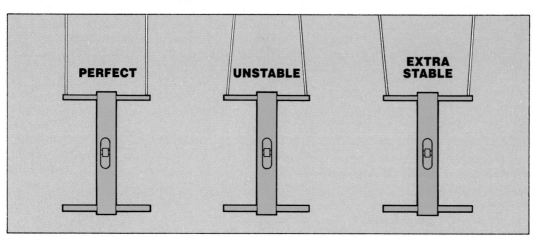

Figure 10. When looking at the glider from the front, handle ropes should hang parallel. If they spread out a little, the swing will be more stable; but don't let them come together.

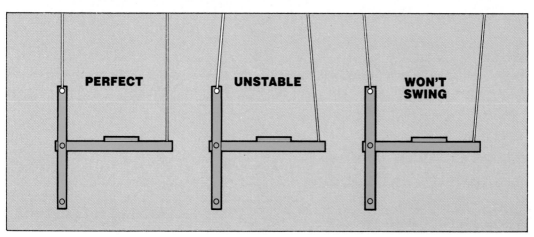

Figure 11. When looking at the swing from the sides, all ropes must hang parallel. Don't let them come together or spread apart.

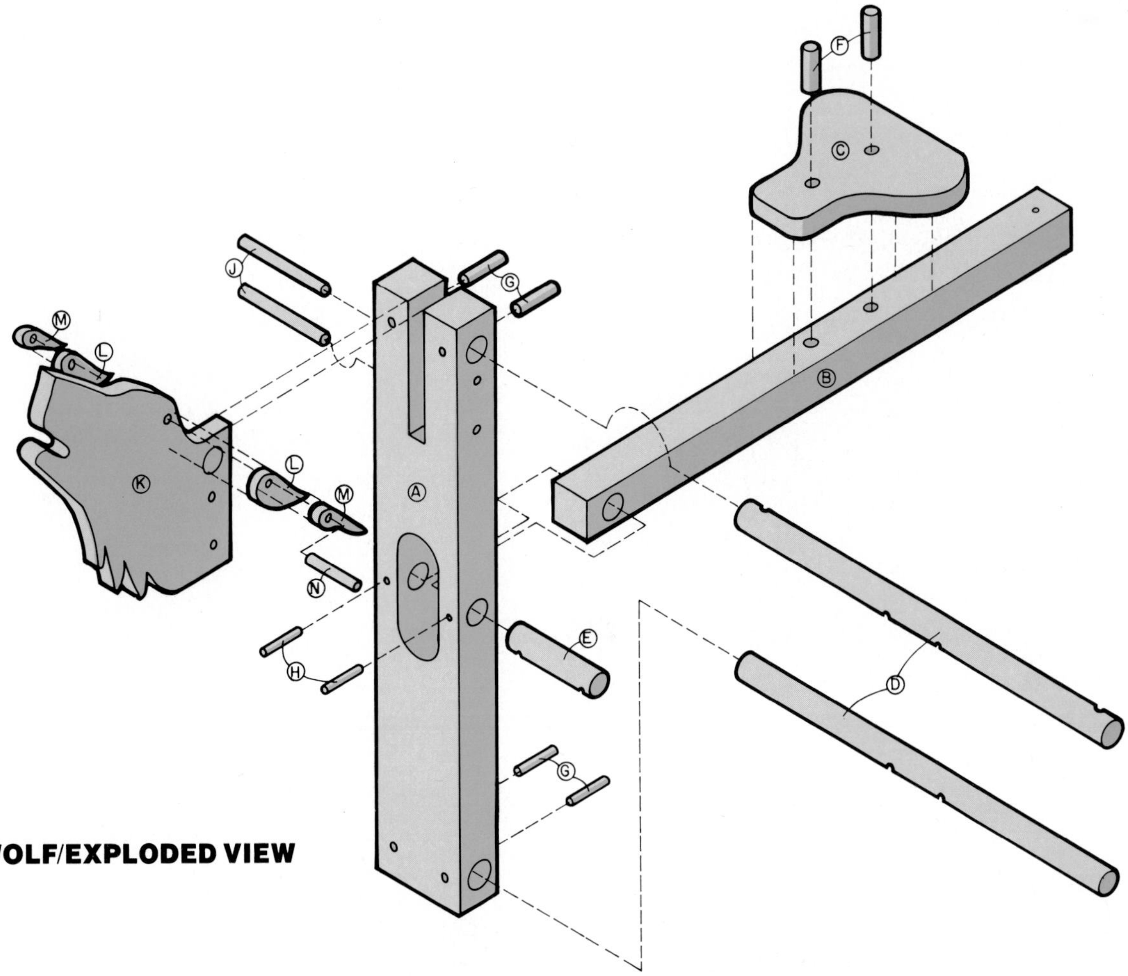

WOLF/EXPLODED VIEW

BILL OF MATERIALS — Animal Gliders

Finished Dimensions in Inches

Swing

A.	Vertical support	1¾ x 4 x 24
B	Horizontal support	1¾ x 1¾ x 24
C.	Seat	¾ x 7 x 7
D.	Handle/footrest (2)	1 dia. x 18
E.	Pivot	1 dia. x 4
F.	Seat dowels (2)	½ dia. x 1¾
G.	Handle/footrest dowels (4)	⅜ dia. x 1¾
H.	Pivot dowels (2)	¼ dia. x 1¾
J.	Head dowels (2)	⅜ dia. x 4

Wolf Head

K.	Head	¾ x 6½ x 14⅛
L.	Inner ears (2)	⅜ x 1⅜ x 3
M.	Outer ears (2)	⅜ x 1 1/16 x 3
N.	Dowel	⅜ dia. x 2¼

Moose Head

K.	Head	¾ x 8⅞ x 13¼
L.	Antlers	¾ x 7¾ x 15¾
M.	Inner ears (2)	⅜ x 1⅜ x 2¾
N.	Outer ears (2)	⅜ x 1⅜ x 2
P.	Ear dowel	⅜ dia. x 2¼
Q.	Antler dowel	¼ dia. x 2½

Horse Head

K.	Head	¾ x 7¾ x 10⅞
L.	Mane (2)	⅜ x 2⅞ x 6¼
M.	Inner ears (2)	⅜ x 1 7/16 x 3¾
N.	Outer ears (2)	⅜ x ¾ x 3¾
P.	Dowel	⅜ dia. x 1½

Elephant Head

K.	Head	¾ x 9¾ x 11¾
L.	Tusks (2)	¾ x 1¾ x 6½
M.	Ears (2)	¾ x 3⅝ x 5⅝
N.	Tusk dowels (2)	⅜ dia. x 2¼
P.	Ear dowels (2)	⅜ dia. x 2½

Ram Head

K.	Head	¾ x 9⅝ x 10¾
L.	Horns (2)	¾ x 6 x 6⅝
M.	Dowels (2)	⅜ dia. x 2¼

Hardware

¼″ Nylon parachute cord (as much as needed)
⅜″ Eye screws (3)
S-hooks (3)

Designed and Built by Nick Engler

Kitchen Organizers

Mix-and-match storage units help to organize the small items in your kitchen.

You've probably seen dozens — maybe hundreds — of project plans for small kitchen accessories. And every one of them was designed to work in someone else's kitchen — except this one!

Here are the plans for five useful storage units for small kitchen paraphernalia: a spoon rack, spice shelf, tea drawers, salt box, and rolling pin holder. Mix and match these units to fit *your* kitchen. Pick two or three units that you need, mount them on a backboard, and hang them up.

These 'kitchen organizers' make great gifts, too. If you know what your relatives and friends need in their kitchen, you can mass produce these units, but still give them personalized gifts.

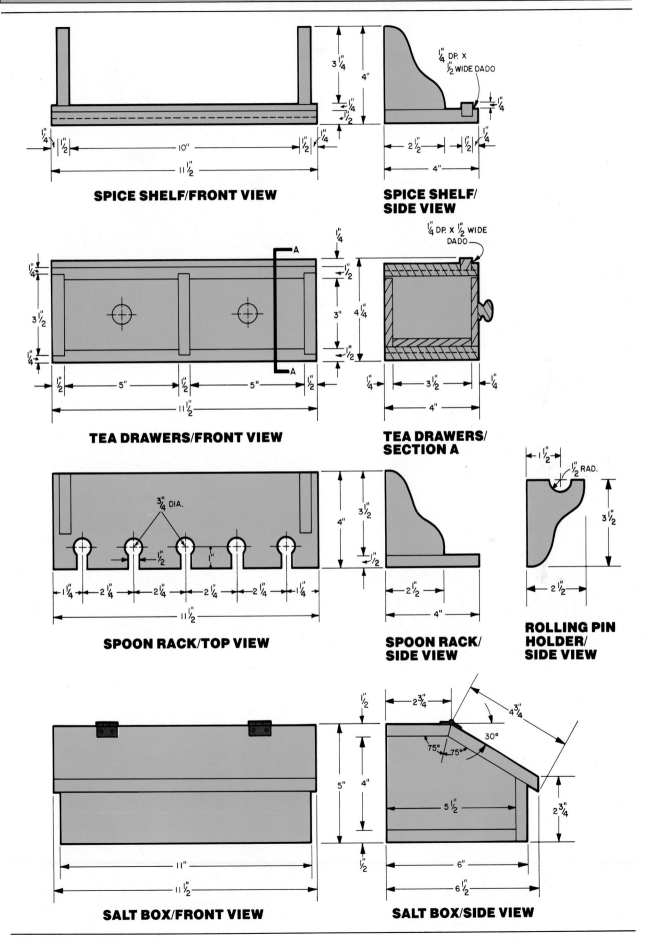

SPICE SHELF/FRONT VIEW

SPICE SHELF/ SIDE VIEW

TEA DRAWERS/FRONT VIEW

TEA DRAWERS/ SECTION A

SPOON RACK/TOP VIEW

SPOON RACK/ SIDE VIEW

ROLLING PIN HOLDER/ SIDE VIEW

SALT BOX/FRONT VIEW

SALT BOX/SIDE VIEW

Making the Storage Units

Each of these units is simple to make. It's also simple to make a lot of them — some of the components in one unit are also used in others. This makes it easier to set up for mass production.

> **Tip ◆** Finish sand all components before you assemble a unit. That will make your sanding chores much simpler.

Spice Shelf — The spice shelf is perhaps the simplest of the components. It consists of a shelf, two brackets, and a rail to keep the spices from falling off. Cut out the brackets on a bandsaw, and make all the other parts on a table saw. Glue the parts together, then reinforce the joints between the brackets and the shelves with wood screws. If you wish, countersink and counterbore the screws so that you can hide the heads with wooden plugs.

Spoon Rack — The spoon rack is made in a similar fashion to the spice shelf. The rack, in fact, is just a shelf with notches. This rack is held by the same brackets as you used to make the spice shelf. To make the notches for the spoons, first drill ¾" holes in the rack. (See Figure 1.) Then cut ½" wide openings to these holes on the bandsaw. (See Figure 2.)

Rolling Pin Holder — The rolling pin holders are just shelf brackets with notches in them to hold the pin. The pin is turned on a lathe. If you'd like to find out how to turn a really fancy pin, see the "Laminated Rolling Pin" chapter in this book.

Tea Drawers — Make two shelves, and cut dadoes in them, as shown in the working drawings. Cut the partitions, and glue them to the shelves to make the case. Cut rabbets in the drawer fronts and backs, and cut grooves near the bottom of all the drawer parts to hold the drawer bottom. Assemble the drawer parts with glue and reinforce the rabbet joints with brads.

> **Tip ◆** Make the drawer parts from aromatic cedar. Tradition has it that food stored in cedar keeps better.

Salt Box — Cut the box parts on your table saw. The front corner of the sides is cut at 30°. You can make these cuts easily with a tapering jig. (See Figure 3.) Rip the top edge of the box front at 30°, and the mating edges of the top and lid at 15°. Assemble the sides, top, and front with glue, then hinge the lid to the top.

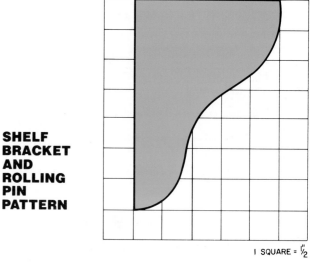

SHELF BRACKET AND ROLLING PIN PATTERN

1 SQUARE = ½"

Mounting and Finishing

As shown in the photograph, all of these units are mounted on backboards that are 12" wide and 14" long. You may want to vary the length of the backboard, depending on how many units you want to mount on a single board and how you want to space them. Drill two ½" holes at a slight angle near the top of each backboard so that you can hang it on a wall.

Glue the units to the boards and let the glue dry. Then reinforce the glue joints with wood screws. Install these screws through the *back* side of the backboard so that they won't show.

Finish sand any parts that still need it, and apply a non-toxic finish to your organizers. You have several choices: mineral oil, 'salad-bowl' finish, or Danish oil. If you use Danish oil, remember that this finish only becomes non-toxic after it has set up for several weeks.

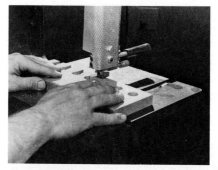

Figure 2. Then open these holes on your bandsaw.

Figure 3. Cut the angled corners in the sides of the salt box using a tapering jig. With this jig, you can cut every side exactly the same.

Figure 1. To make the notches in the spoon rack, first drill ¾" holes near the front of the rack.

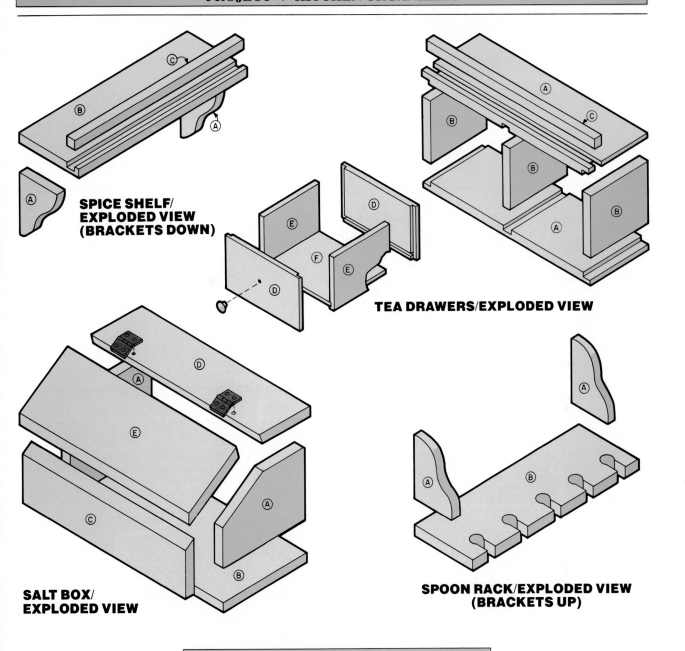

**SPICE SHELF/
EXPLODED VIEW
(BRACKETS DOWN)**

TEA DRAWERS/EXPLODED VIEW

**SALT BOX/
EXPLODED VIEW**

**SPOON RACK/EXPLODED VIEW
(BRACKETS UP)**

BILL OF MATERIALS — Kitchen Organizers

Finished Dimensions in Inches

Tea Drawers

A.	Top/bottom (2)	½ x 4 x 11½
B.	Partitions (3)	½ x 3½ x 4
C.	Rail	½ x ½ x 11½
D.	Drawer front/back (4)	¼ x 3 x 5
E.	Drawer sides (4)	¼ x 3 x 3¾
F.	Drawer bottoms (2)	⅛ x 3¾ x 4¾

Spice Shelf

A.	Brackets (2)	½ x 2½ x 3½
B.	Shelf	½ x 4 x 11½
C.	Rail	½ x ½ x 11½

Spoon Rack

A.	Brackets (2)	½ x 2½ x 3½
B.	Rack	½ x 4 x 11½

Rolling Pin Holder

A.	Brackets (2)	½ x 2½ x 3½
B.	Rolling pin	2½ dia. x 16

Salt Box

A.	Sides (2)	½ x 4 x 5½
B.	Bottom	½ x 5½ x 11
C.	Front	½ x 2¾ x 11
D.	Top	½ x 2¾ x 11½
E.	Lid	½ x 4¾ x 11½

Hardware

Small drawer pulls (2), for tea drawers
Decorative hinges and mounting screws (1 pair), for salt box

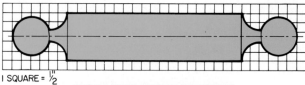

I SQUARE = ½"

ROLLING PIN PATTERN

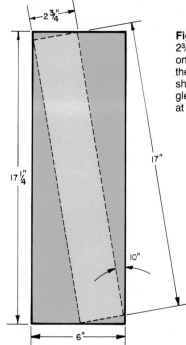

Figure 1. Lay out a 2¾" x 17" rectangle on the wide face of the turning block, as shown. The rectangle should be tilted at 10°.

2¾"

17¼"

17"

10"

6"

Laminated Rolling Pin

Different sorts of wood make this a different sort of rolling pin.

Figure 2. Cut out the rectangle on the bandsaw. In the finished turning block, the layers of wood will appear to be set at an angle.

T he principle is as simple as it is fascinating: Intersect a cylinder with a plane and you'll get a circle, an ellipse, or a cone, depending on the angle of intersection.

In this turning project, the rolling pin is the cylinder and the planes are layers of different woods. The shapes and designs occur because the layers of wood were set at a slight angle to the axis of rotation when the pin was turned.

To duplicate this effect, first glue up several layers of wood to make a turning block 2¾" x 6" x 17¼". Alternate colors of wood — light, dark, light, dark — so that the individual layers are distinct from each other. Be careful that all the surfaces join evenly, and let the glue set up for *at least* 24 hours.

Tip ◆ You may use plywood in this project as long as you use 'lumber-core' plywood, or a similar material with no 'voids' between the plies.

Lay out a 2¾" x 17" rectangle on the 6" face of the block, tilting the rectangle at 10°. (See Figure 1.) Cut out this rectangle on the bandsaw to make a smaller turning block. The layers of wood will appear to be set at an angle in the finished block. (See Figure 2.) Turn this block on a lathe to make a rolling pin. As you work the turning block down to a cylinder, the various layers of wood will begin to form ellipses, cones, and other geometric shapes.

Designed and Built by Rude Osolnik

Acorn Bed

Distinctive finials give this bed a distinctive charm.

Often, the finial — the decorative knob at the end of a spindle — can tell you something about the piece of furniture it belongs to. For instance, some eighteenth and nineteenth century craftsmen developed singular finials that they incorporated into their work as a way of signing their name. Experts on Shaker furniture can tell where a Shaker chair was made by the shape of the finials — each community had its own individual design.

One of the most distinctive finials to be developed in this country was the upside-down acorn. Perhaps the abundance of oak in America suggested the design to colonial woodworkers. The acorn design quickly became popular throughout the colonies, so much so that folks began calling pieces topped with these finials 'acorn' furniture.

Here's an excellent example of this furniture — an acorn bed, designed and built by master woodturner Rude Osolnik.

As designed, the bed will accommodate a standard-size double mattress. Before beginning this project, it would be wise to measure your bedding and adjust the dimensions accordingly.

Making the Flat Parts

To reproduce Rude's acorn bed, start by building the flat parts — the aprons and headboard. First, choose the stock. The boards you select for the aprons — particularly the side aprons — should be *absolutely* clear, free of knots and other grain defects that may cause the wood to crack or split. Remember, the side aprons will support the entire weight of the box springs, mattress, and whoever is sleeping on that mattress.

You'll have to glue up the stock for the headboard; it isn't likely that you'll find a board 22½″ wide. You can get by with using wood with a little character in this part — burls, curls, solid knots — but the ends of the headboard stock must be clear. These ends will become tenons that join to the bedposts. If the grain isn't clear, the tenons may snap.

Tip ◆ It goes without saying that the wood grain in all the flat parts should run horizontally, so that the aprons and tenons have maximum strength.

31

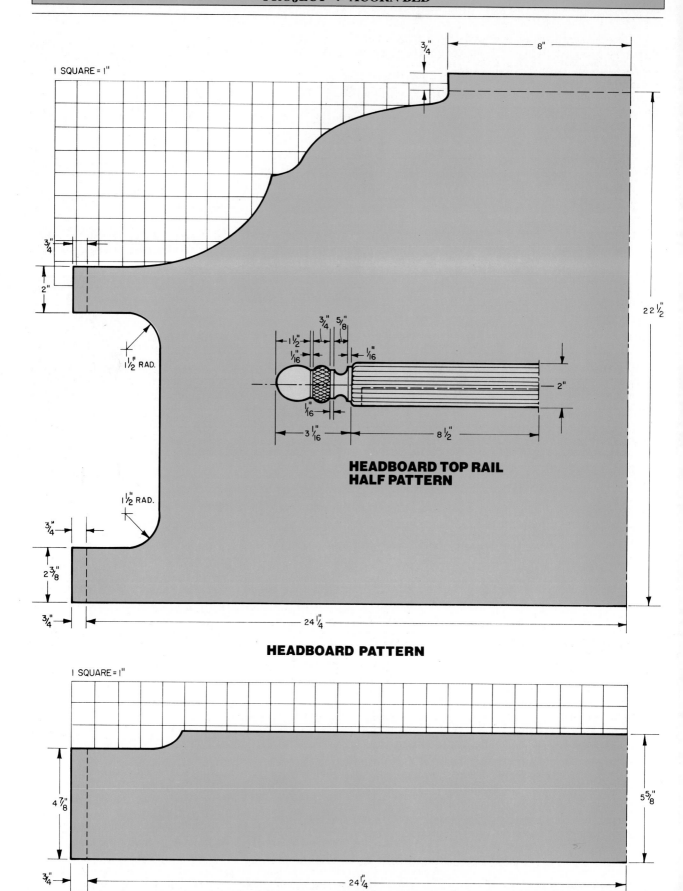

**HEADBOARD TOP RAIL
HALF PATTERN**

HEADBOARD PATTERN

HEADBOARD APRON PATTERN

Enlarge the patterns in the working drawings and trace them on the headboard, head apron, and foot apron. Cut out the patterns with a jigsaw, bandsaw, or sabre saw. You'll probably find that a sabre saw is easiest. You can lay the large boards on your workbench, and prop them up off the bench top with wood scraps. That way, the blade of the sabre saw won't cut into the workbench while you're sawing. (See Figure 1.)

Making the Bedposts

Most home workshop lathes have a 'throw' of 34" or less, so you probably won't be able to turn the bedposts in one piece. That's alright; there's a simple way to join two or more shorter spindles to make one long spindle.

Study the bedpost working drawings. The best place to join the posts would be between two of the beads, just below the long fluted section. (See Figure 2.) Cut the stock for each post accordingly. For example, if you decide to join the posts between the first and second beads (from the bottom), cut the stock for the head bedposts in 23" and 28" lengths. This will give you several extra inches, top and bottom.

Find the exact center of the stock, and drill 15/16" holes, 3" deep in one end of each board, where you want to join them. Cut a 1" dowel, 6" long and carefully sand down the outside of the dowel until it fits snugly in the holes. The reason for drilling small holes and sanding the dowel to fit is that most commercial 1" dowels aren't quite 1" in diameter. And the dowel must fit the holes with no slop.

Cut a second dowel, just 4" long, and fit this dowel to the same holes. This dowel will become your 'turning plug' — you'll plug the hole with this dowel while you're turning the stock. For the time being, set the turning plug aside.

Temporarily, join the two parts of the bedposts with the 6" dowel. Lay out the joinery, disassemble the post, then cut the mortises in the bedposts *before* you turn them. Make sure all the tenons fit properly. If you attempt to cut the joinery after you turn the posts, you'll find it almost impossible to cut the joints accurately.

Take the bedpost sections apart again and insert the turning plug in one hole. Find the exact center of the plug — a center finder will help you do this accurately. (See Figure 3.) Then mount the stock on the lathe, with the turning plug

Figure 1. Use a sabre saw to cut the shape of the headboard. To keep the saw blade from biting into your workbench, prop the stock up off your workbench top with scraps of wood.

Figure 2. Perhaps the best place to join the bedpost sections is between the beads just under the flutes. Use 1" dowels, sunk at least 3" into each section.

Figure 3. Use a center finder to locate the exact center of the turning plug.

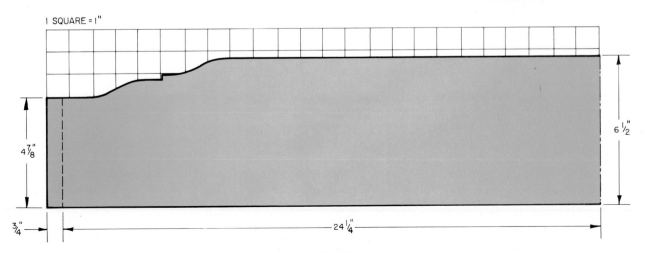

I SQUARE = 1"

4 7/8"

6 1/2"

3/4"

24 1/4"

FOOTBOARD APRON PATTERN

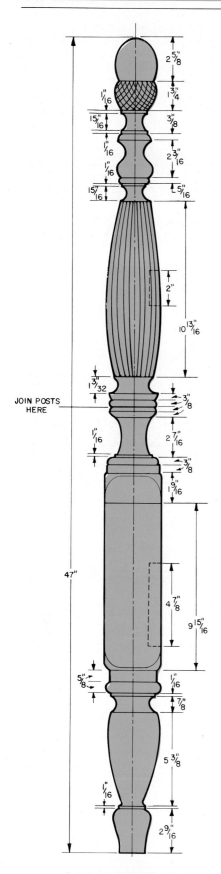

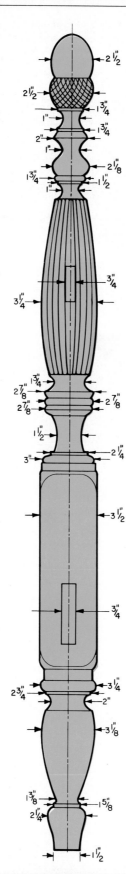

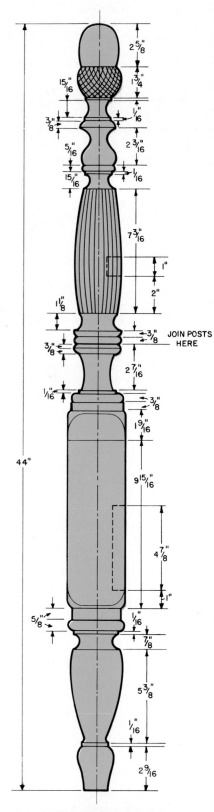

**HEADBOARD BEDPOST
DETAIL
VERTICAL DIMENSIONS**

**HEADBOARD BEDPOST
DETAIL
HORIZONTAL DIMENSIONS**

**FOOTBOARD BEDPOST
DETAIL
VERTICAL DIMENSIONS**

engaging the *tailstock* center. (See Figure 4.) Turn the stock at a low speed. Repeat this process for all eight bedpost sections, using the same turning plug over and over.

The fluting on the upper sections of the bedpost, the head rail, and the foot rail is optional. But if you want to do it, there are several methods you can use. Rude used a molder, and ground his own knives to make the flutes. This is a bit tricky, however. An easier, safer way is to use a 'scratch' fluting tool and a special jig. The jig performs two functions. It indexes the spindle so that you can scratch one flute, turn the spindle *exactly 15°*, and cut another. The jig also guides the fluting tool so that each flute is perfectly straight. In making the jig, be careful to position the guide so that it holds the point of the fluting tool directly above the axis of the spindle.

To make the fluting tool, first get some 'scratch stock'. Any high carbon steel approximately $1/16''$ thick will do. The fluting tool used here was made from a strip of steel cut from an old scraper. You can also use an old hand saw blade. Grind two $1/2''$ coves in the steel so that they make a point in the middle, as shown in Figure 5. Hone the fluting tool blade with a gouge slip; then put a burr on the edges, just as you would when sharpening a scraper. Mount the blade in a handle.

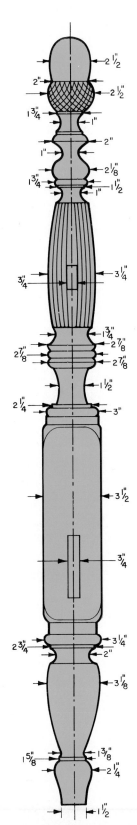

Figure 4. Mount the bedpost on the lathe, with the turning plug installed in one end. The plug should engage the tailstock center.

Figure 5. To cut the flutes in the spindles, make a fluting tool as shown here.

**FOOTBOARD BEDPOST
DETAIL
HORIZONTAL DIMENSIONS**

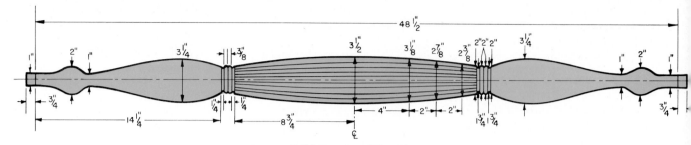

FOOT RAIL DETAIL

To use the fluting tool, first mount the spindle in the jig. Hold the fluting jig firmly against the guide and position the point on the spindle where you want to start cutting the flute. Slowly draw the fluting tool along the spindle, pressing down lightly. The tool will scratch a fine line in the spindle. If you're satisfied that the line is straight and that it begins and ends where you want it to, reposition the tool and make another stroke. Use a little more pressure this time, and scratch the line a little deeper. Repeat until you've cut the flute. Then turn the spindle 15°, and cut another flute. When you've finished, clean up the flutes with hand chisels.

Assembly

Rude designed this as a 'knock-down' bed. The side aprons can be easily removed from the footboard and headboard so that the bed can be transported. In order to make knock-down furniture, you need some special knock-down fittings. These fittings can be purchased from several mail order houses, such as:

The Woodworker's Store
21801 Industrial Blvd.
Rogers, MN 55374

The Wise Company
6503 St.Claude Ave.
Arabi, LA 70032

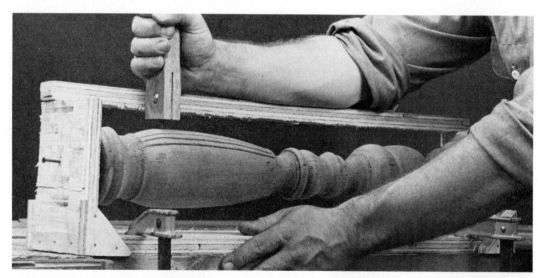

Figure 6. Scratch the flutes in the spindle, lightly pressing down on the fluting tool as you draw it against the spindle. Hold the handle of the tool firmly against the guide to keep the flutes straight.

Figure 7. Mortise the female part of the bed fastener into the bedpost, then drill holes behind the slots to accommodate the male tabs.

Figure 8. When properly installed, the bed fastener plate should be flush with the surface of the bedpost, and the tabs should be fitted to the end of the aprons.

Screw the male parts of these fittings directly to the ends of the side aprons. The female parts must be mortised into the bedposts, and holes drilled behind the slots so that the tabs will properly engage the plates. (See Figures 7 and 8.)

Tip ◆ When you're fitting the side aprons to the bedposts, remember that there's such a thing as a right bedpost and left bedpost. This will determine the location of the knock-down plates on each post.

Once the knock-down fittings have been installed, remove the side aprons from the bedpost and set the aprons aside. Then glue the headboard, head apron, and head posts together. Set this assembly aside, and glue the foot rail, foot apron, and foot posts together.

When the glue is dry, carefully remove any glue beads with a chisel. Finish sand, and apply a finish to all parts. Finally, install bed spring supports on the inside of the side aprons. These brackets support the box springs with no need for wooden slats. (They are available from the same suppliers previously mentioned.) If you're building a single bed, use three brackets per side (six total). If you're building a double bed, use four. Queen- and king-size beds will require five.

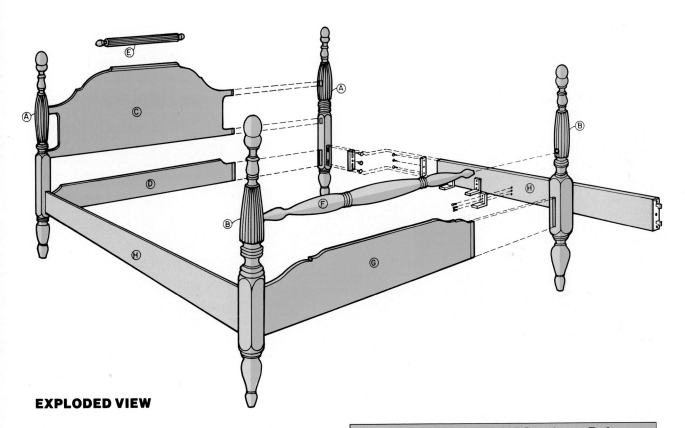

EXPLODED VIEW

BILL OF MATERIALS — Acorn Bed

Finished Dimensions in Inches

A.	Head Bedposts (2)	3½ x 3½ x 47
B.	Foot Bedposts (2)	3½ x 3½ x 44
C.	Headboard	¾ x 22½ x 50
D.	Head Apron	¾ x 5⅝ x 50
E.	Head Rail	2 dia. x 24
F.	Foot Rail	3¼ dia. x 50
G.	Foot Apron	¾ x 6½ x 50
H.	Side Aprons	¾ x 4⅞ x 72

Hardware

Knock-Down Bed Fasteners and Mounting Screws (4) Bed Spring Supports and Mounting Screws (6-10)

Designed and Built by Harry Cooper

Hallway Ensemble

Dress up your hallway with a matched set of mirrors.

There's nothing better than getting big returns on small investments. The matched set of mirrors that you see here will do just that for you. For a modest investment of your time and materials, you get a big return on looks. This 'hallway ensemble' really dresses up the entrance to your home.

The ensemble is the creation of Harry Cooper of Vine Grove, Kentucky. It was one of his more popular designs — Harry sold enough of these framed mirrors to pay for some of the power tools in his shop. That's another good return on a modest investment.

Making the Mirrors and Shelf

To make these frames look as good as possible, use good wood when you're making them. Choose a rich-looking hardwood that compliments any other furniture or trim you may have in your hallway.

Rip and cut all the parts to size, then cut the side contours on the bandsaw. Using a jigsaw or a sabre saw, make piercing cuts to form the openings in the three mirror frames. (See Figure 1.) Clean up all edges, inside and outside, with sandpaper and a rasp.

Rout the outside *and* inside edges of the mirror frames with a piloted bit. Harry used an ogee bit to shape the edges as you see them here. Also rout the three outside edges of the shelf, shaping the *bottom* corners; and the three free edges of

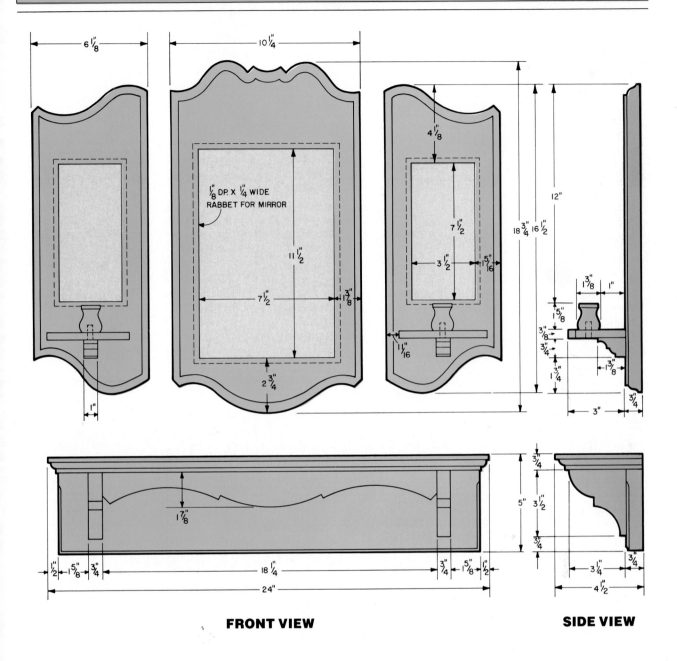

FRONT VIEW

SIDE VIEW

the shelf mount, shaping the outside corner. When you shape the shelf mount, raise the ogee bit about ³/₁₆″ so that you only cut the cove part of the ogee. (See Figure 2.)

Rout the inside back edge of the mirror frames with a straight bit to make rabbets ⅛″ deep and ¼″ wide. Square the corners where the rabbets meet with a hand chisel.

Turn the candle holders on a lathe, if you want. Or, you can purchase ready-made hardwood candle holders from several direct mail companies. Here are two addresses:

The Woodworkers' Store   Woodworker's Supply
21801 Industrial Blvd.   5604 Alameda NE
Rogers, MN 55374   Albuquerque, NM 87113

Figure 1. To make the mirror opening, use a jigsaw or a sabre saw to make a piercing cut.

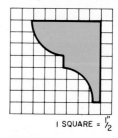

Figure 2. When you rout the edges of the shelf mount, raise the bit so that you only cut the cove part of the ogee.

SHELF BRACKET PATTERN

CANDLE HOLDER PATTERN

I SQUARE = ½"

I SQUARE = ½"

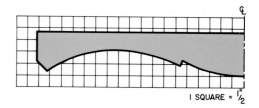

I SQUARE = ½"

VALANCE PATTERN

Glue together all the shelf and candle ledge parts, then reinforce the glue joints with finishing nails. Drive these nails in from the backs of the frames or mount so that the heads don't show. Dowel the candleholders to the candle ledges. Sand all surfaces smooth, then apply a finish.

Place the mirrors in the frames. Harry designed the frames so that he could use inexpensive mirror tiles. These are available at most discount department stores and some paint stores. Tack sheets of ⅛" thick hardboard to the backs of the frames to hold the mirrors in place. With the mirrors in place, install the hangers on the backs of the frames and the shelf assembly.

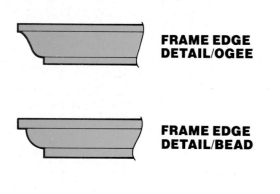

FRAME EDGE DETAIL/OGEE

FRAME EDGE DETAIL/BEAD

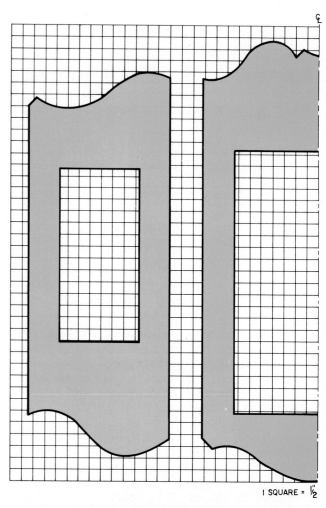

I SQUARE = ½"

FRAME PATTERNS

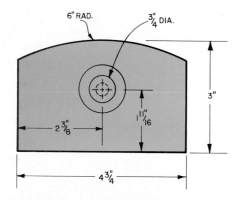

6" RAD.

¾" DIA.

3"

2 ⅜"

1 ¹¹⁄₁₆"

4 ¾"

CANDLE LEDGE LAYOUT

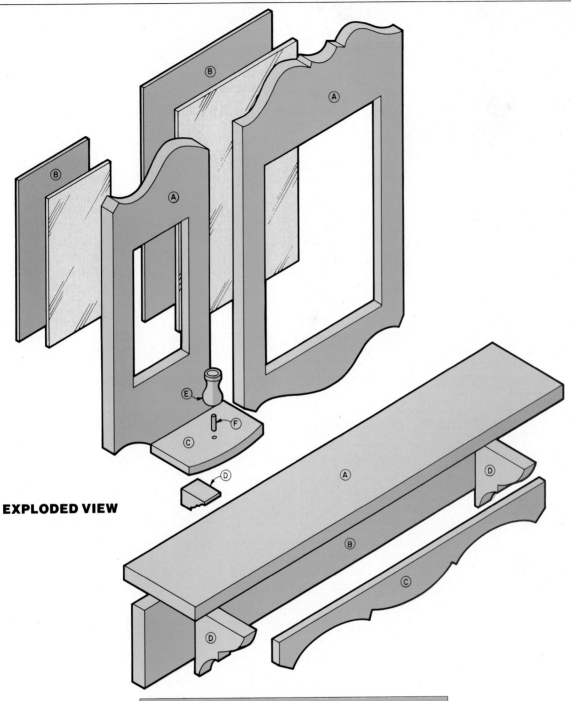

EXPLODED VIEW

BILL OF MATERIALS — Hallway Ensemble

Finished Dimensions in Inches

Center Mirror

A.	Frame	¾ x 10¼ x 18¾
B.	Mirror back	⅛ x 9⅛ x 13

Side Mirrors

A.	Frames (2)	¾ x 6⅛ x 16½
B.	Mirror backs (2)	⅛ x 5 x 9¼
C.	Candle ledges (2)	⅜ x 3 x 4¾
D.	Brackets (2)	¾ x 1 x 1⅜
E.	Candle holders (2)	1⅜ dia. x 1⅝
F.	Dowels (2)	⅜ dia. x 1

Shelf

A.	Shelf	¾ x 4½ x 24
B.	Shelf mount	¾ x 4¼ x 23
C.	Valance	½ x 1⅞ x 18¼
D.	Brackets (2)	¾ x 3¼ x 3½

Hardware

4d Finishing nails (1-2 dozen)
⅝" Brads (2 dozen)
Hangers (5)
4" x 8" Mirrors (2)
8" x 12" Mirror

Designed and Built by Nick Engler

Pie Safe

Punched tin adds a touch of country to your kitchen.

Not so very long ago, most kitchens were used for baking every day. Pies, breads, and pastries would come out of the oven, then put in a 'pie safe' to cool. The pie safe was a cabinet designed especially to circulate fresh air, while keeping the bugs off the baked goods. To

our modern minds, the easiest way to keep out the bugs and let in the air is to use screen wire. But screen or 'fly wire' as it was called in some parts, was scarce and expensive. So the cabinetmakers punched small holes in sheets of tin, then mounted these sheets in the door panels (and sometimes the side panels) of the pie safe.

The punched tin you see in this project is mostly decorative. However, in all other respects, this pie safe is quite functional in the most modern kitchen. The open area between the upper and lower cabinets will accommodate a microwave oven. (See Figure 1.) The drawer is mounted on a full-extension slide, and has a large work surface on top of the drawer. This surface scoots from side to side to let you access the drawer space beneath it. (See Figure 2.) The

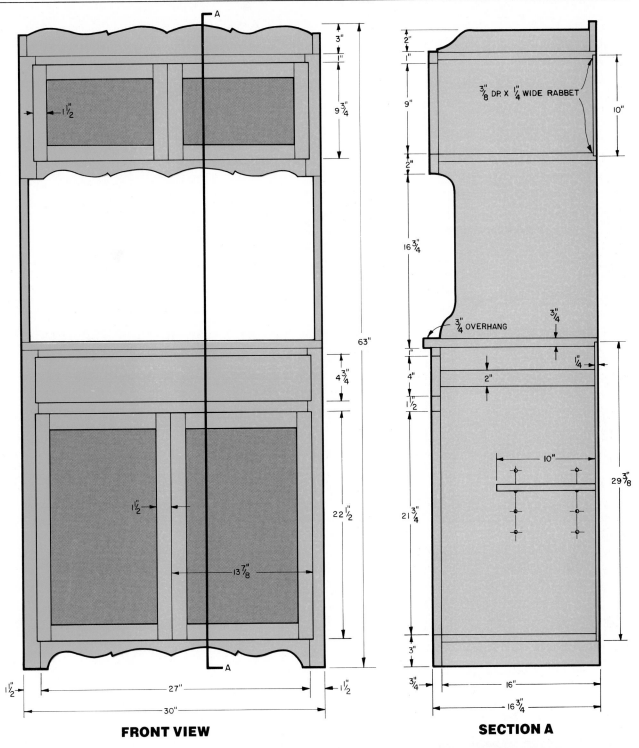

FRONT VIEW

SECTION A

Figure 1. The open space between the two cabinets is large enough to mount a microwave oven.

Figure 2. The drawer pulls out to reveal a work surface and cutting board. This board slides back and forth so that you can access the drawer space underneath.

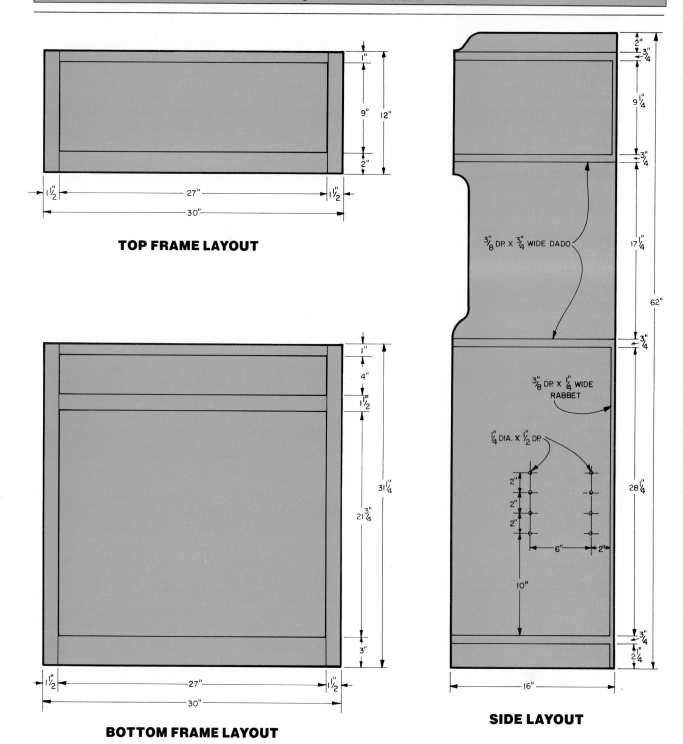

TOP FRAME LAYOUT

BOTTOM FRAME LAYOUT

SIDE LAYOUT

bottom cabinet has an adjustable half-shelf so that you can store large, medium, and small kitchen appliances and accessories.

Making the Case

Begin this project by gluing up stock for the sides and shelves. Set these aside so that the glue can set up, and make the top and bottom frames. Cut the decorative design in the backstop, the valance, and the skirt on a bandsaw. Set the backstop aside for the time being.

Tip ◆ The design shown here is a standard colonial/country furniture design. If you want to change the appearance of this piece to blend with more modern surroundings, cut a simpler design.

Dowel the top and the bottom frames together. Put two dowels in the ends of frame members that are 1½″ wide or wider, but just use one dowel in the ends of the 1″ members. (See Figure 3.) As you fit the frames together, the valance

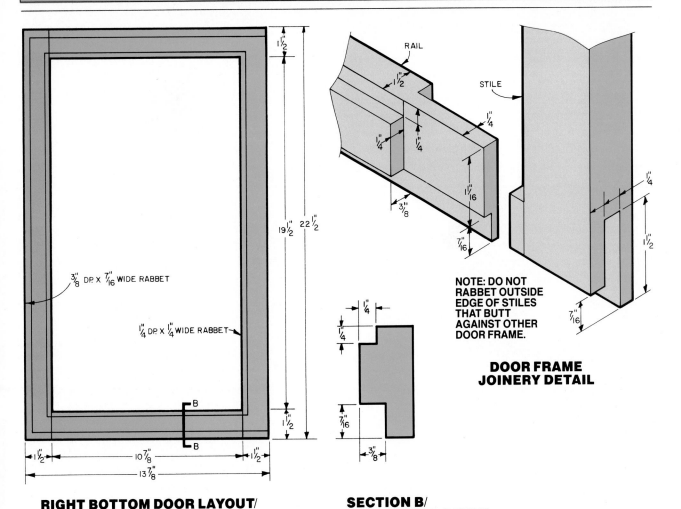

$\frac{3}{8}''$ DP. X $\frac{7}{16}''$ WIDE RABBET

$\frac{1}{4}''$ DP. X $\frac{1}{4}''$ WIDE RABBET

$1\frac{1}{2}''$

$19\frac{1}{2}''$ $22\frac{1}{2}''$

$1\frac{1}{2}''$

$1\frac{1}{2}''$ $10\frac{7}{8}''$ $1\frac{1}{2}''$

$13\frac{7}{8}''$

B

B

RAIL

STILE

$1\frac{1}{2}''$

$\frac{1}{4}''$

$\frac{1}{4}''$ $\frac{1}{4}''$

$1\frac{1}{16}''$

$\frac{3}{8}''$

$\frac{7}{16}''$

$1\frac{1}{16}''$

$\frac{1}{4}''$

$1\frac{1}{2}''$

$\frac{7}{16}''$

NOTE: DO NOT RABBET OUTSIDE EDGE OF STILES THAT BUTT AGAINST OTHER DOOR FRAME.

DOOR FRAME JOINERY DETAIL

$\frac{1}{4}''$

$\frac{1}{4}''$

$\frac{7}{16}''$

$\frac{3}{8}''$

RIGHT BOTTOM DOOR LAYOUT/ BACK VIEW

SECTION B/ DOOR FRAME MEMBER DETAIL

becomes the lower member of the top frame, and the skirt becomes the lower member of the bottom frame.

Cut the sides and shelves to size, then cut the rabbets and dadoes in these parts. (See Figure 4.) Also drill a series of ¼" holes in the sides, as shown in the working drawings. These holes will hold pin-style shelf supports, which will in turn hold the adjustable shelf. Finally, cut the notches in the work shelf with a bandsaw or hand saw.

Dry assemble the sides, shelves, backstop, and frames to make sure that everything fits properly. Once you're satisfied that the fit is good, take the cabinet apart and finish sand all parts. Then reassemble the case with glue and wood screws.

Making the Drawer and Doors

As mentioned previously, the drawer is mounted on a full-extension slide. These slides make the mounting of the drawer very easy. All you have to do is screw one end of the slide to the case, and the other end to the drawer. However, this does require some careful planning.

All extension slides take up a certain amount of room. The ones that were used in this project were ½" wide. That meant that the drawer had to be built 1" narrower than the width of the drawer opening, so that there was adequate room for a slide on either side. It also meant putting ¾" thick shims or 'slide mounts' on the sides of case, just behind the

Figure 3. Put just one dowel in the ends of the upper frame members, since these are just 1" wide. Put two dowels in all the other frame members.

Figure 4. If you have a table saw with a rip fence that can be positioned up to 30" away from the blade, you can use it to cut all the dadoes in the sides. If not, you'll have to cut some of the dadoes with a hand-held router.

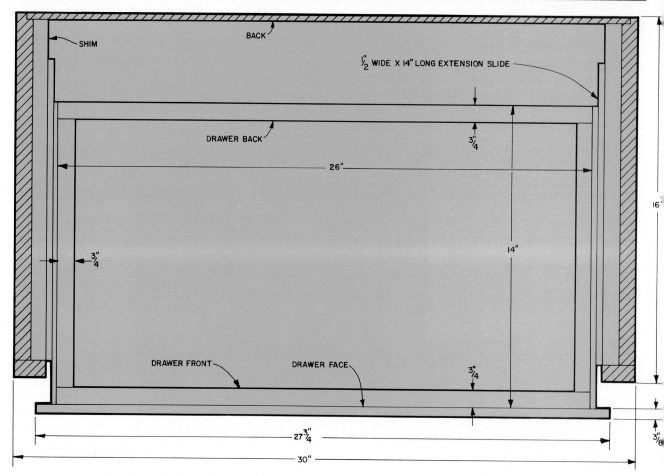

**DRAWER LAYOUT/TOP VIEW
(DRAWER PARTIALLY OPEN)**

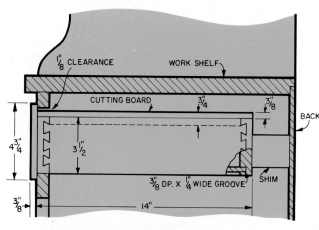

**DRAWER LAYOUT/SIDE VIEW
(DRAWER CLOSED)**

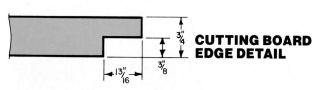

**CUTTING BOARD
EDGE DETAIL**

drawer opening. These shims were necessary because the slides have to be mounted on a surface that's flush with the drawer opening.

Before you cut the pieces for your drawer, purchase the extension slides so that you know just how much space they require. If they require something other than ½", you'll have to adjust the dimensions of the drawer parts accordingly. These slides are available from many home centers and hardware stores, or you can buy them through the mail from:

The Woodworker's Store
21801 Industrial Blvd.
Rogers, MN 55374

The drawer is just a simple box with a ⅜" thick face. Use a router and a jig to dovetail the drawer front, back, and sides together. (See Figure 5.) If you don't have a dovetail jig, you could also cut a lock joint on your table saw. (See Figure 6.) Cut a groove around the bottom edge of the drawer front, back, and sides to accept the drawer bottom. Then assemble the drawer parts with glue. *Do not* attach the drawer face at this time; wait until after you've mounted the drawer.

While the glue is setting up on the drawer, make the doors. Join the door stiles to the rails with a slot mortise and tenon. Make the slot by passing the ends of the stiles over a saw blade. (See Figure 7.) A tenoning jig will help to keep the stiles square to the blade. To cut the full width of the slots, make one pass over the blade; reverse the stiles in the jig, and make a second pass. Cut the tenons by passing the ends of the rails over a dado blade. (See Figure 8.) Cut one side of the tenon; flip the rails over, and cut the other side.

Glue the door frame parts together, making sure that the doors are absolutely square. After the glue has set up, rout rabbets on all the inside faces, where shown in the working drawings. The rabbets on the inner edges of the doors will be used to mount the metal panels. The rabbets on the outer edges of the doors are so the door can be partially inset into the case. The only edges that don't get rabbeted are the outer edges where the doors meet.

Finish sand the drawer, drawer face, and door frames. If you haven't already done so, glue the slide mounts to the sides just behind the drawer opening. Mount the drawer in the opening, following the instructions that come with your extension slides. When the drawer is properly mounted, there should be a ⅜″ space between the top of the drawer and the lower edge of the upper bottom frame rail. This space will allow you to mount a sliding cutting board in the drawer, if you so wish.

Once the drawer is mounted, carefully measure where the drawer face should be positioned. Then glue the drawer face to the drawer front.

Mount the doors to the case with self-closing hinges for inset doors. These hinges are available from most hardware stores, or you can buy them through the mail from the Woodworker's Store, mentioned previously. With the doors and the drawers mounted, attach the pulls.

When you've completed and assembled all the wooden parts of the pie safe, and you're satisfied that they all work together, remove all the hardware. Finish sand any wooden parts that still need it, and apply a water resistant finish.

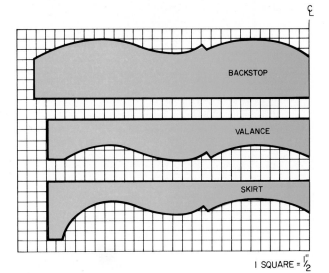

BACKSTOP

VALANCE

SKIRT

1 SQUARE = 1½″

BACKSTOP, VALANCE & SKIRT PATTERNS

Punching the Tin

While the finish is drying, make the punched tin panels for the doors. True tin is a little hard to come by these days, so unless you live in a large city with a tin supplier, you're probably limited to four choices: galvanized sheet steel, aluminum, brass, or copper. If you opt for galvanized sheet metal or aluminum, you can give it an antique tin look by rubbing it with gun blueing. As shown, the 'tin' panels in this

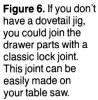

Figure 5. Use a dovetail jig to join the drawer front, back, and sides.

Figure 6. If you don't have a dovetail jig, you could join the drawer parts with a classic lock joint. This joint can be easily made on your table saw.

Figure 7. Cut the slot mortises in the stiles with a saw blade. A tenoning jig helps to keep the stile square to the blade.

Figure 8. Make the tenons in the rails with a dado. Cut both the inside and outside faces of the rails to form the tenon.

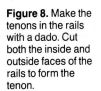

Figure 9. Attach the pattern to the sheet metal with rubber cement or spray adhesive. Then tap the awl into the metal until the point just comes through the other side, creating a small hole. Repeat until you've completed the pattern.

UPPER DOOR PANEL PATTERN

project are actually sheet copper. The copper is expensive, but it looks great.

To 'punch' sheet metal, you first need to make a long, sharp awl. A nail set isn't long enough; you'll find it tires your hands quickly. Purchase a 6″ pin punch and sharpen the end of it with your grinder or belt sander. The extra length will give you the leverage you need to easily remove the awl from the metal after you punch a hole.

Lay out your pattern on a piece of paper and copy the pattern over several times. There's a pattern included with the working drawings, but you may find others that are more to your liking. Attach the pattern to the sheet metal with rubber cement or spray adhesive, then lay the sheet on a scrap of plywood or hardboard. Then begin punching. Tap the awl into the metal until the point just begins to break through and creates a small hole; remove the awl, and repeat at the next point in your pattern. (See Figure 9.) Get comfortable before you start this step; it takes a *long* time.

> **Tip ◆** As you work, the metal will want to curl up on you. You can prevent this by tacking down the corners of the sheet to the plywood backing.

When you've finished punching the patterns, remove the remains of the paper and wash the metal off with acetone. This will remove any rubber cement or adhesive still on the metal. Straighten the sheets, if necessary, then mount them in the door frames with glazing points.

LOWER DOOR PANEL PATTERN

Finally, reassemble the doors and drawer to the case, and install all the hardware. Nail the top and bottom back sheets in place with small brads. Then, if you're so inclined, bake a pie to celebrate the completion of your pie safe.

BILL OF MATERIALS — Pie Safe

Finished Dimensions in Inches

A.	Sides (2)	¾ x 16 x 62
B.	Shelves (3)	¾ x 16 x 29¼
C.	Work shelf	¾ x 17½ x 30
D.	Half shelf	¾ x 10 x 28½
E.	Backstop	¾ x 3 x 28½
F.	Top frame stiles (2)	¾ x 1½ x 12
G.	Bottom frame stiles (2)	¾ x 1½ x 31¼
H.	Top frame/bottom frame upper rails (2)	¾ x 1 x 27
J.	Bottom frame middle rail	¾ x 1½ x 27
K.	Valance	¾ x 2 x 27
L.	Skirt	¾ x 3 x 27
M.	Top door stiles (4)	¾ x 1½ x 9¾
N.	Bottom door stiles (4)	¾ x 1½ x 22½
P.	Door rails (8)	¾ x 1½ x 13⅞
Q.	Drawer face	⅜ x 4¾ x 27¾
R.	Drawer front/back (2)	¾ x 3½ x 26

S.	Drawer sides (2)	¾ x 3½ x 13¼
T.	Drawer bottom	¼ x 13¼ x 25¼
U.	Cutting board	¾ x 14 x 16
V.	Top back	¼ x 10 x 29¼
W.	Bottom back	¼ x 29¼ x 29⅜
X.	Shims (2)	¾ x 2 x 15¾

Hardware

14″ Full-extension slides with mounting screws (1 pair)
Self-closing hinges for ⅜″ inset doors, with screws (4 pair)
Door/drawer pulls (6)
Pin-style shelf supports (4)
#8 x 1¼″ Flathead wood screws (2-3 dozen)
1″ Brads (2-3 dozen)
11⅜″ x 20″ sheets of tin, copper, or brass (2)
11⅜″ x 7¼″ sheets of tin, copper, or brass (2)

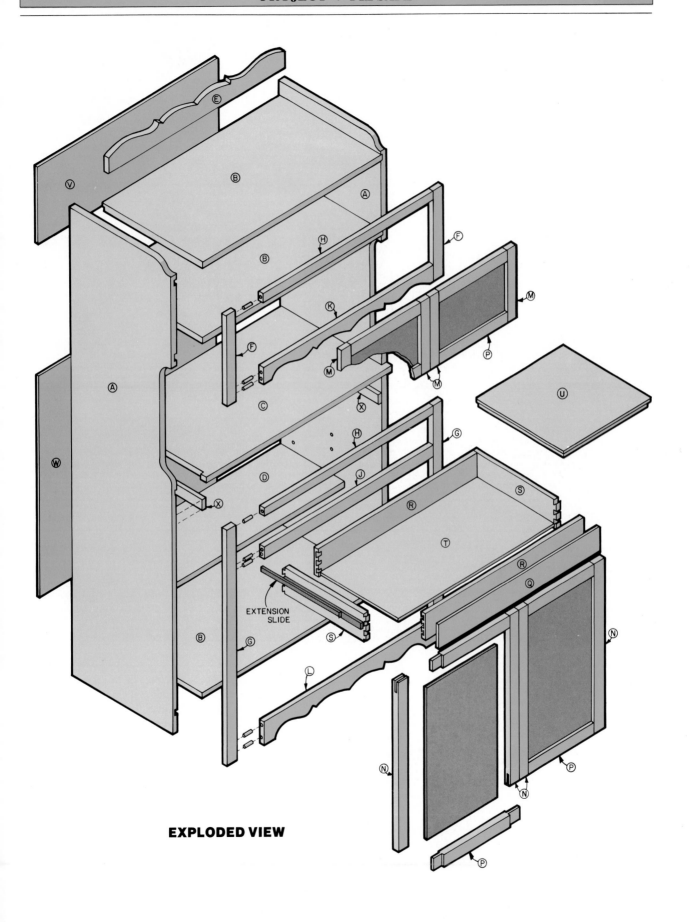

EXTENSION SLIDE

EXPLODED VIEW

Designed and Built by Harry Cooper

Doll Cradle

This doll-sized cradle is just the place for a cherished playmate to rest her head.

Every doll needs a cradle — just ask any child. How else do you rock your playmate to sleep? This colonial-design cradle makes a wonderful place for a doll to bed down.

This project was designed by Harry Cooper, a prolific woodworker from Vine Grove, Kentucky. Although Harry pretends to be retired, he turns out dozens of projects from his home shop. This cradle is just one of his designs. Harry explains that several of the details on this doll cradle are optional, such as the edge treatment or the contours of the headboard. "If you don't like them," says Harry, "just change them to suit yourself."

Another option you have when building this project is the dimensions. Harry designed this cradle so that it was exactly *half* as big as a full-size cradle. Should you want to make this project for a full-size baby, simply use 1″ thick stock and increase all the other dimensions in the plans by two.

Making the Cradle

Cut all parts to size. Rip the bottoms of the sides, headboard, and footboard at 10°. Also, taper the ends of these pieces at 10°. This tapering can be done easily with a tapering jig. (See Figure 1.)

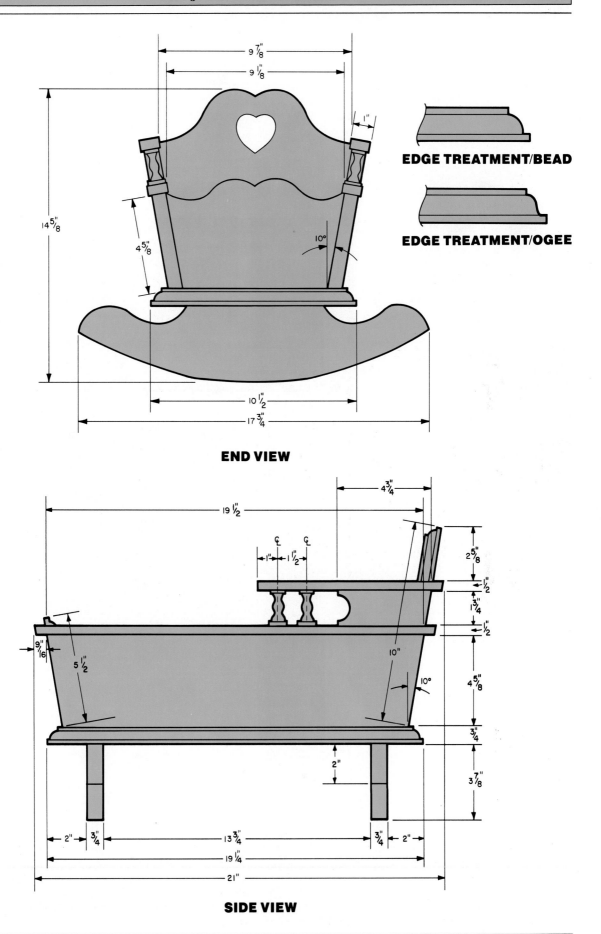

EDGE TREATMENT/BEAD

EDGE TREATMENT/OGEE

END VIEW

SIDE VIEW

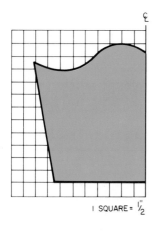

I SQUARE = 1/2"

**FOOTBOARD
PATTERN**

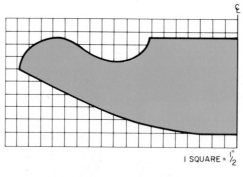

I SQUARE = 1/2"

ROCKER PATTERN

I SQUARE = 1/8"

**SPINDLE
PATTERN**

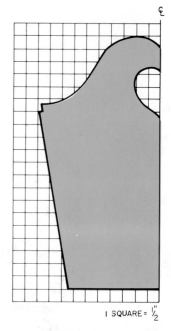

I SQUARE = 1/2"

**HEADBOARD
PATTERN**

Using a bandsaw or a jigsaw, cut the outside patterns in the sunshields, headboard, footboard, and rockers. The wood grain in the rockers should be running *horizontally* — lengthwise through the rockers. If the wood grain is oriented improperly, the ends of the rockers may break off sooner or later.

Turn the galley spindles on your lathe. You can also purchase these spindles from several different mail order sources, such as:

The Woodworkers' Store
21801 Industrial Blvd.
Rogers, MN 55374

To cut out the decorative hole in the headboard, make a piercing cut with a jigsaw or sabre saw. Sand all the contoured edges, inside and out, to remove any mill marks.

If you wish, shape the edges of the base, the top edges of the headboard and footboard, and the inside edge of the decorative hole in the headboard. (See Figure 2.) Use a router and a bit with a pilot. Harry uses a piloted ogee bit to shape the edges of his cradles.

Finish sand all surfaces, then assemble the rockers, base, and stretchers with glue and wood screws. While the glue is drying on this assembly, glue and nail the sides, headboard,

and footboard together. Sand all the corners flush, and cover the heads of any screws or finishing nails that you don't want to show. Then put the two assemblies together with glue and nails.

Drill holes in all the rails for the spindles. Notch the side rails so that they fit around the headboard, then attach these rails to the sides with glue and brads. Attach the sunshields, spindles, and sunshield rails in the same manner.

Finish the cradle with a non-toxic finish. You can use mineral oil, 'salad-bowl dressing', or Danish oil. If you use Danish oil, remember that this finish doesn't become non-toxic until it has set up for a few weeks.

Figure 1. Use a tapering jig to cut the ends of the headboard, footboard, and sides at 10°.

Figure 2. Use a piloted bit to shape both the inside and outside edges of the headboard and footboard contours.

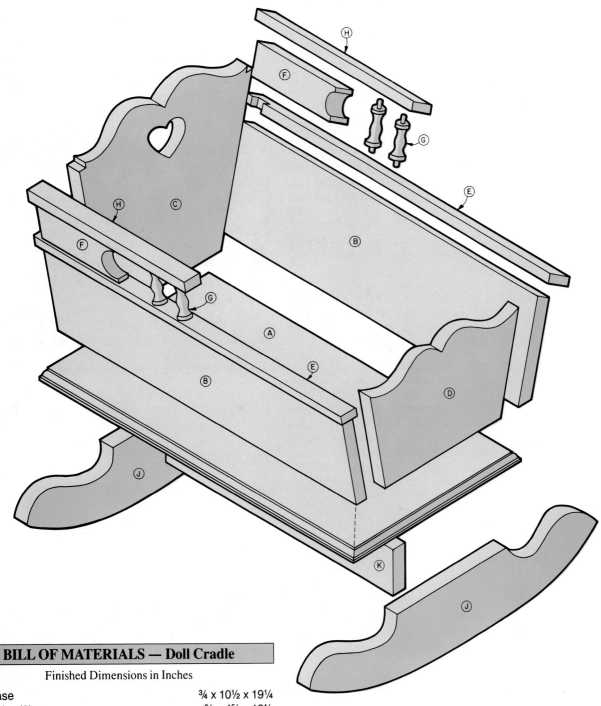

BILL OF MATERIALS — Doll Cradle

Finished Dimensions in Inches

A.	Base	¾ x 10½ x 19¼
B.	Sides (2)	¾ x 4⅝ x 19½
C.	Headboard	¾ x 10 x 10⅞
D.	Footboard	¾ x 5½ x 10
E.	Side rails (2)	½ x 1 x 20⅝
F.	Sunshields (2)	¾ x 1¾ x 4¾
G.	Spindles (4)	⅞ dia. x 1¾
H.	Sunshield rails (2)	½ x 1 x 9½
J.	Rockers (2)	¾ x 3⅞ x 17¾
K.	Stretcher	¾ x 2 x 13¾

Hardware

#8 x 1¼" Flathead wood screws (8)

4d Finishing nails (2 dozen)

1" Brads (16)

EXPLODED VIEW

Enlarging Patterns with a Photocopier

Enlarging patterns is always something of a bother. The pantograph is awkward, and the squares method takes too long. Well, now there's a little help from a new technological marvel — the variable reducing/enlarging photocopier.

Many small 'quick print' shops have these machines. Call around until you find one, then have them enlarge the patterns you want by photocopying them straight out of the book. All you need to do is figure the *percentage* of enlargement required.

◆ For example, let's say that you want to enlarge a pattern to 12″ long. It's printed in the book 2½″ long. Simply divide the size you need by the size in the book.

$$12 \div 2.5 = 4.8$$

You need to enlarge the pattern 480%.

Most photocopiers will only enlarge up to 140%. So what do you do? Enlarge the patterns several times, photocopying the photocopies until you get it as big as you need it. (See Figure A.) To figure out how many times you need to enlarge a pattern, and at what percentage, first find out what is the maximum enlargement of the machine. Let's say it's an average machine and its enlargement capacity is 140%. Multiply 1.4 times itself until you get a number bigger than 4.8.

$$1.4 \times 1.4 \times 1.4 \times 1.4 \text{ (four times)} = 5.378$$

Drop down to three times, so that you get a number *smaller* than 4.8.

$$1.4 \times 1.4 \times 1.4 \text{ (three times)} = 3.842$$

If you enlarge the pattern three times at 140%, you'll end up with a 384% enlargement. That isn't quite as big as you need, so to find the percentage of the final enlargement, divide the percentage you need by 384.

$$480 \div 384 = 1.25$$

Make the last enlargement at 125%, and you'll have the 480% enlargement that you wanted. For those of you that have a mind for numbers, here's the equation:

$$\frac{A}{(B)^C} \times 100 = X$$

Where:

A = Percentage enlargement needed.

B = Maximum enlargement percentage of the copier.

C = Number of times that you enlarge the pattern at the maximum percentage without exceeding the percentage enlargement needed.

X = Percentage of the final enlargement.

◆ If the enlargement starts getting larger than the paper in the photocopier, break the pattern into segments and enlarge those. Then assemble the entire pattern with tape.

◆ One more tip concerning photocopied patterns. You can transfer the pattern to the wood by simply ironing the pattern with a dry iron!

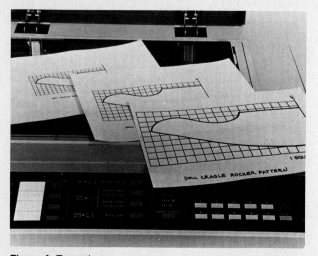

Figure A. To get the size enlargement you need, you may have to copy the pattern over several times on the photocopier.

Designed and Built by Thomas Stender

Blanket Chest

Dovetail joinery makes this simple chest a true classic.

The blanket chest — sometimes called the six-board chest — is possibly the oldest American furniture form. It was indispensable to the early settlers of this country.

The design is wonderfully utilitarian. This simple box can be used for dozens of purposes. It was used by the colonists first as a suitcase. They packed up their belongings in chests like these to ship them across the Atlantic, then overland to their final destination. Once they arrived at their new wilderness home, the owners continued to store their personal effects in these chests. They lived 'out of their suitcases', so to speak, since they had no dressers or closets. The six-board chests often did double-duty as beds, benches, and sideboards. These chests were large enough for a child or

a small adult to sleep on, wide enough for anyone to sit on, and they made a handy place to set things when you were short of table space. Sometimes, they were used for protection — colonists hid behind them or in them during Indian raids. Now and then, you can find an old, old chest that still bears the scars of such attacks.

As the colonies began to prosper, and the colonists acquired more and more furniture, the role of the six-board chest became more limited. By the late eighteenth century, they were most commonly used to store linens and bedding. Sometimes, the colonists would line their old chests with cedar to keep the moths out and help prevent mildew. They became true 'blanket' chests.

The chest you see here was designed and built by Thomas Stender, a professional cabinetmaker who specializes in classical furniture. He built this chest along classical lines. In keeping with tradition, the sides and ends are dovetailed together. (See Figure 1.) The dovetail was the strongest corner joint the colonists could make. This strength was necessary for the chest to survive all its different roles.

They aren't necessary today, of course. But they serve another purpose. The dovetails add grace and beauty to what would otherwise be an austere piece of furniture.

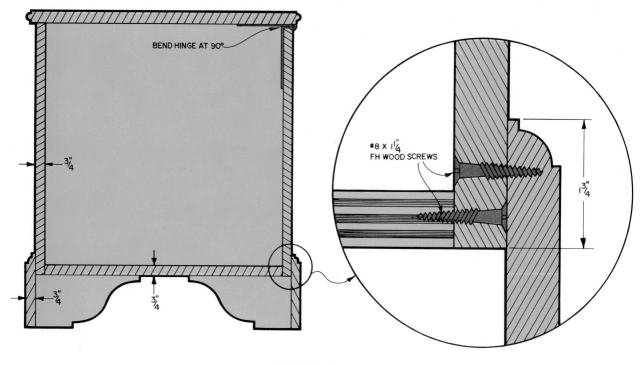

BEND HINGE AT 90°

#8 X 1¼"
FH WOOD SCREWS

1¾"

¾"

¾"

¾"

SECTION A

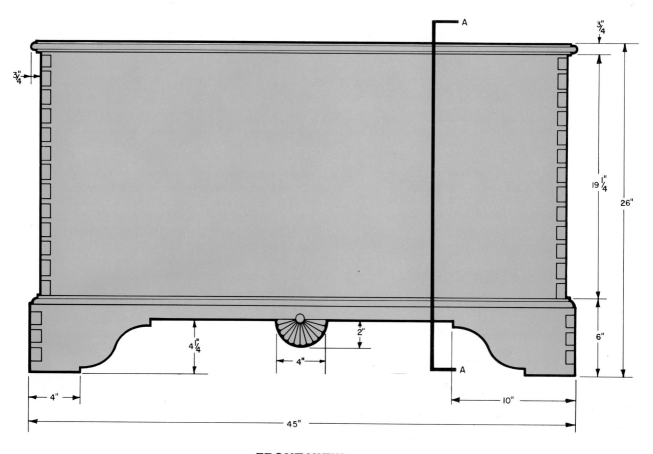

A

¾"

¾"

19¼"

26"

6"

2"

4¼"

4"

4"

10"

45"

FRONT VIEW

Choosing and Gluing Up Stock

This project requires six wide boards — wider than what you can normally find at a lumberyard. You can make one of these pieces — the bottom — from plywood, but you'll have to glue up stock for the other five.

Before gluing up the stock, give some careful thought to the wood you're going to use. The lid board is not reinforced; other than the hinge strap, there is nothing to keep it from cupping. To be sure that the lid will remain fairly flat over the years, you should use a wood that doesn't expand and contract a great deal with changes in humidity and temperature. Avoid open-grain woods — these absorb the moisture in the air more readily than close-grain woods. Tom made this chest from sugar maple; hard maple or cherry would also be good choices.

Make sure that the wood has been properly dried before you use it. The moisture content should be 10% or less. Kiln-dried lumber may serve you best, since it's dried to 7%-8%. If you use air-dried lumber, refer to the chapter on "Drying Your Own Lumber" in the **Techniques** section to see how to calculate the moisture content.

If you can get it, use quarter-sawn or rift-sawn lumber. These types of lumber are cut *perpendicular* to the annual growth rings in the tree. It's these rings that are responsible for cupping. The rings seem to want to straighten out. Consequently, the wood cups in the opposite direction than the growth rings are curved. In quarter-sawn and rift-sawn lumber, the growth rings curve through the thickness of the board, not the width. (See Figure 2.) The curves of the rings are much shorter, and the tendency of the wood to cup is much decreased.

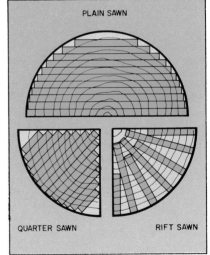

Figure 1. The sides and ends of the blanket chest are dovetailed together.

Figure 2. In quarter-sawn and rift-sawn lumber, the annual growth rings run perpendicular to the width of the board. In plain-sawn lumber the growth rings run through the width, making it prone to cupping.

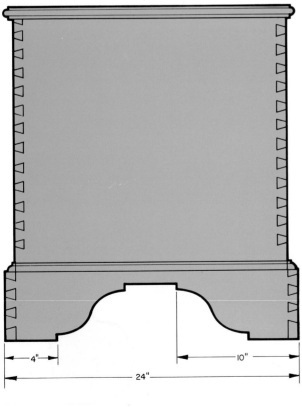

SIDE VIEW

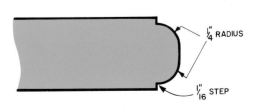

LID EDGE PROFILE

If you use plain-sawn lumber, take some extra care when you glue up the stock for the sides, ends, and lid. Make sure that the growth rings in the sides and ends all curve in the same direction, towards the *outside*. (See Figure 3.) The wood will want to cup towards the inside, but this tendency is easily controlled by the joinery. The dovetail joints at the corners will keep the sides and ends flat.

When you're gluing up the stock for the lid, *alternate* the direction of the rings — one up, one down, one up, etc. Use fairly narrow boards, no wider than 5"-6". This way, if the wood does cup, the whole lid won't cup in one direction. The surface may get a little 'wavy', but it will still lay fairly flat on the chest.

Tip ◆ No matter what kind of wood you use, don't glue it up immediately upon bringing it into your shop. Let it sit for a few weeks and give it time to adjust to new temperature and humidity levels.

Making the Chest

Cut the parts of the chest to size, then cut the dovetails in the sides, ends, and skirts. For a detailed explanation of how to make these dovetails, see "The Dovetail Joint" chapter in the **Techniques** section. Remember, cut the tails in the end pieces, and the pins in the side pieces.

Tip ◆ You may find it difficult cutting dovetails in these large pieces on the bandsaw. If this is the case, use a dovetail saw or a hand-held sabre saw.

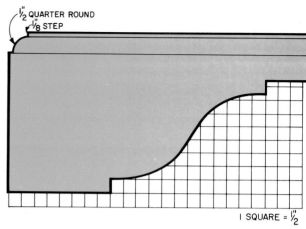

FOOT PATTERN

I SQUARE = 1/2"

Dry assemble the sides, ends, bottom, and skirts to check the fit. When you're satisfied with the way all the parts fit together, disassemble them.

Shape the skirts as indicated in the working drawings. First, shape the top edge with a 1/2" quarter-round shaper cutter or router bit. Using a bandsaw, cut the design in the skirts. If you wish, carve a small shell in the front skirt. The shell carving is a traditional classic motif that was used often in furniture making during the eighteenth century.

Sand all the parts of the chest, then reassemble them with glue and wood screws. The ends and sides don't have to

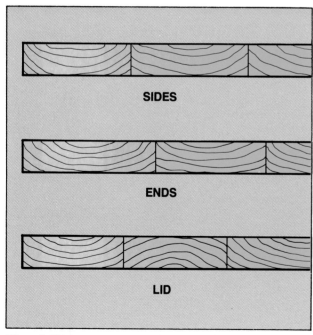

SIDES

ENDS

LID

Figure 3. Glue up the sides and ends so that the growth rings are all oriented in the same direction. Glue up the lid so that the direction of the rings alternates.

Figure 4. Attach the bottom to the chest by passing screws through from the *outside* of the sides and ends. Attach the skirt by passing screws through from the *inside*. The skirts will hide the bottom screws, and no screw heads should be visible from the outside.

be screwed together, of course, since they are held together by dovetails. However, the bottom is held in place with screws, as are the skirts. Attach the bottom first, passing the screws through the sides and ends from the outside. Then put the skirt pieces in place, and attach them by passing the screws through the sides and ends from the *inside*. (See Figure 4.) This way, the skirt will cover the screws that hold the bottom in place, and no screws will be visible from the outside.

There are several ways to hinge the lid to the chest. Perhaps the easiest is to cut a long ⅛″ deep mortise along the edge of the back side and install a piano hinge. There are also several makes of 'concealed' hinges for full overlay doors and lids that would work. Some of these are available through the mail; others you may be able to find in a hardware store.

To keep this project authentic, Tom decided to use cast iron strap hinges, such as might have been made by colonial blacksmiths. However, in order to get this hinge to work properly and to keep it concealed *inside* the chest, he had to put a 90° bend in one strap. (See Figure 5.) To make this bend, heat up the metal strap with a welding torch. When it glows a dull red, bend it over with a long pair of tongs. Let the metal cool, then repaint it a flat black.

After you've hinged the lid to the chest, remove the hardware. Finish sand any parts that still need it. Apply finish to the wood parts, and reinstall the hardware.

> **Tip ◆** Apply just as many coats of finish to the inside of the chest as you did to the outside. This will help keep the wood from changing shape as the weather changes.

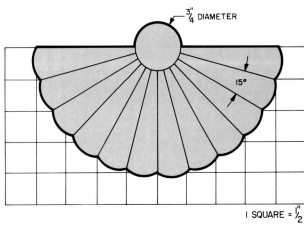

SHELL PATTERN

Lining the Chest

If you wish, line the chest with ¼″ thick cedar boards. The technique is simple — line the bottom first, then the sides and ends. Tack the cedar in place with brads. There's no sense in trying to use glue since you've already sealed the inside of the chest and the glue won't penetrate the pores of the wood. Cut out the cedar boards around the hinges, and chamfer the edges of the cutouts. (See Figure 6.)

Do not apply a finish to the cedar. This will defeat the whole purpose of the cedar lining. A finish will seal in the oils that give the cedar its aroma. If the oils are sealed in, the cedar loses its ability to repel insects and freshen the linens.

Figure 5. If you use cast iron strap hinges, as Tom did, you'll need to put a 90° bend in one strap on each hinge.

Figure 6. Cut out the cedar lining to go around the hinges.

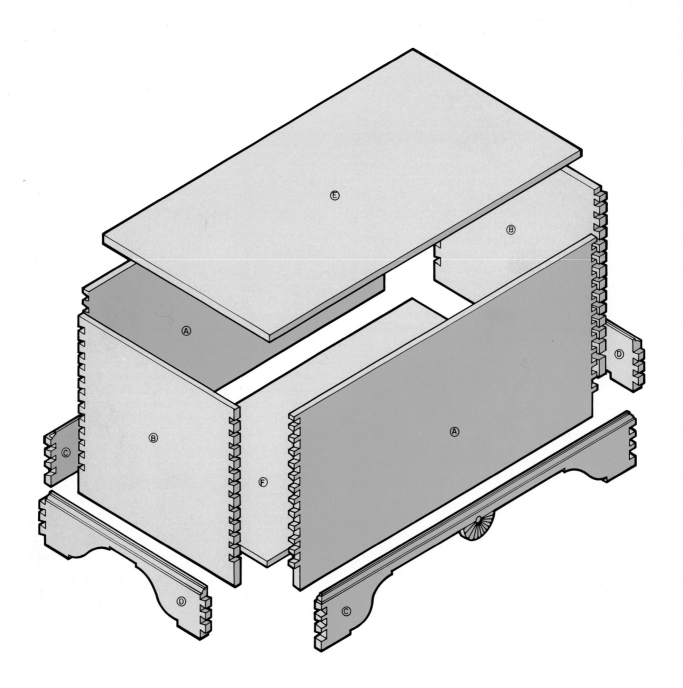

EXPLODED VIEW

BILL OF MATERIALS — Blanket Chest	
Finished Dimensions in Inches	
A. Front/Back (2)	¾ x 21 x 43½
B. Ends (2)	¾ x 21 x 22½
C. Front/Back Feet (2)	¾ x 6 x 45
D. End Feet (2)	¾ x 6 x 24
F. Bottom	¾ x 21 x 42
G. Cedar Lining (optional)	¾ x 3⅜ x 756 (total)

Hardware

Wrought iron strap hinges and mounting screws (1 pair)

Designed and Built by Nick Engler

Writing Table

A slight bevel on the front edge of this desk helps to make writing more comfortable.

I f you've ever been forced to sit at a desk for a long time — typing reports, paying bills, or writing chapters for woodworking yearbooks — then you know how poorly designed most desk tops really are. The edge of the desk catches you somewhere between your wrist and your forearm. It doesn't bother you at first, but after a while, that edge presses against your arm like a blunt knife.

I put up with ordinary desks and typing tables for a long time. But recently, I designed and built a desk that makes writing for long stretches or doing the monthly balancing act with the checkbook much more endurable. The front edge of the desk you see here is *beveled* at the same angle that my arm hits it when I'm resting my fingers on the computer keys. With this setup, my wrist is supported by a flat surface — not a knife's edge. Build one of these and try it for yourself. You won't believe the difference that simple little change makes.

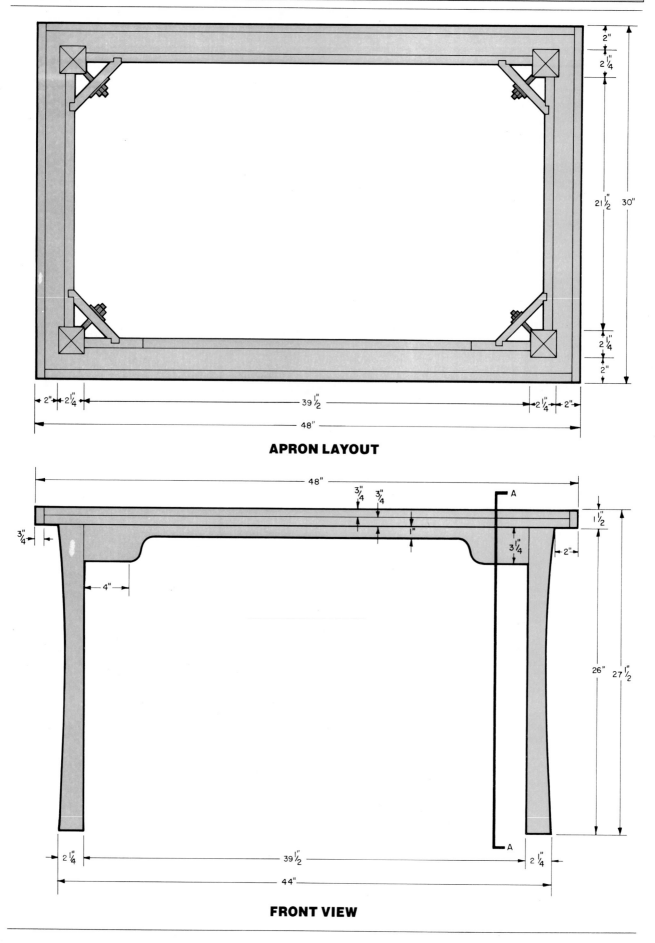

APRON LAYOUT

FRONT VIEW

Making the Top

Make the top of the table from hardwood-veneered plywood. You can make the table from solid wood, but plywood will save you some headaches later on. It doesn't expand and contract with the weather nearly as much as solid wood. The top will remain flat longer, and the joints between the top and the side moldings won't be strained by changes in temperature and humidity.

Cut the plywood top and the moldings to size, and set them aside. Glue up the stock for the beveled front edge, then rip the edge at 15°. You'll find it's easier and safer to make this rip cut on a bandsaw. (See Figure 1.)

Dowel the top, moldings, and front edge together. Note that all dowel holes are *blind* — you shouldn't be able to see any of them once the top is assembled. To properly position these blind holes, use dowel centers and work in this sequence: First drill dowel holes in all edges of the top, and in the ends of the front edge, where shown in the working drawings. Put dowel centers in the holes in the front and back of the top, and press the back molding and the front edge in place. The centers will leave small indentations where you want to drill the matching dowel holes. (See Figure 2.)

Drill the holes in the front edge and back molding, then *dry* assemble these parts to the top. *Do not* use glue at this time. With these parts assembled, put dowel centers in the holes in the sides of the top and the ends of the front edge.

Figure 1. Rip the beveled front edge on a bandsaw, with the table tilted at 15°.

Figure 2. Use dowel centers to help locate the dowel holes in the moldings and front edge.

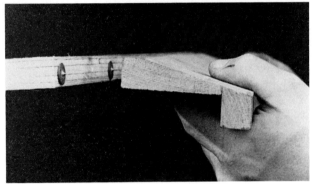

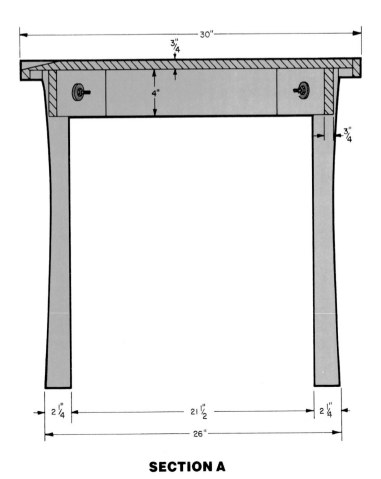

SECTION A

FRONT APRON LAYOUT

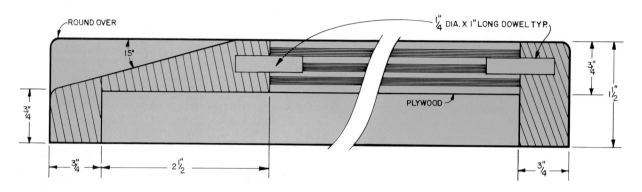

ROUND OVER

15°

¼" DIA. X 1" LONG DOWEL TYP.

PLYWOOD

¾"

1½"

¾"

2½"

¾"

¾"

¾"

FRONT EDGE AND MOLDING DETAIL

Press the side moldings in place, then drill dowel holes wherever the centers left an indentation.

Dry assemble all parts to check the fit. When you're satisfied that everything fits correctly, reassemble the parts with glue. Clamp the molding and the edge to the top, and let the glue cure under pressure.

> **Tip ◆** If you don't have bar clamps long enough to clamp up the top assembly, you can make one long bar clamp out of two shorter ones. Just hook the sliding faces together as shown. (See Figure 3.)

Making the Apron

As designed, this is a 'knock-down' table. The legs can be detached so that you can store or move the table easily. The legs mount to the aprons with 'hanger bolts' and 'hanger blocks'. You can buy hanger bolts in most hardware stores, but hanger blocks are a little harder to come by. You can get them through the mail from some of the bigger hardware suppliers, or you can make your own.

To make a hanger block, you have to make four cuts in each end of the block, all at 45°. Adjust your table cut to the proper angle, then make the V-grooves near the end on the blocks. (See Figure 4.) Use the rip fence as a guide.

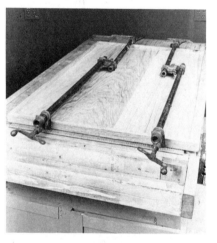

Figure 3. You can make one long bar clamp out of two short ones. Just hook the sliding faces together.

Figure 4. Making the V-groove in the hanger block requires two separate cuts, both at 45°. Use the rip fence as a guide.

Figure 5. After cutting the V-groove, make the 'short' miter on the ends of the blocks.

Figure 6. After cutting the 'short' miter, cut the 'long' one. The rip fence must be positioned very accurately when you make these last two cuts. You want a double miter on the end of the block, but you don't want to shorten the block with the miter cuts.

After you've made the grooves, miter the ends. This miter requires two separate cuts — a 'short' miter and a 'long' miter. (See Figures 5 and 6.) Once again, use the rip fence as a guide. To complete the hanger blocks, drill a hole in the center of each block for the hanger bolts.

> **Tip** ◆ The rip fence must be positioned *very* accurately for these two miter cuts. If the fence is too close to the blade, you'll shorten the block on the second-to-the-last pass, and the last miter cut will be way off.

Cut the aprons to length. Make the cutout in the front apron on your bandsaw, and round over the bottom edge of the cutout with a rasp or ¼" quarter-round shaper cutter. Using a dado blade, cut dadoes in the inside faces of all the aprons to fit the hanger blocks.

The apron is screwed to the top, and the screws sit in screw pockets on the inside faces of the aprons. These pockets must be made before you assemble the aprons.

To make a screw pocket, tilt the table of your drill press at 15°. Using a ½" brad-point bit or Forstener bit, drill a 'pocket' in the inside face of the apron. (See Figure 7.) *Do not* drill all the way through the wood. Stop the hole ½"-¾" above the work surface. Change to a ³⁄₁₆" bit — this bit is about the same diameter as the screw shank. Complete the hole with the smaller bit. The shank hole should emerge from the center of the top edge of the apron. (See Figure 8.)

Finish sand the aprons, then assemble the aprons and hanger bolts with glue and wood screws. Then set the assembly aside for the glue to dry.

Making the Legs

Cut the legs to length, and drill a hole in the inside corner for the hanger bolts. However, *do not* install the hanger bolts just yet.

As shown, the legs have a 'reverse' taper cut into the two 'outside' faces. Make this taper with a compound cut on your bandsaw. Cut the first curve, tape the waste back to the leg, and cut the second curve. (See Figure 9.) Sand the millmarks from the curves by 'rocking' a belt sander back and forth along the length of the leg.

> **Tip** ◆ You can change the entire appearance of the table by simply changing the legs. A straight leg or an ordinary table will give the table a country look. Turned legs let it fit in among colonial and classical surroundings.

Figure 7. With a ½" bit, drill screw 'pockets' on the inside faces of the aprons. Stop the holes ½"-¾" above the work surface, and switch to a ³⁄₁₆" bit. Complete the holes with a smaller bit.

Figure 8. In a screw pocket, the large hole should be slightly bigger than the screw head, and the small hole should be the same size as the screw shank. The shank hole should emerge from the center of the top edge of the apron.

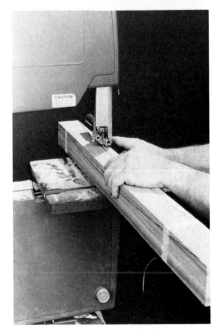

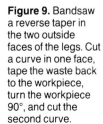

Figure 9. Bandsaw a reverse taper in the two outside faces of the legs. Cut a curve in one face, tape the waste back to the workpiece, turn the workpiece 90°, and cut the second curve.

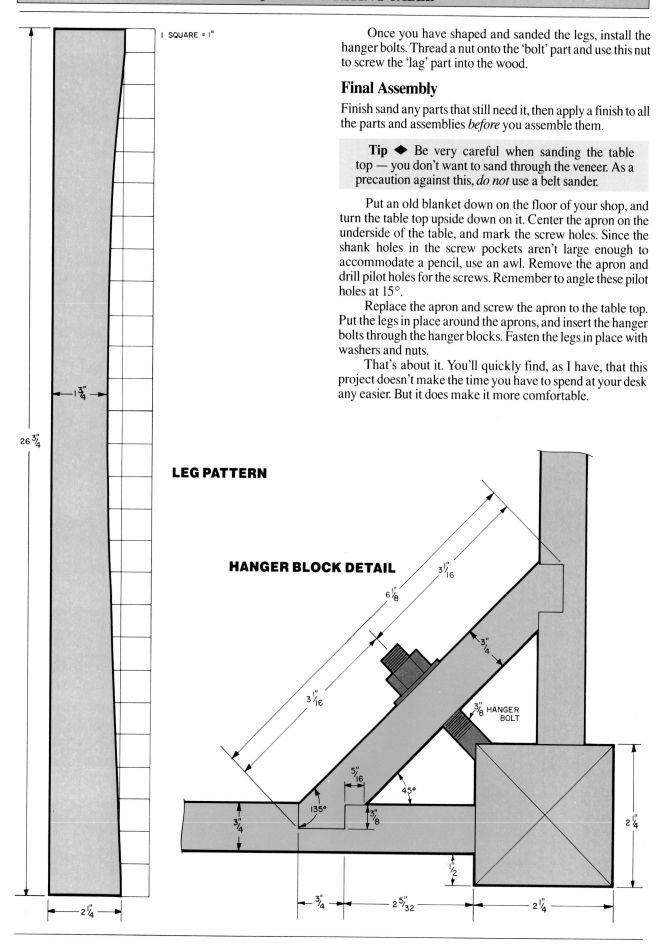

I SQUARE = I"

LEG PATTERN

HANGER BLOCK DETAIL

Once you have shaped and sanded the legs, install the hanger bolts. Thread a nut onto the 'bolt' part and use this nut to screw the 'lag' part into the wood.

Final Assembly

Finish sand any parts that still need it, then apply a finish to all the parts and assemblies *before* you assemble them.

> **Tip** ◆ Be very careful when sanding the table top — you don't want to sand through the veneer. As a precaution against this, *do not* use a belt sander.

Put an old blanket down on the floor of your shop, and turn the table top upside down on it. Center the apron on the underside of the table, and mark the screw holes. Since the shank holes in the screw pockets aren't large enough to accommodate a pencil, use an awl. Remove the apron and drill pilot holes for the screws. Remember to angle these pilot holes at 15°.

Replace the apron and screw the apron to the table top. Put the legs in place around the aprons, and insert the hanger bolts through the hanger blocks. Fasten the legs in place with washers and nuts.

That's about it. You'll quickly find, as I have, that this project doesn't make the time you have to spend at your desk any easier. But it does make it more comfortable.

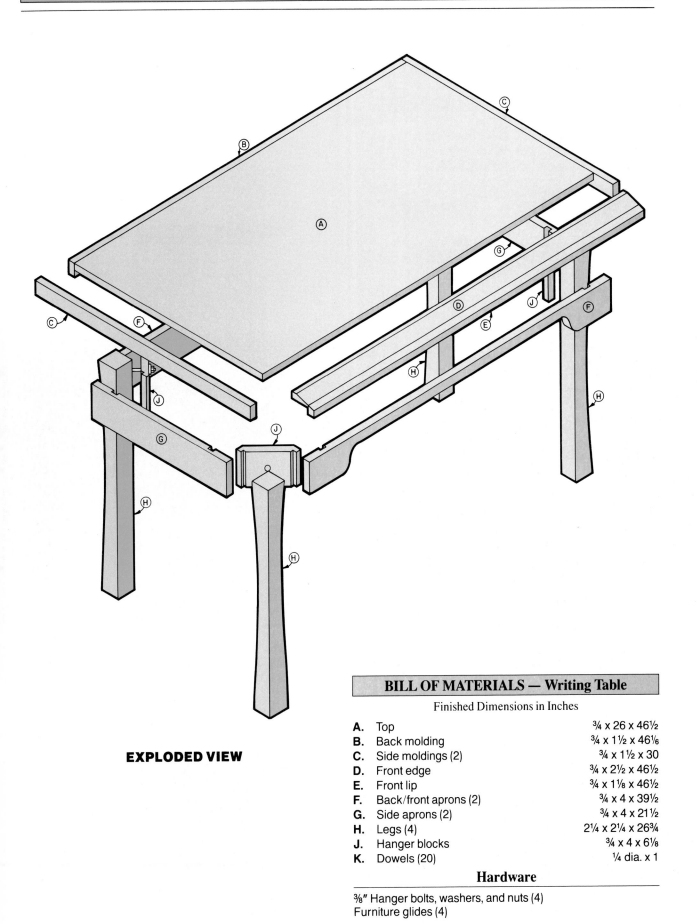

EXPLODED VIEW

BILL OF MATERIALS — Writing Table

Finished Dimensions in Inches

A.	Top	¾ x 26 x 46½
B.	Back molding	¾ x 1½ x 46⅙
C.	Side moldings (2)	¾ x 1½ x 30
D.	Front edge	¾ x 2½ x 46½
E.	Front lip	¾ x 1⅛ x 46½
F.	Back/front aprons (2)	¾ x 4 x 39½
G.	Side aprons (2)	¾ x 4 x 21½
H.	Legs (4)	2¼ x 2¼ x 26¾
J.	Hanger blocks	¾ x 4 x 6⅛
K.	Dowels (20)	¼ dia. x 1

Hardware

⅜" Hanger bolts, washers, and nuts (4)
Furniture glides (4)

Designed and Built by Nick Engler

Storage Shed/Greenhouse

This small building can be built as a shed, a greenhouse, or both!

If you have a backyard, you've probably thought about putting up a storage shed. People who have backyards tend to accumulate things like lawn mowers, rakes, shovels, barbecue grills, etc. Sooner or later, people who have backyards put up a storage shed to hold all their backyard stuff.

If you have a backyard *and* you like to grow things, you've probably thought about putting up a greenhouse. People who like to grow things in their backyards like to have a greenhouse so that they can extend the growing season.

The trouble is, you may not have the room or time to build both. Well, here's the solution to your problem. By changing the plans a little to suit your own needs, you can build this backyard building as a storage shed, a greenhouse, or both.

Laying the Foundation

The building is light enough that it doesn't need a heavy-duty foundation. When I put this building up a few years ago, I simply laid some concrete blocks on a bed of gravel. The building is still level, and it hasn't blown away.

Stake out a rectangle 8′ x 10′ where you want to build. If you're building a greenhouse, the 8′ dimension should face east and west, and the 10′ dimensions north and south. Dig a

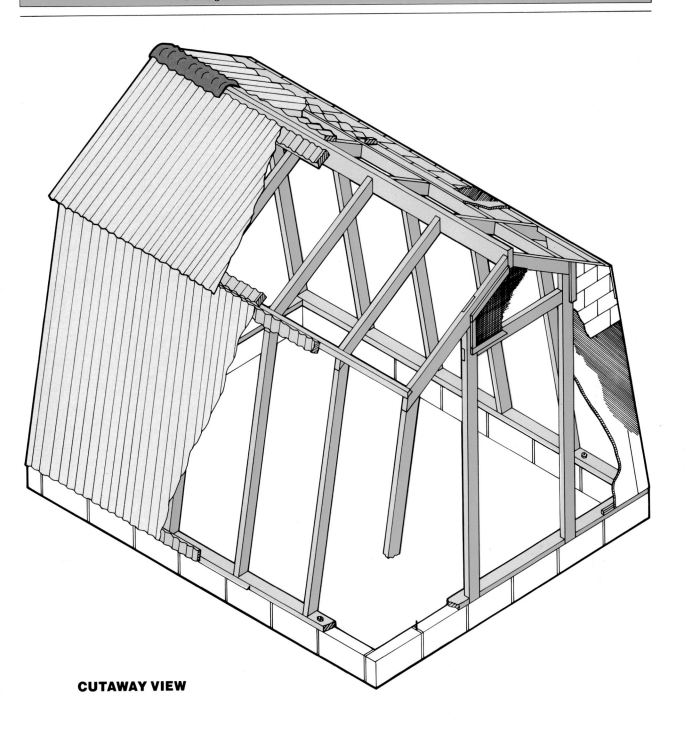

CUTAWAY VIEW

trench 6″ wide and 12″ deep around the perimeter and fill it with 8″ of gravel for drainage. Working with a level, lay 4″ x 8″ x 16″ solid concrete blocks on top of the gravel to make a foundation.

> **Tip ◆** Put the corner blocks in place first and make sure they're level to each other. Then fill in the sides. (See Figure 1.)

If you wish, lay mortar in between the blocks and set anchor bolts in the mortar to hold the base plate to the foundation. (I skipped the anchor bolts, myself. Unless the soil is unstable, the building will stay put without them.)

Figure 1. Put the corner blocks in the foundation first and make sure they're level to one another. Then fill in the sides.

NOTE: Corrugated Fiberglass Glazing and purlins needed only if building Greenhouse/Shed combination.

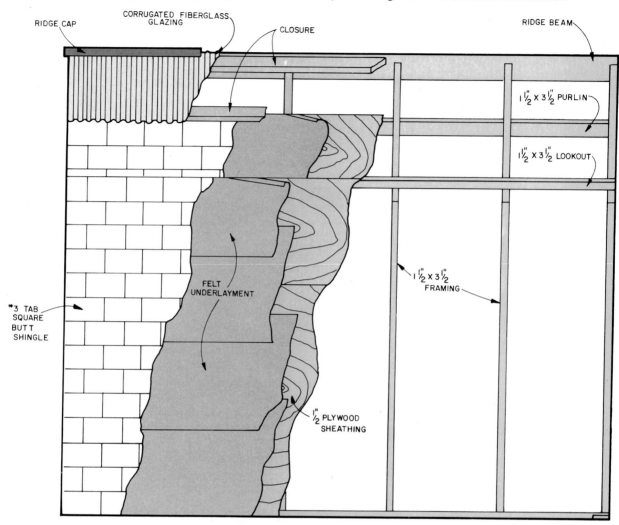

RIDGE CAP

CORRUGATED FIBERGLASS GLAZING

CLOSURE

RIDGE BEAM

$1\frac{1}{2}'' \times 3\frac{1}{2}''$ PURLIN

$1\frac{1}{2}'' \times 3\frac{1}{2}''$ LOOKOUT

$1\frac{1}{2}'' \times 3\frac{1}{2}''$ FRAMING

FELT UNDERLAYMENT

#3 TAB SQUARE BUTT SHINGLE

$\frac{1}{2}''$ PLYWOOD SHEATHING

STORAGE SHED/SIDE VIEW

Figure 2. Cut all dadoes, rabbets, and lap joints in the frame members with a dado blade.

Building the Frame

Cut all the frame members to size at the proper angles. Rip all $1\frac{1}{2}'' \times 1\frac{1}{2}''$ stock (for the door frame and shelf supports) and $\frac{3}{4}'' \times 1\frac{1}{2}''$ stock (for molding, door jamb, window and vent frames, and filler) and $\frac{3}{4}'' \times \frac{3}{4}''$ stock (for window and vent jambs and nailing blocks). Paint all stock with waterproofing stain and set it aside to dry.

Cut all the lap joints, dadoes, and rabbets in the frame members where indicated in the working drawings. (See Figure 2.) This joinery is important; it adds a great deal of strength to the finished structure.

Nail the base plate members together with 8d nails. Since these nails are longer than the lap joints you're driving them through, peen them over on the underside. Drill holes in the base plate for the anchor bolts, if you're using them, then set the base plate in place.

Tip ◆ Use galvanized nails throughout this project. They'll last long in the weather, and they won't stain the wood.

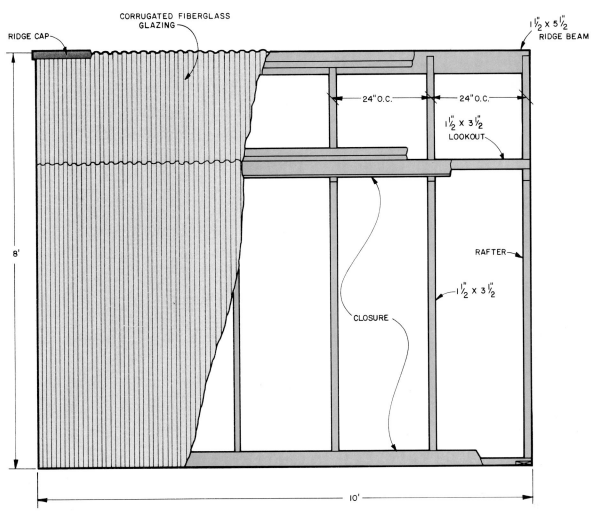

RIDGE CAP

CORRUGATED FIBERGLASS GLAZING

$1\frac{1}{2}'' \times 5\frac{1}{2}''$ RIDGE BEAM

24" O.C.   24" O.C.

$1\frac{1}{2}'' \times 3\frac{1}{2}''$ LOOKOUT

RAFTER

$1\frac{1}{2}'' \times 3\frac{1}{2}''$

CLOSURE

8'

10'

GREENHOUSE/SIDE VIEW

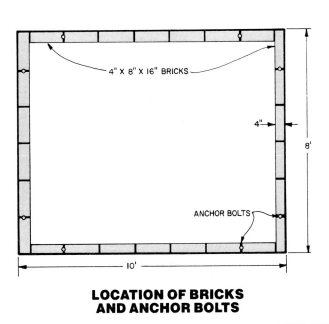

4" X 8" X 16" BRICKS

4"

8'

ANCHOR BOLTS

10'

LOCATION OF BRICKS
AND ANCHOR BOLTS

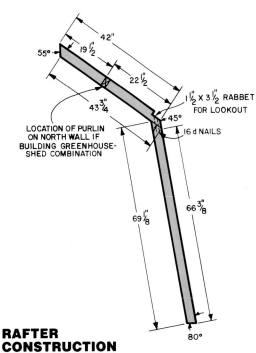

55°

42"

$19\frac{1}{2}$

$22\frac{1}{2}$

$1\frac{1}{2}'' \times 3\frac{1}{2}''$ RABBET FOR LOOKOUT

$43\frac{3}{4}''$

45°

16 d NAILS

LOCATION OF PURLIN ON NORTH WALL IF BUILDING GREENHOUSE-SHED COMBINATION

$69\frac{1}{8}''$

$66\frac{3}{8}''$

80°

RAFTER
CONSTRUCTION

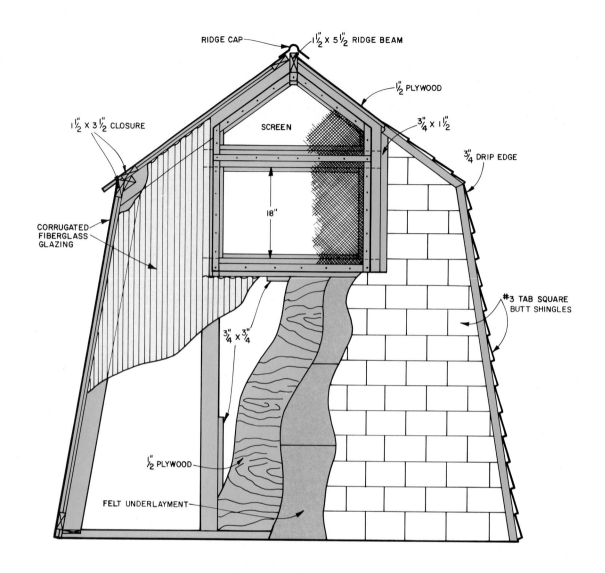

RIDGE CAP

1½" x 5½" RIDGE BEAM

½" PLYWOOD

1½" x 3½" CLOSURE

SCREEN

¾" x 1½"

¾" DRIP EDGE

CORRUGATED
FIBERGLASS
GLAZING

18"

#3 TAB SQUARE
BUTT SHINGLES

¾" x ¾"

½" PLYWOOD

FELT UNDERLAYMENT

**GREENHOUSE/SHED
WINDOW END VIEW**

Figure 3. Assemble the rafters by nailing the upper rafter to the lower one.

Assemble the rafters, nailing the upper rafter to the lower one with 16d nails. (See Figure 3.) Drill undersized pilot holes for the nails to keep the wood from splitting. Once you've assembled the rafters, assemble the front and back frames with #12-1¼" flathead wood screws. Don't attach the shelf supports at this time.

Attach the front and back frame to the base plate. Arm braces staked to the ground will keep them upright while you work. (See Figure 4.) With the front and back frames in place, nail the ridge beam to the frames with 16d nails. Then toenail the rafters to the ridge beam and base plate. (See Figure 5.)

When the rafters are in place, nail the lookouts to them. If you're building a storage shed, nail purlins between the upper rafters where shown. When the lookouts and the purlins are in place, you can remove the arm braces.

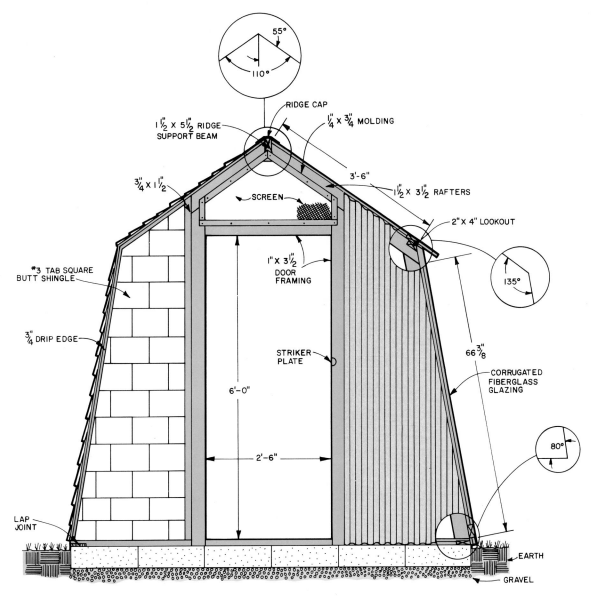

55°

110°

RIDGE CAP

$1\frac{1}{2}$" X $5\frac{1}{2}$" RIDGE SUPPORT BEAM

$\frac{1}{4}$" X $\frac{3}{4}$" MOLDING

3'-6"

$\frac{3}{4}$" X $1\frac{1}{2}$"

$1\frac{1}{2}$" X $3\frac{1}{2}$" RAFTERS

SCREEN

2" X 4" LOOKOUT

#3 TAB SQUARE BUTT SHINGLE

1" X $3\frac{1}{2}$" DOOR FRAMING

135°

$\frac{3}{4}$" DRIP EDGE

STRIKER PLATE

66$\frac{3}{8}$"

CORRUGATED FIBERGLASS GLAZING

6'-0"

80°

2'-6"

LAP JOINT

EARTH

GRAVEL

GREENHOUSE/SHED
DOOR END VIEW

Figure 4. Attach the front and back frames to the base plate. Vertical members fit in the dadoes; rafters are toenailed.

Figure 5. Toenail the rafters to the ridge beam and the base plate. A second pair of hands comes in handy for this step.

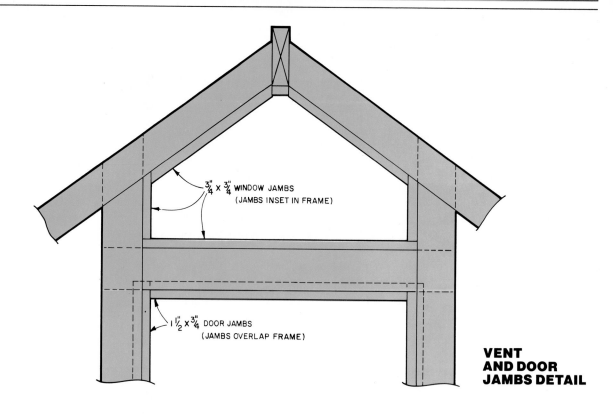

$\frac{3}{4}" \times \frac{3}{4}"$ WINDOW JAMBS
(JAMBS INSET IN FRAME)

$1\frac{1}{2}" \times \frac{3}{4}"$ DOOR JAMBS
(JAMBS OVERLAP FRAME)

**VENT
AND DOOR
JAMBS DETAIL**

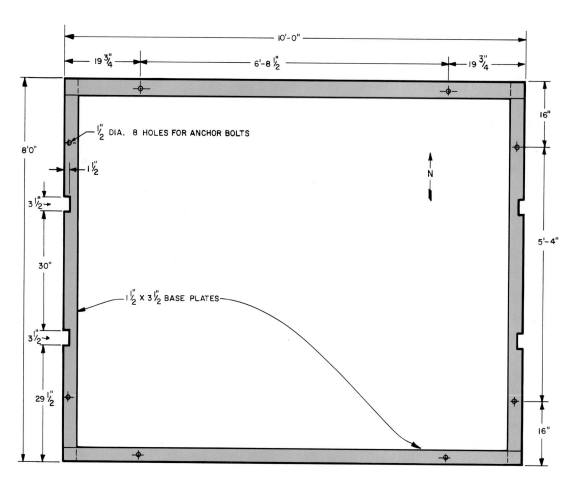

10'-0"

19$\frac{3}{4}$ 6'-8$\frac{1}{2}$ 19$\frac{3}{4}$

16"

$\frac{1}{2}"$ DIA. 8 HOLES FOR ANCHOR BOLTS

8'0"

1$\frac{1}{2}$

3$\frac{1}{2}$

5'-4"

30"

N

3$\frac{1}{2}$

$1\frac{1}{2}" \times 3\frac{1}{2}"$ BASE PLATES

29$\frac{1}{2}$

16"

BASE PLATE DETAIL

If you are building a greenhouse, nail closure strips to the ridge beam, lookouts, and along the bottom of the rafters, just above the base plate. (See Figure 6.) If you're building a storage shed, cover the rafters with ½″ exterior plywood. Nail the plywood on the side walls directly on top of the rafters. However, when covering the front and back walls, use cleats and *inset* the plywood in the frame. (See Figure 7.) Finish the frame by nailing the jambs in place. The door jamb is nailed to the *inside* of the front frame; the window and vent jambs are *inset* in the frame. (The vents are for the greenhouse. If you're building a storage shed, just fill in the vent spaces with plywood.)

Although most of the stock has been painted once, repaint the entire finished frame with waterproofing stain. This will seal the exposed cut ends and provide extra protection from the weather.

Roofing and Glazing

If you're building a storage shed, cover all the plywood surfaces with tarpaper. Cover the front and back walls with shingles, starting at the bottom and working your way up. Use ⅝″ long roofing nails, so that the heads don't come through the plywood on the inside. Nail drip edges along the roof line to cover the shingles on the front and back, then finish by putting shingles on the side walls. (See Figure 8.)

Tip ◆ Don't use black or dark-colored shingles. The shed will heat up like an oven if you do.

If you're building a greenhouse, nail the fiberglass panels to the upper rafters first. (See Figure 9.) Use special nails with rubber seals to attach the panels. Be sure that the upper panels overhang about 2″, so that they will cover the

Figure 6. If you're building a greenhouse, attach closure strips to the ridge beam, lookouts, and along the base of the rafters.

Figure 8. Put shingles on the front and back walls first. Nail drip edge along the roof line, then put shingles on the side walls.

Figure 7. Here's a close-up of the frame, showing how the different parts fit together. The one side of this building serves as a shed, so it's covered with plywood. Notice that the plywood on the side wall is nailed on top of the rafters, while the plywood on the front is inset between the frame members. Also notice that the door jamb is nailed to the inside of the frame, while the upper vent jamb is inset in the frame.

Figure 9. Attach the upper panels first. These panels should overhang the lookouts by about 2″, so that they will cover the lower panels.

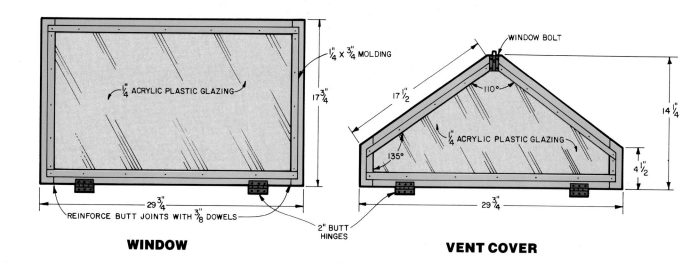

WINDOW

- 1¼" × ¾" MOLDING
- 1¼" ACRYLIC PLASTIC GLAZING
- 17¾"
- 29¾"
- REINFORCE BUTT JOINTS WITH ⅜" DOWELS
- 2" BUTT HINGES

VENT COVER

- WINDOW BOLT
- 17½"
- 110°
- 135°
- ¼" ACRYLIC PLASTIC GLAZING
- 14¼"
- 4½"
- 29¾"

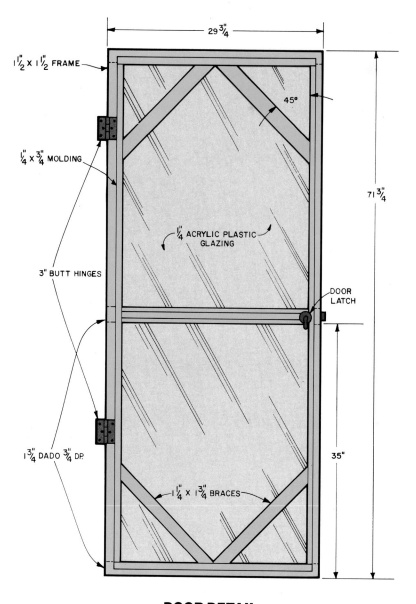

- 29¾"
- 1½" × 1½" FRAME
- 45°
- ¼" × ¾" MOLDING
- ¼" ACRYLIC PLASTIC GLAZING
- 71¾"
- 3" BUTT HINGES
- DOOR LATCH
- 35"
- 1¾" DADO ¾" DP.
- 1¼" × 1¾" BRACES

DOOR DETAIL

lower panels when you attach them. If you're building both a shed and a greenhouse, let the panels overlap the shingles just above the purlins. As you put the upper panels in place, cover the roof peak with aluminum ridge cap. (See Figure 10.)

> **Tip ◆** To cut the fiberglass panels smoothly, turn the blade of your saw around so that the teeth are pointing in the wrong direction.

When you've got the upper panels in place, nail the lower panels to the rafters. Finally, cover the front and back sides wherever you want glazing. However, don't cover the vents or window.

Adding the Door, Window, and Vents

Cut the pieces for the door frame from 1½" x 1½" stock, and make the dadoes and rabbets in the vertical members where shown. Assemble the frame with #12 x 1¼" flathead wood screws. If you're building a storage shed, cover the door with plywood and stain it or paint it. If you're building a greenhouse, cover it with fiberglass glazing.

> **Tip ◆** If you want more security, you can make a solid door from ¾" plywood or lumber. However, remember that this sort of door will be heavier and you'll have to use heavy-duty hinges.

Cut the window frame from ¾" x 1½" stock and dowel it together with ⅜" dowels and waterproof glue. When the glue is dry, rabbet around the inside edge and install clear plastic glazing. Even if you're making a storage shed, I suggest you make a clear window that opens. This will provide for some extra light and ventilation.

The vents are for the greenhouse only. They let the heat escape to keep your plants from burning up. Like the window frame, cut the vent frames from ¾" x 1½" stock and dowel it together. Rabbet the inside edge and install glazing.

Install hinges, latches and window bolts to the completed door, window, and vents. Hang the door on its hinges in the shed/greenhouse frame. Chisel out the frame member where the latch strikes, and install a striker plate.

Hang the window with the hinges towards the ground. Use turn buttons on either side of the window to hold it closed. Gravity will hold it open.

Like the windows, the vents are installed with the hinges down. To hold the vents closed, drill a hole in the ridge beam for the window bolts. To hold them open, and to keep them from flopping all the way down, attach cup hooks to the ridge beam, and screw eyes to the vent frames. Tie a short length (about 14") of string to the hooks and eyes. (See Figure 11.)

Complete the exterior of the building by stapling screen to the frame outside the window and vents. Nail ¼" x ¾" strip molding around the screen to cover the edges.

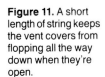

Figure 10. Cover the roof peak with aluminum ridge cap.

Figure 11. A short length of string keeps the vent covers from flopping all the way down when they're open.

Figure 12. The shelves in this shed/greenhouse are adjustable. You can remove them or add them as needed.

Adding Shelving

Whether you're building a greenhouse or a shed, you'll need shelving inside this structure. I've designed a simple system of adjustable shelving to accommodate whatever you have to store — or grow. (See Figure 12.)

Dig holes 12″ deep and 6″ in diameter in the floor of the building where the ends of the vertical shelf support will be buried. Use a plumb bob to locate these holes. Cut the vertical and horizontal shelf supports for the four middle shelf support assemblies from 1½″ x 1½″ stock. Nail the upper ends of the vertical supports to the rafters, then nail the horizontal shelf supports in place between the vertical supports and the rafters. If the wood tends to split, drill pilot holes.

Partially fill the holes around the lower ends of the vertical shelf supports with gravel for drainage, then fill the rest of the holes with earth and tamp it down. Check your work with a level to be sure that the vertical supports remain level.

Cut the horizontal shelf supports for the two *end* shelf support assemblies from ¾″ x 1½″ stock. Nail these to the front and back wall frames.

If you're building a storage shed, cut a length of board or plywood to lay across the shelf supports. If you're building a greenhouse, cut ¾″ x ¾″ strips of wood. Arrange these strips on the supports with spaces in between. This will let the sunlight through the shelves to the plants beneath them.

This chapter was adapted from a project plan originally published by Shopsmith, Inc. Our thanks for their permission to use it here.

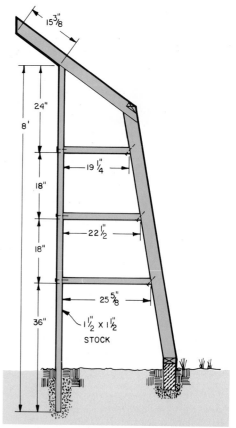

SHELF SUPPORTS DETAIL

BILL OF MATERIALS
Storage Shed/Greenhouse

Shopping List for Lumber and Building Materials*

2 x 4 x 10′	18 pieces	2d Finishing nails	½ lb.
2 x 4 x 8′	8 pieces	Aluminum nails with rubber seals	200 pieces
2 x 6 x 10′	1 piece		
½″ x 4′ x 8′ C-DX plywood	4 sheets	⅝″ Roofing nails	2 lbs.
Redwood closure	60 linear feet	⅜″ Staples	¼ box
1½″ x 1½″ (2 x 2)	94 linear feet**	#12 x 1¼″ Flathead wood screws	54 pieces
¾″ x 1½″ (1 x 2)	87 linear feet**	3″ Butt hinges and screws	1 pair
¾″ x ¾″ (1 x 1)	102 linear feet**	2″ Butt hinges and screw	3 pair
¼″ x ¾″	18 linear feet**	Turn buttons and screws	2 pieces
4″ x 8″ x 16″ Concrete blocks	26 pieces	Cup hooks	2 pieces
2′ x 12′ Corrugated clear fiberglass panels	7 pieces	Eye screws	2 pieces
Aluminum window screen	12 square feet	String	28 inches
Ready-mix mortar	1 bag (70 lbs. — optional)	Door latch	1 piece
Clear silicone caulk	2 tubes	Striker plate and screws	1 piece
Waterproofing stain	1 gallon		
24″ Aluminum ridge cap	5 pieces		

Hardware

½″ x 6″ Hex-head bolts, washers and nuts	8 pieces (optional)
16d Common nails	4 lbs.
8d Common nails	1 lb.

* The list given here is to make the project as shown in the photos — half storage shed, half greenhouse. If you wish to build one or the other, adjust the list accordingly.

** It's more economical to rip this material from standard dimension lumber than it is to buy it. Purchase six extra 2 x 4 x 8's and three 1 x 12 x 8's. This will allow you a little stock for wastage.

Designed by Nick Engler, Built by Adam Blake

Stacking Bookcase

These easy-to-build shelving units have built-in bookends.

The number of books I have in my home never remains constant. I'm always buying new books, and giving old ones away. This creates a few problems.

First of all, since the number of books doesn't remain constant, neither does the amount of shelf space I need to store and display my books. And secondly, the books that I do have never fit the shelves exactly. If I organize the books the way I want them, then there's a lot of books flopping over near one end of the shelves or the other for want of a bookend.

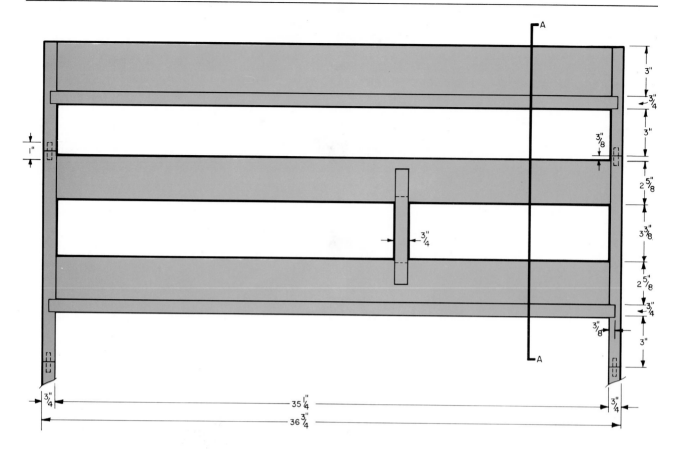

FRONT VIEW

Here's a 'stacking' bookcase that solves both of these problems. You can add or subtract shelves as you need them, *and* each shelf has built-in bookends to make it easier for you to organize your library.

Building the Shelving Units

The shelving units are just five pieces of wood — two sides, shelf, and two stretchers. The top unit is just four pieces —sides, shelf, and backstop. The joinery is simple; the shelves are dadoed into the sides, and the stretchers are butted to the sides and shelf.

To build several of these units, set up to mass produce the pieces. Figure out how many linear feet you need of 10", 6½", 3", and 2⅝" wide stock. Glue up the wide stock, if you need to, then rip all stock to size. Remember that one edge of the stretchers must be beveled at 20°.

To cut the stock to the proper lengths, use a stop block clamped to your rip fence. (See Figure 1.) Clamp this stop block to the fence, as close to the front of the table as possible. (If the block is too far forward, the wood will bind and kick back as you cut it.) Adjust the position of the rip fence so that the face of stop block is as far away from the blade as the lengths you want to cut. Put a board against your miter gauge, butt one edge against the stop block, and feed the board forward into the blade while holding it securely against the gauge. Repeat as many times as necessary. All the lengths you cut should be exactly the same — until you change the position of the rip fence again.

Figure 1. Use a stock block clamped to your rip fence to quickly measure and cut duplicate lengths of wood. This block should be as close to the front of the table as possible.

Figure 2. To keep a dado blade from tearing or chipping the wood at the end of a cut, score the outline of the dado with an awl or pocket knife on the edge of the board.

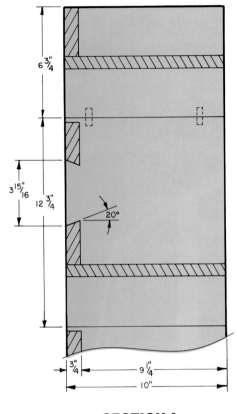

SECTION A

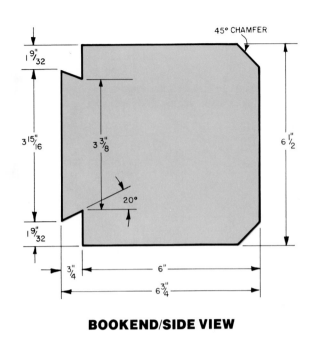

BOOKEND/SIDE VIEW

After you've cut all the parts, make all the dadoes. Mount a dado cutter to your table saw, and set the rip fence to guide the stock into the cutter.

Tip ◆ To keep the dado blade from tearing out the wood at the end of the cut, score the edges of the dado with an awl or pocket knife. (See Figure 2.)

Dowel the ends of the sides so that they can be stacked one on top of the other. This demands some very careful measuring. Carefully mark where each dowel hole should be drilled, and doublecheck your measurements before drilling. Use a doweling jig to help position the holes precisely.

Sand all parts, and assemble them with glue and wood screws. Countersink and counterbore the wood screws, then hide the heads with wooden plugs.

While the glue on the shelving units is setting up, shape the bookends on the bandsaw. Cut a 20° 'dovetail' on the back end of each bookend to match the bevels on the edges of the stretchers. (See Figure 3.) These dovetails fit in between the stretchers and hold the bookends in place. To move the bookends, just slide them back and forth along the stretchers. To remove a bookend or put one in place, just give it a little twist. (See Figure 4.)

Finish the units with a penetrating finish, such as Danish oil or tung oil. When the finish has set up, rub all the units down with a good paste wax. This will help keep the bookends operating smoothly.

Figure 3. Cut the dovetails in the ends of the bookends on a bandsaw.

Figure 4. To install the bookends in the shelving units, or to remove them, just give them a twist.

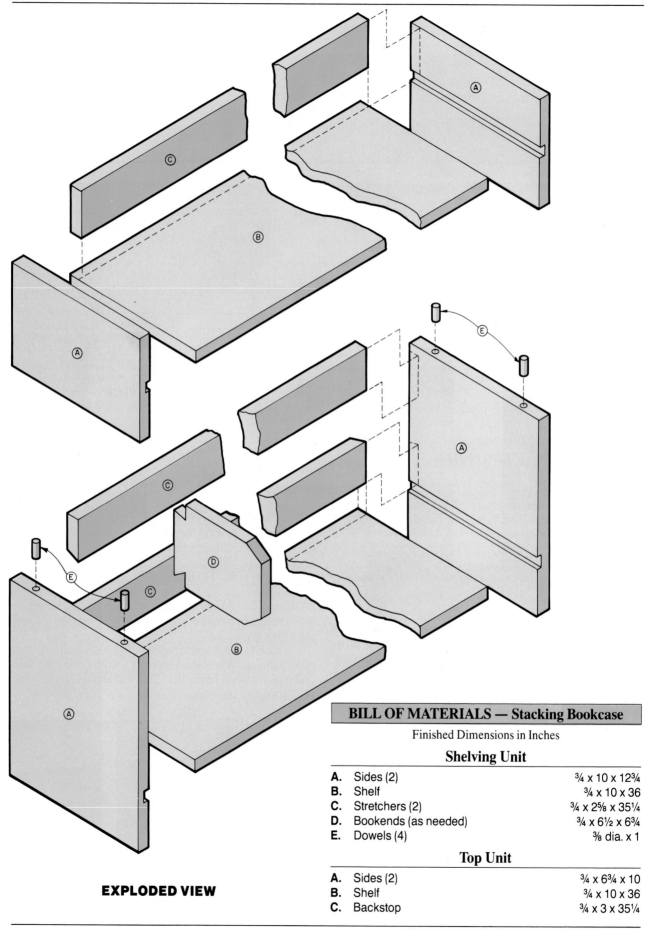

EXPLODED VIEW

BILL OF MATERIALS — Stacking Bookcase

Finished Dimensions in Inches

Shelving Unit

A.	Sides (2)	¾ x 10 x 12¾
B.	Shelf	¾ x 10 x 36
C.	Stretchers (2)	¾ x 2⅝ x 35¼
D.	Bookends (as needed)	¾ x 6½ x 6¾
E.	Dowels (4)	⅜ dia. x 1

Top Unit

A.	Sides (2)	¾ x 6¾ x 10
B.	Shelf	¾ x 10 x 36
C.	Backstop	¾ x 3 x 35¼

Reproduced from a Shaker design by Bob Pinter

Shaker Sewing Stand

A simple Shaker design makes a wonderfully versatile piece of furniture.

Bob Pinter, the woodworker who crafted this elegant sewing stand, tells me that there is no better way to gain an appreciation for Shaker furniture than to duplicate a Shaker piece. The timeless Shaker design is wonderful to look at, but you really don't understand the why's and wherefore's of the design until you work your way through a project. Then you begin to notice the little details, the graceful touches that make up the design. "By the time you're finished," says Bob, "You think, 'the woodworker who built this piece really knew his wood.'"

Bob built this table after studying a picture in John Kassay's classic book on Shaker furniture. The original was probably built by a Shaker brother in the first half of the nineteenth century. These tables were particularly popular during that period because the floors of the houses were rarely level. A standard four-legged table often needed a chock under one leg, but a three-legged table would automatically compensate for any irregularities in the floor.

Making the Tripod

Cut the legs out on a bandsaw, according to the pattern in the working drawings. Remember the grain should run lengthwise along the legs so that they're as strong as possible.

Turn the centerpost on a lathe to a 2½" cylinder. *Do not* turn the shapes yet; just round the post on the lathe. It's

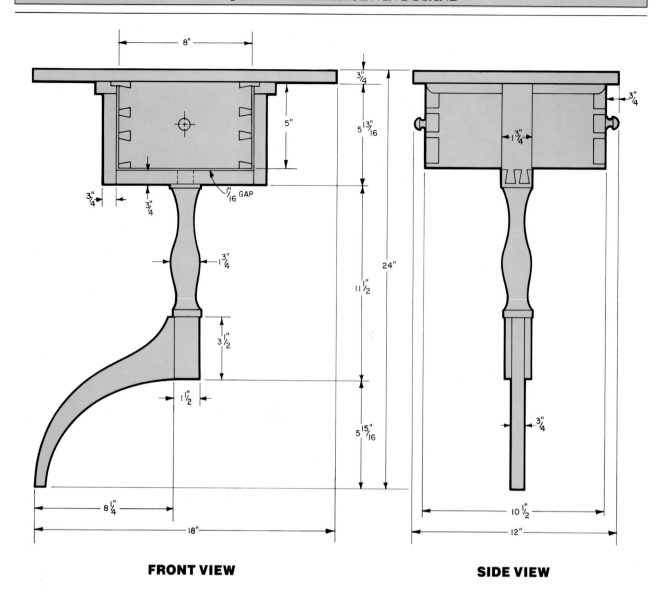

FRONT VIEW

SIDE VIEW

much easier to cut the joinery for the legs when the post is a simple cylinder.

The legs are joined to the post by mortises. There are two methods you can use to cut these mortises. No matter what method you use, you'll have to make a cradle for the post, as shown in the working drawings. This cradle holds the post and keeps it from turning while you cut the joinery.

If you have an overarm router, or a router attachment for your drill press, mount a ¾" straight bit in the router chuck. Clamp a guide fence to your worktable. Position this fence so that the centerpost will be directly under the router chuck when you hold the cradle up against the fence. Turn on the machine and rout a shallow groove 3½" long and ⅛" deep in one end of the post. Lower the bit another ⅛", and make another pass. Continue until you have cut a mortise ¾" deep. (See Figure 1.) Then square up the top corners of the mortise with a chisel. (See Figure 2.) Turn the post 120° in the cradle and make another mortise. Continue until you've cut three mortises.

You can also use a drill press and ¾" drill bit to make the mortises. The procedure is similar; you must attach a guide

fence to the drill press table to keep the post properly positioned under the bit. To make each mortise, drill a series of overlapping holes. (See Figure 3.) Then clean up the edges and the corners with a hand chisel.

Figure 1. With the centerpost clamped securely in a cradle, rout three mortises in the bottom end. *Router guard removed for clarity.*

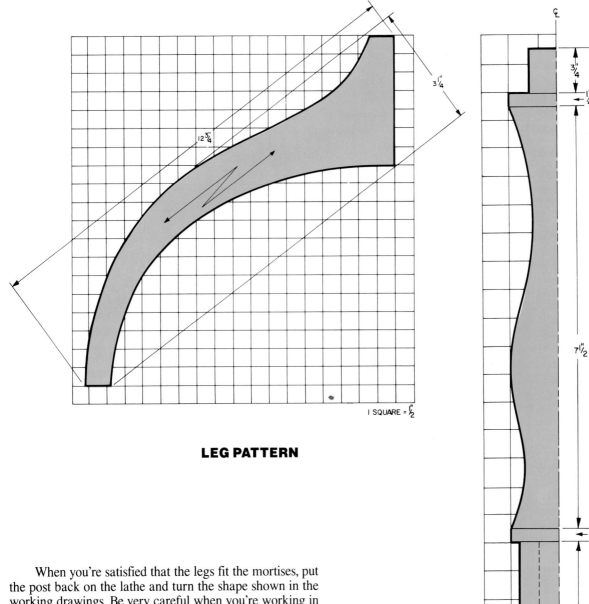

LEG PATTERN

1 SQUARE = 1/2"

When you're satisfied that the legs fit the mortises, put the post back on the lathe and turn the shape shown in the working drawings. Be very careful when you're working in the area where you cut the mortises. Feed the lathe chisels into the wood very slowly so that you don't chip out the wood.

Figure 2. Square up the upper corners of the mortises with a chisel.

CENTERPOST PATTERN AND LAYOUT

1 SQUARE = 1/2"

Tip ◆ To keep the wood from chipping, and to make the post more secure on the lathe, temporarily fill the mortises with ¾″ thick scraps. You can hold these fillers in place with just a dot or two of white glue on the bottom of the mortises, then remove them later with a chisel.

While you're set up for lathe turning, make the drawer pulls. You'll need two of them — one to mount on either end of the drawer. This particular drawer is designed to open towards the back *or* the front.

Making the Drawer and Top

The top portion of this project consists of a U-shaped bracket, a drawer, drawer guides, and, of course, a table top.

Make the top first. Glue boards edge to edge, if you need to, to get the full width. Make sure that the end grain of all the boards is all cupping in the same direction; and that when you mount the table top to the drawer guides, the end grain curves *up*. This way, the top will remain flat and even through changes in temperature and humidity. Round over the edge of the top on the underside with a ½″ quarter-round shaper cutter or router bit.

Make the drawer guides and the bracket as a unit. Cut rabbets on the inside edges of the drawer guides and the upper ends of the bracket arms. Then cut dadoes in the guides to accept the bracket arms. The rabbet in the guides and the arms should match up. Dovetail the bracket parts together, as shown. To see how to make the dovetails, look over "The Dovetail Joint" chapter in the **Techniques** section.

The ends and sides of the drawer are dovetailed together, using the same techniques as you used to join the bracket's parts — there are just more dovetails to make. Once again, refer to the chapter mentioned previously to see how to make these dovetails. The drawer bottom rests in stop grooves in the other drawer parts. Make these stop grooves with a router, or a router attachment on your drill press. (See Figure 4.) When you've finished machining all the drawer parts, glue the drawer glides to the drawer sides.

Assembly

Dry assemble all parts to check the fit — legs, post, bracket, drawer, and table top. When you're satisfied that they fit, disassemble the table and finish sand all parts. Bob Pinter never touches his woodworking projects with 50# or 80# sandpaper. Instead, he scrapes all parts smooth, then starts with 100# and works his way up to 250#. This makes a real difference in the way his projects look. The extra care in sanding really brings out the grain. When you're finished sanding, reassemble the parts with yellow glue.

Tip ◆ *Do not* glue the table top to the drawer guides. Instead, drill ¼″ holes in the guides and attach the top with #8 x 1¼″ roundhead wood screws and washers. The oversize holes will let the top expand and contract with the weather.

When you assemble the bracket to the tripod stand, arrange it so that one leg points straight out towards the front of the piece. When the drawer is in place, the tip of the leg should be centered under the drawer pull. There is a reason for this. If you want to place the sewing table against a wall, the two legs that aren't centered under a pull become the back legs. This arrangement looks better, and it allows you to get the back edge of the table top flush up against the wall, if you so wish.

When you've assembled the table like you want it, and all the glue has set up, remove all glue beads and do touch-up sanding wherever it's needed. Bob finished this project with three coats of Deft, rubbing out each coat with 0000 steel wool. This gives a good, durable finish that's not only pleasant to look at, but a pleasure to touch.

That's it. It's not a complex project; there aren't a lot of parts. But it does take some care and patience to put together correctly. That's one of the beauties of Shaker design — to build Shaker furniture correctly almost demands a peaceful, unhurried approach. It's a pleasant change from what we're used to in our lives.

Figure 3. If you're using a drill bit to make the mortises, drill a series of ¾″ holes, then clean up the edges with a chisel.

Figure 4. Rout the stop grooves in the drawer ends and sides. These grooves must be 'stopped' on both ends so that they don't show when you assemble the drawer.

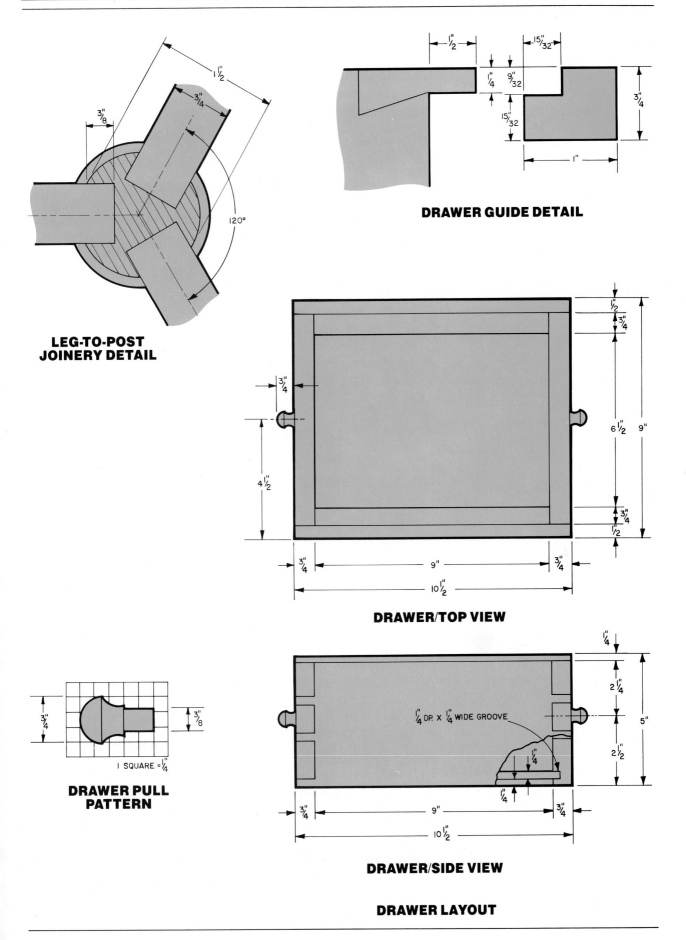

**LEG-TO-POST
JOINERY DETAIL**

DRAWER GUIDE DETAIL

DRAWER/TOP VIEW

I SQUARE = ¼"

**DRAWER PULL
PATTERN**

¼" DP. X ¼" WIDE GROOVE

DRAWER/SIDE VIEW

DRAWER LAYOUT

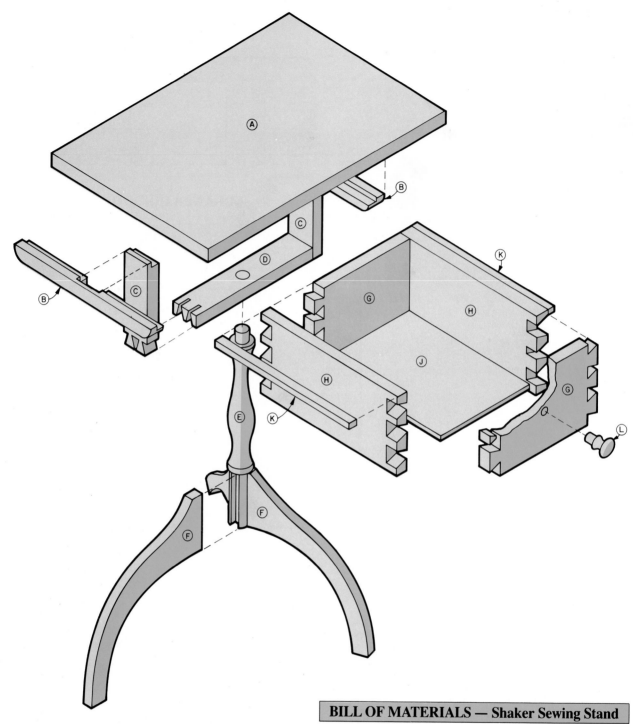

EXPLODED VIEW

A.	Top	¾ x 12 x 18
B.	Drawer guides (2)	¾ x 1 x 10½
C.	Bracket arms (2)	¾ x 1¾ x 5¹³/₁₆
D.	Bracket stretcher	¾ x 1¾ x 9⅝
E.	Centerpost	1¾ dia. x 12¼
F.	Legs (3)	¾ x 3¼ x 12¾
G.	Drawer ends (2)	¾ x 5 x 8
H.	Drawer sides (2)	¾ x 5 x 10½
J.	Drawer bottom	¼ x 7 x 9½
K.	Drawer glides (2)	¼ x ½ x 10½
L.	Drawer pulls (2)	¾ dia. x 1¼

Designed and Turned by Nick Engler

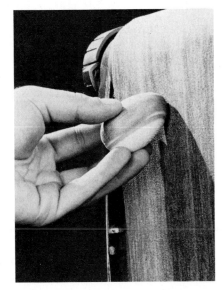

I SQUARE = 1/4"

EGG PATTERN

Cedar Eggs

Turned cedar scraps keep your linens fresh.

I hate to throw wood scraps away, and I feel doubly so about cedar scraps. I just can't bring myself to pitch something that smells so good in the garbage. So I'm constantly looking for things you can do with small pieces of cedar. Here's one possibility: Cedar eggs!

What do you use them for? Put a couple of them in each drawer, and they'll help keep your clothes and linens fresh.

To make the eggs, first glue up the scraps to make a turning block about 1½″ square. Let the glue dry for at least twenty-four hours, then turn the block down to a rough egg shape. Cedar has a lot of knots, so take it slow and easy as you turn. Finish sand all but the ends of the egg right on the lathe. (See Figure 1.)

Cut the waste stock off both ends with a bandsaw or coping saw. Then round the ends of the egg on the 'soft' side of your belt sander. (See Figure 2.) This is the side that doesn't have any backing. Finish up with a little hand sanding. *Don't* apply a finish. You don't want to seal in that wonderful cedar smell.

Figure 1. Turn the block to an egg shape and sand all but the ends on the lathe.

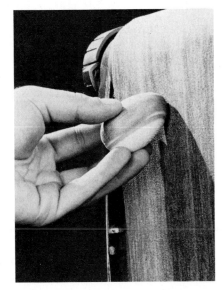

Figure 2. Sand the ends of the egg on the 'soft' side of your belt sander.

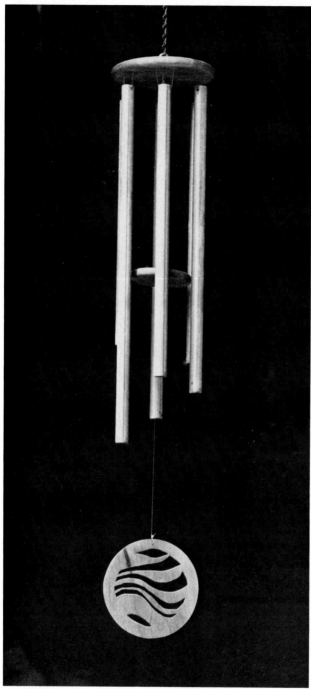

Designed by Linda Watts, Built by Adam Blake

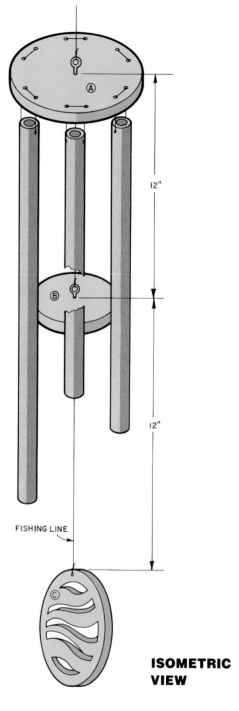

**ISOMETRIC
VIEW**

Chimes of Parthenope

Make beautiful music from shop scraps.

In Greek mythology, the Siren Parthenope threw herself into the sea after her songs failed to lure Ulysses to his doom. The Sirens, you may remember from your high school days, lived upon an island surrounded by treacherous rocks and shoals. They enticed sailors with irresistible songs, then took great delight when the ships foundered and sank.

The music of these wind chimes isn't quite so dangerous, but it is irresistible in a soothing sort of way. The chimes are tuned to the Pentatonic scale — the musical scale of ancient Greece. Unlike many wind chimes, which simply provide pleasant background noise, these chimes sometimes actually seem to pick out a song.

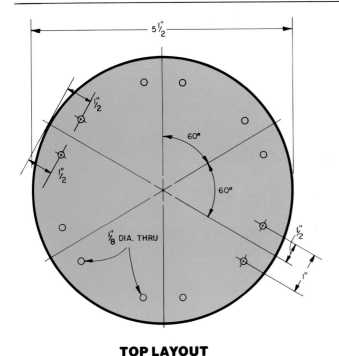

TOP LAYOUT

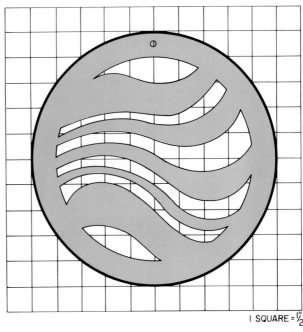

SAIL PATTERN

I SQUARE = ½"

Making the Chimes

Cut the wooden top and clapper from ⅜" thick stock, and the sail from ¼" thick stock. Since this project will hang outdoors, use a wood that weathers well. Cedar and redwood are both good choices. So are some of the exotic woods, such as rosewood, teak, and cocobolo. These woods are saturated with natural oils that fend off moisture. If you have any scraps of teak laying about, you might want to use them up in this project.

Drill holes in the top, where shown on the working drawings. Then 'pressure turn' the top and the clapper on a lathe, to round the edges and also to make sure that these parts are perfectly circular. To do a pressure turning, first cut two 'pressure blocks'. These blocks should be somewhat smaller than the piece to be turned, and they should have a small brad or nail protruding from the center. Place the turning between the blocks, lining up the points of the brads with the center of the turning. Then squeeze the blocks and the turning together between the turning centers of your lathe. (See Figure 1.) The centers act like a vise to keep the turning in place while you shape it.

Trace a design on the sail, and cut it out on a jigsaw. Saw the interior designs by making 'piercing' cuts. Drill a small hole in the waste; thread the jigsaw blade through the hole; mount the blade in the jigsaw; and make the cut. (See Figure 2.) The design you see here is meant to represent the waves that surrounded the islands of the Sirens, but you may have other designs that you'd rather use.

Cut the chimes from electrical conduit pipe, and drill holes in the top ends. The lengths shown in the working drawings will produce a rough Pentatonic scale, but you'll have to enlist the help of someone with a musical ear if you want to 'fine tune' the chimes. Have them listen carefully as you strike each length of pipe with a scrap of wood. If the pipe

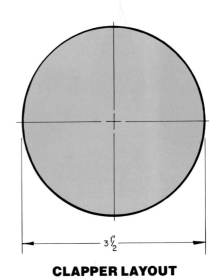

Figure 1. 'Pressure' turn the top and the clapper between two scrap blocks on your lathe.

CLAPPER LAYOUT

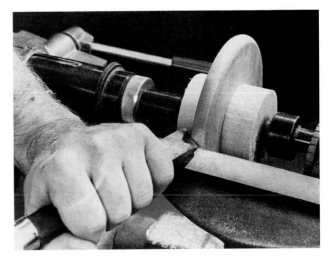

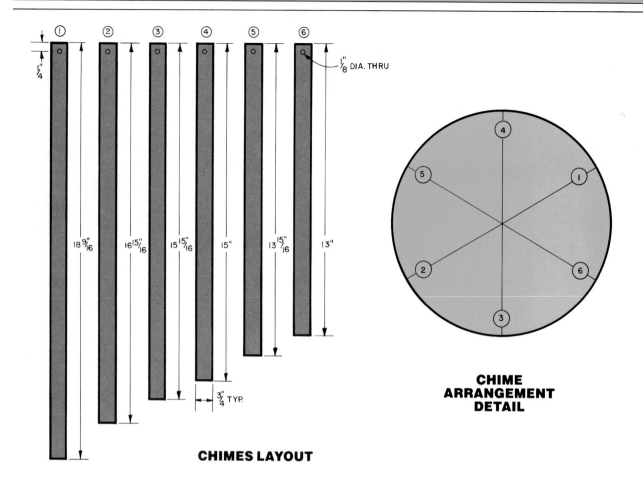

CHIMES LAYOUT

CHIME ARRANGEMENT DETAIL

is flat, you can raise the pitch by grinding a little off one end. If it's sharp, you have to cut a new pipe to replace it, slightly longer than the original.

Install eye screws into the top and bottom surface of the top and the clapper. Since you have to thread two screws through the same hole — each from a different direction — clip off part of the thread so that they don't interfere with each other. Hang the top by a chain, then hang the clapper and the sail beneath it with nylon fishing line.

Hang the chimes around the circumference of the top with nylon line. To get the chimes to balance, hang the longest and the shortest next to each other. Directly opposite the shortest chime, hang the second shortest. Opposite the longest, hang the second longest. Then hang the third longest between the shortest and the second longest, and the third shortest between the longest and second shortest. Got all that? If you don't, try some different arrangements until you find one that balances reasonably well.

Put a dab of epoxy glue on all the knots in the fishing line to make sure the knots stay knotted. Hang the chimes where they will catch the breeze, then try to steer clear of the rocks.

Figure 2. Cut the design in the sail by making piercing cuts on your jigsaw.

BILL OF MATERIALS — Chimes	
Finished Dimensions in Inches	
A. Top	5½ Dia. x ⅜
B. Clapper	3½ Dia. x ⅜
C. Sail	5 Dia. x ¼

Hardware

Conduit pipe	¾ x 13
Conduit pipe	¾ x 13¹⁵⁄₁₆
Conduit pipe	¾ x 15
Conduit pipe	¾ x 15¹⁵⁄₁₆
Conduit pipe	¾ x 16¹⁵⁄₁₆
Conduit pipe	¾ x 18⁹⁄₁₆
³⁄₁₆" Screw eyes (4)	
Fishing line (48")	

Designed and Built by Nick Engler

Backyard Cart

This roll-around cart dresses up your garbage cans.

Many of us who live in suburban or rural neighborhoods are plagued with raccoons or dogs. Every so often — usually on the morning right before the trash pick-up — you find your garbage cans overturned by some animal. Well, here's a simple cart that helps keep the lids on your cans.

Even if you aren't bothered by animals, you may want to build this cart to 'dress up' your cans. Who wants to stare at beat up aluminum or cracked plastic trash containers? This wooden enclosure helps to make your backyard a more pleasant place.

Making the Frame

When you purchase the wood for this project, buy cedar, redwood, or 'pressure-treated' lumber. These materials will withstand the weather much better than ordinary lumber, and they don't require yearly coats of stains or varnish. Also purchase *galvanized* nails to assemble the project. Ordinary nails will rust and stain the wood.

TOP LAYOUT/BOTTOM VIEW

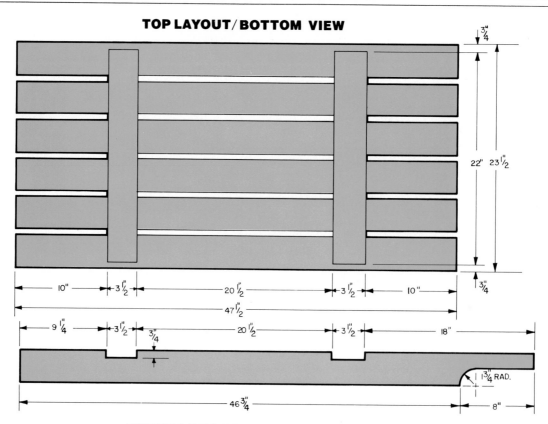

UPPER LONG FRAME MEMBER LAYOUT

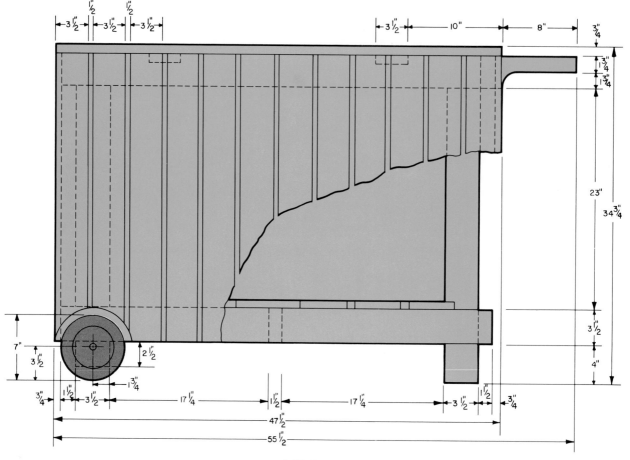

SIDE VIEW

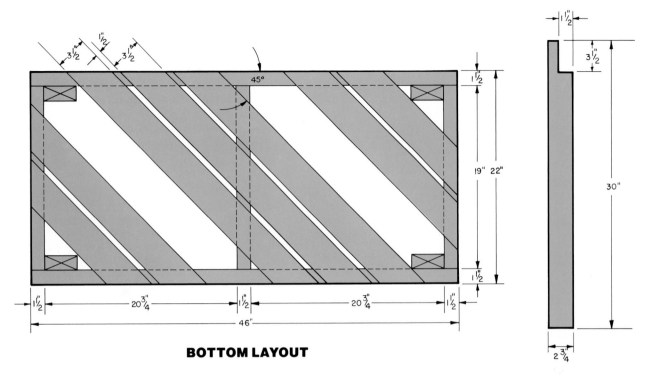

BOTTOM LAYOUT

**OUTSIDE END
BATTEN LAYOUT**

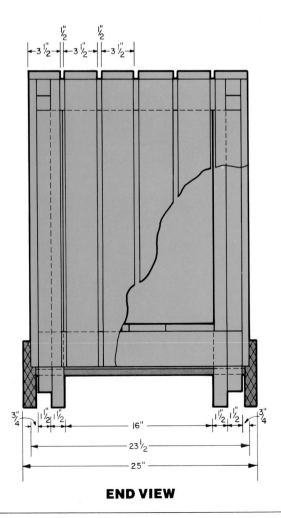

END VIEW

Tip ◆ If it's important to you that this cart be portable, use redwood or cedar to build it. Pressure treated lumber is much heavier than the other two woods.

As shown in the working drawings, this cart will hold two standard (22 gallon) metal trash cans. If your cans are a different size, or you want the cart to hold more than two cans, you will have to adjust the dimensions. However, be forewarned that the completed cart is fairly substantial with just two cans. If you add another can or two, it may become too heavy to wheel around easily.

Begin the project by making the upper and lower frames. These frames are exactly the same, except that the long members — rails — of the upper frame extend to make 'handles'. Pare these handles down to comfortable dimensions on the bandsaw, then round over the edges with a spokeshave or rasp. Also, cut notches in the upper frame rails to fit the top battens.

Cut the four legs, and attach the spacers to the two front legs. Then drill holes through the legs and the spacers for the axle. Make these holes about ¹/₁₆″ larger than the axle, so that you can slip it in and out easily.

Join the legs to the upper and lower frames. Check that all parts of the frame are square, then attach the floor boards to the lower frame. These floor boards are mounted on a diagonal to help reinforce the frame and keep it square. (See Figure 1.)

Tip ◆ If you're bothered by raccoons, cover the lower frame with hardware cloth, then nail the floor boards to it. This will keep the raccoons from squeezing up through the floor boards.

Making the Cart Mobile

Insert the metal axle in the axle holes. Place two flat washers, one on either end of the axle, to prevent the wheels from rubbing against the spacers. Place the wheels on the axles, and then two more washers.

Hold the wheels on the axles with cap nuts. These nuts are simply pounded on the ends of the axles; they don't need to be threaded. (See Figure 2.) Get a helper to hold an anvil or nailing block against one end of the anvil while you pound the cap nut onto the other end.

Completing the Enclosure

Cut the battens to length, and nail them in place all around the frame. Shape the ends of the battens where necessary to accommodate the wheels and the handles. (See Figure 3.)

To help space the battens evenly, make a jig as shown here and in the working drawings. (See Figure 4.) Remember that this jig will work for an entire row of battens *only* if all the battens are *exactly* 3½″ wide. This is rarely the case with building materials. You'll probably have to adjust the position of the last two or three battens in a row to compensate.

Place the top battens in the notches of the upper frame rails. Position the top boards over the top battens, and nail them in place. Clinch the nails over on the underside.

Hinge the top to one side of the cart, and mount a hasp to the other side. Install two lengths of chain to help keep the top from flopping back against the side of your house or garage when you open the top. Finally, put your trash cans in place and wheel the cart to wherever you think it looks best.

Figure 3. Shape the ends of the battens to accommodate the wheels, as shown. You'll also have to shape the battens to fit around the handles.

Figure 4. Use this simple jig to help evenly space the battens.

Figure 1. Nail the floor boards to the lower frame on a diagonal. This helps to keep the frame square.

Figure 2. Hold the wheels on the axle with cap nuts. These nuts are simply hammered in place.

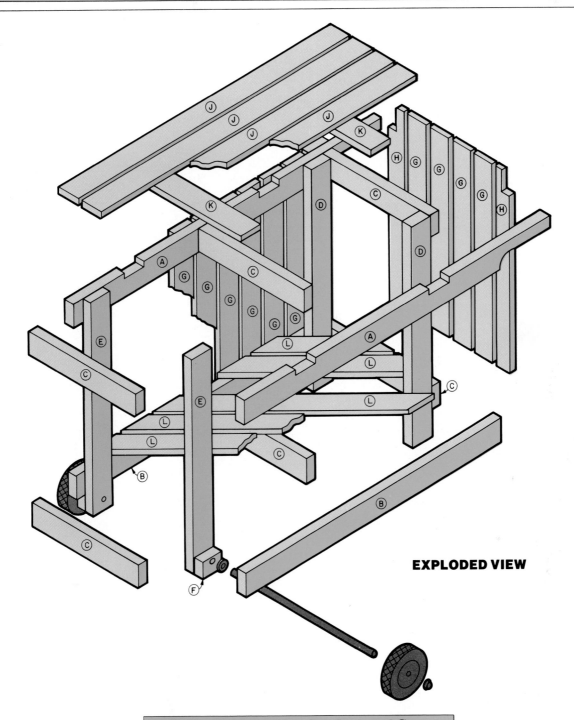

EXPLODED VIEW

BILL OF MATERIALS — Backyard Cart

Finished Dimensions in Inches

A.	Upper Long Frame Members (2)	1½ x 3½ x 54¾
B.	Lower Long Frame Members (2)	1½ x 3½ x 46
C.	Short Frame Members (6)	1½ x 3½ x 19
D.	Long Uprights (2)	1½ x 3½ x 34
E.	Short Uprights (2)	1½ x 3½ x 33
F.	Spacers (12)	1½ x 3½ x 2½
G.	Battens (32)	¾ x 3½ x 30
H.	Outside End Battens (4)	¾ x 2¾ x 30
J.	Top Battens (6)	¾ x 3½ x 47½
K.	Crosspieces (2)	¾ x 3½ x 22
L.	Floor Boards (total)	¾ x 3½ x 194½

Hardware

8d Galvanized nails (1-2 lbs.)
16d Galvanized nails (1-2 lbs.)
½" x 26" Steel axle
7" Wheels (2)
½" Washers (4)
½" Cap nuts (2)
3" Strap hinges and mounting screws (1 pair)
Hasp and mounting screws

Design by Nick Engler and Jim McCann,
Built by Jim McCann

Reference Bookstand

This classy stand makes it easier to page through bulky reference volumes.

As a workshop writer, there are several books that I like to keep on 'combat alert' status — a thesaurus, a one-volume "comprehensive" encyclopedia, several textbooks on cabinetmaking and carpentry, and (of course), an unabridged dictionary. (Try looking up "dado" in an abridged dictionary sometime. Mr. Abridged thinks it's the middle part of a pedestal.)

The publishers who sold me these tomes all assured me that these were "desktop" reference works. Oh, sure. For people with steel-trussed desks, perhaps. Both the dictionary and the encyclopedia came with free bodybuilding courses. And the other books are smaller by only a few tons.

Until recently, it was quite a chore hauling these books off and on their bookshelves all day long. Then one day, while visiting my local library, I was struck with a sudden burst of inspiration. (That is to say, I ripped off a good idea.) With yet another burst of inspiration, I cajoled a good friend of mine — Jim McCann, a whiz at precision joinery — to help design and build it.

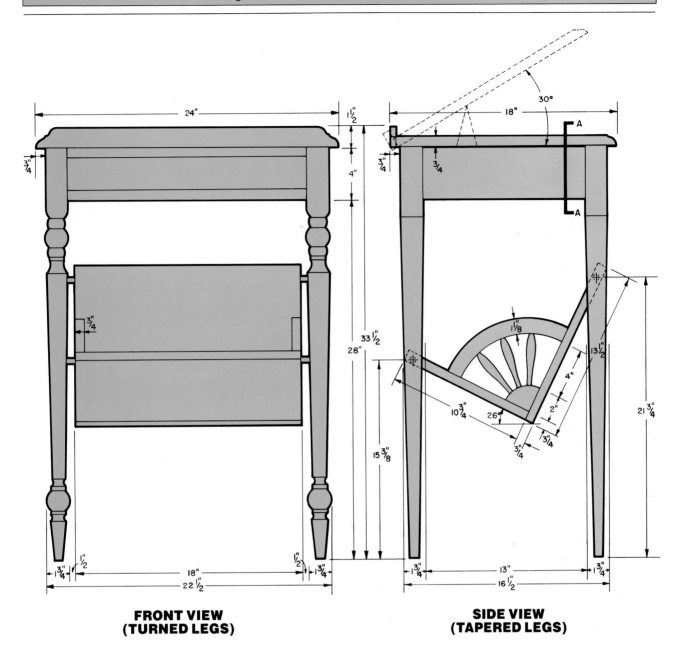

**FRONT VIEW
(TURNED LEGS)**

**SIDE VIEW
(TAPERED LEGS)**

You see the results of my inspiration and Jim's craftsmanship here. This bookstand holds all my bulky reference volumes 'at ready', where I can find them quickly. The top of the stand is waist-high and it tilts slightly, holding the books at a comfortable height and angle for browsing. Under the top is a small drawer for a traditional magnifying glass, and under that a 'floating' shelf to keep the reference books when you're not using them.

Design and Construction

As you can see from the drawings, Jim's bookstand is really a small side table with a tilting top. Except for the drawer, most of the joinery in this project is mortise-and-tenon joints and a few dowel joints — the legs are held to the apron by mortises and tenons, the storage shelf is doweled to the legs so that it seems to 'float' between them. The top is hinged to the front of the table, and tilts up to a comfortable reading angle. It's held in the tilted position by a single adjustable support centered beneath the top. (See Figure 1.)

Figure 1. The top is supported at a variety of angles by a triangular support block. This block fits in the dowel holes in the top support rail.

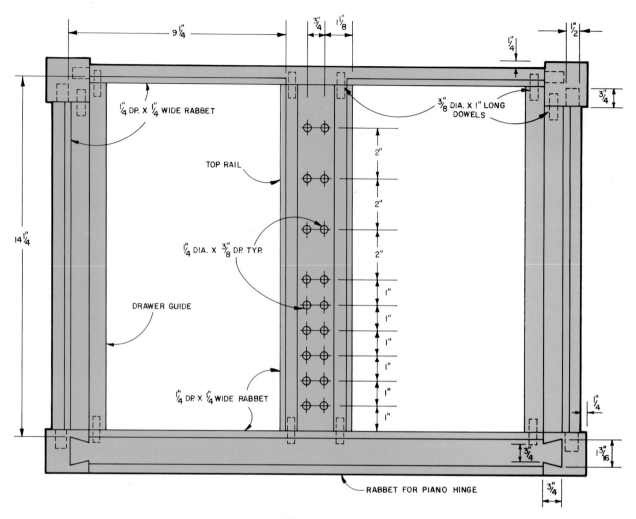

TOP VIEW
(DUST SHIELDS AND TOP REMOVED)

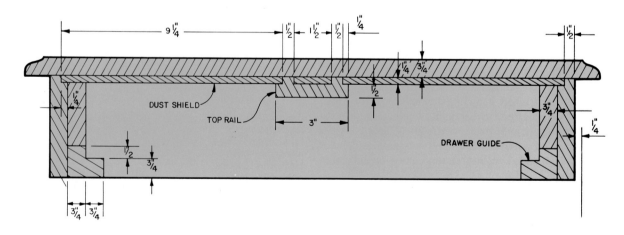

SECTION A

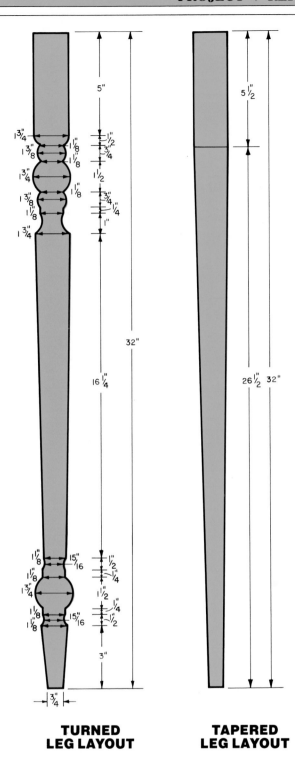

**TURNED
LEG LAYOUT**

**TAPERED
LEG LAYOUT**

Figure 2. Put all the legs together and mark the innermost corners. Then lay out the joinery on the ends.

Figure 3. Cut the joinery in the legs *before* you turn them. Make the mortises by drilling a series of holes. Stop blocks at either end of the fence ensure that all the mortises are exactly the same.

LR	RR
LF	RF

design, you make the legs no wider than 2″. The height of the stand draws attention to the legs, and fat legs make the piece look disproportionate and awkward.

Machining the Legs and Aprons

The assembly of the stand is pretty straightforward. Cut all parts to size, contour and sand them, then put them together. However, there's a little more to it than that. There are several different assemblies here that must all be built separately, then come together all at the same time. Let me give you some helpful hints:

◆ You can lose your religion making the mortises, tenons, and the dowel holes in the aprons and legs. It's sometimes difficult to get these joints to line up correctly. In a situation like this, careful planning and measuring can save a lot of swearing. Clamp all four legs together in a square and mark the innermost corner of each leg with initials for the leg positions — LF is left front, RR is right rear, etc. Then lay out all the joinery on the ends of the legs. (See Figure 2.) This helps you keep track of what goes where.

◆ As you mark the joints, remember that the front legs and the rear legs are mirror images of each other. Also remember to mark and drill the holes in the legs for the dowels that will support the shelf.

The design of the table can be adapted easily from either contemporary to classical by simply changing two elements: the shape of the legs and the edge treatment on the top. I've shown two possibilities in the drawings, one with turned legs and the other with tapered legs. Each has a different top treatment to match. The construction will work just as well with straight legs, cabriole legs, legs with reverse tapers and any number of top designs. Shape the legs and the top to suit your own tastes. However, Jim suggests that, whatever your

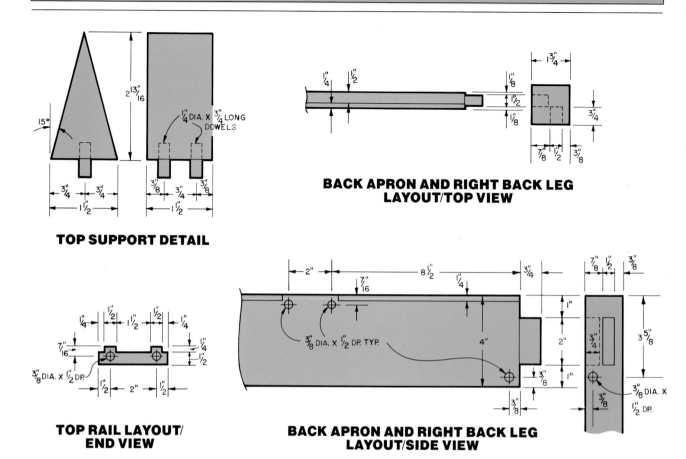

TOP SUPPORT DETAIL

**BACK APRON AND RIGHT BACK LEG
LAYOUT/TOP VIEW**

**TOP RAIL LAYOUT/
END VIEW**

**BACK APRON AND RIGHT BACK LEG
LAYOUT/SIDE VIEW**

Let's begin machining with the legs. Before you turn them, cut the joinery in each leg. Make the mortises by drilling a series of holes, then cleaning up the sides of the mortises with a chisel. (See Figure 3.) Remember to drill the dowel holes for the shelf supports and the drawer supports. It's much harder to cut accurate joints after the legs are square because that flat surface of the legs has been pared away, for the most part. When it comes time to mount the front legs on the lathe, cut temporary plugs for the dovetail mortises in the tops. (See Figure 4.)

Cut matching tenons in the aprons. Cut the dovetail in the ends of the top apron rail on your bandsaw. Cut the tenons in the other apron parts on your table saw, using a dado cutter. Round the ends of each tenon to match the mortises. (See Figure 5.) Then pare down the sides of each tenon with a hand chisel until the tenon slips easily into its mortise. (See Figure 6.) The fit should be snug, with no slop, but not too snug. If you can push the parts together without using a mallet, then the fit is right.

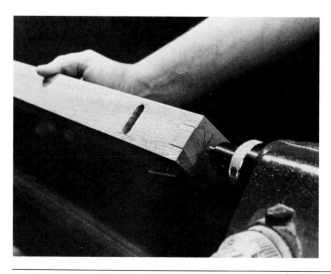

Figure 4. To mount the front legs on the lathe, cut a temporary plug for the dovetail mortises.

Figure 5. Use a rasp to round the tenons to fit the mortises.

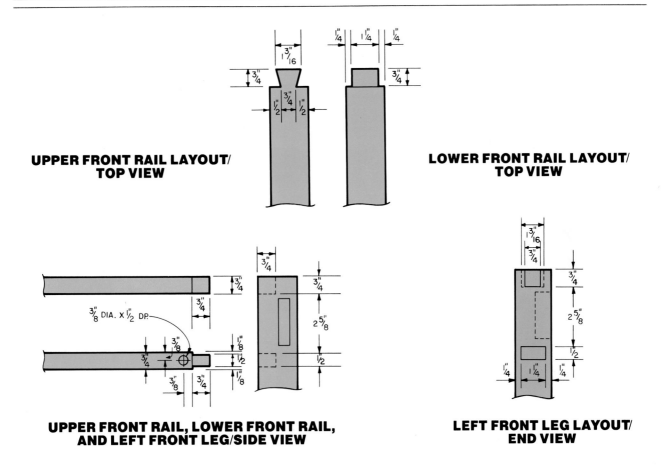

**UPPER FRONT RAIL LAYOUT/
TOP VIEW**

**LOWER FRONT RAIL LAYOUT/
TOP VIEW**

**UPPER FRONT RAIL, LOWER FRONT RAIL,
AND LEFT FRONT LEG/SIDE VIEW**

**LEFT FRONT LEG LAYOUT/
END VIEW**

As shown in the drawings, they are 32″ long and 1¾″ square. The average homeshop lathe has a 'throw' of just 32″-34″, so you don't have much extra room to play with, no more than an inch on each end. A long, slender turning like this will begin to 'whip' on the lathe as you pare down the diameter of the spindle. To prevent this, use a 'steadyrest' to support the spindle in the middle. (See Figure 7.)

Tip ◆ Use a 'storystick' to help turn each leg exactly the same. See the chapter on "Lathe Duplication" in the **Techniques** section.

Making the Shelf

While you're working on the lathe, also make the spokes for the shelf 'wheels'. Set these spokes aside and lay out the arcs

Figure 6. Pare away the sides of the tenons with a hand chisel until they fit the mortises properly. The fit should be snug, with no slop, but not too snug.

Figure 7. Use a steadyrest to prevent the legs from whipping when you turn them.

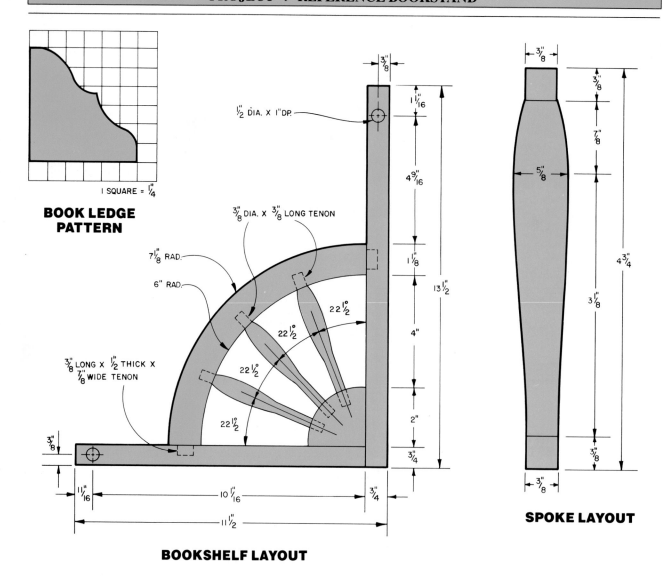

BOOK LEDGE PATTERN

1 SQUARE = 1/4"

BOOKSHELF LAYOUT

SPOKE LAYOUT

of the wheels and hub on the face of the stock. Carefully measure and mark the holes for the spokes and the tenons on the stock. *Do not* cut the curve of the wheels at this time.

Cut the tenons in the wheel stock with a dado cutter. Set your miter gauge to 45° and use the gauge to feed the stock over the cutter. Use the rip fence and a rip fence extension to guide the stock as you cut the shoulder of the tenons. (See Figure 8.) Then tape the wheel pieces together and the hub pieces together to make two 'pads'. Since this project requires two identical wheels and hubs, you can machine each pad at the same time.

Cut the hubs and the inside curve of the wheels on a bandsaw. (See Figure 9.) Then drill holes for the spokes in all pieces. First, drill the middle holes in the wheel with the table square to the drill bit. Then tilt the table to 22½°, and drill the outside holes in both the wheels *and* the hubs. (See Figures 10 and 11.) Reset the table to 45° and drill the middle holes in the hubs. (See Figure 12.) Finally, saw the tenons to their proper dimensions, and cut the outside curve in the wheels. (See Figure 13.)

Make the mortises in the shelf bottom and back in the same manner that you drilled the mortises in the legs. Dowel the shelf bottom to the back, then dry assemble all the shelf parts — bottom, backs, hubs, spokes, and wheels. If you're satisfied with the fit of the joints, reassemble the parts with glue. After the glue has set up, drill the holes in the edges of the shelf back and bottom for the shelf supports. (See Figure 14.)

Making the Drawers and Other Parts

The sides of the drawer are attached to the front with half-blind dovetails. These can be made simply by using a router and dovetail template. If you don't own a router or a template, you can also use a bandsaw, drill, and elbow grease. See the chapter on "The Dovetail Joint" in the **Techniques** section.

Cut the other joinery in the drawer with a dado or table saw. Dry assemble the parts to check the fit, then glue them up.

Glue up L-shaped brackets for the drawer guides, and a U-shaped bracket for the top support rail. Bore dowel holes in the ends of the brackets and rail, as shown in the working

Figure 8. Cut the tenons in the wheel stock *before* you cut the curves. Use the miter gauge and a rip fence extension to help guide the stock.

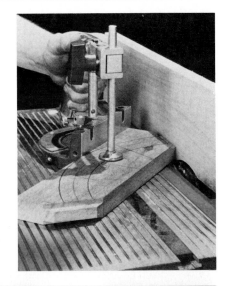

Figure 9. After you've cut the shoulders of the tenons, tape the wheel stock together in a 'pad'. Pad saw the inside curves.

Figure 10. Drill the 'outside' spoke holes in the wheel stock with the drill press table tilted to 22½°.

Figure 11. Leave the table tilted to 22½° and drill the outside holes in the hubs.

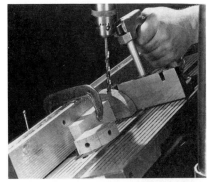

Figure 12. Tilt the table to 45°, and drill the inside holes in the hubs.

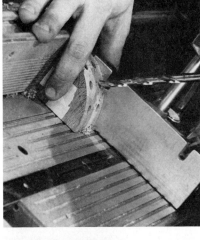

Figure 13. With the wheel stock still taped up in a pad, cut the tenons to the proper dimensions, and cut the outside curve.

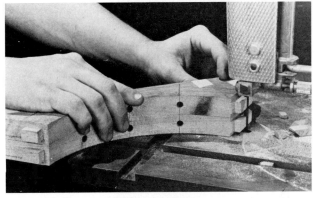

Figure 14. After you've glued up the shelf, bore the holes for the shelf supports.

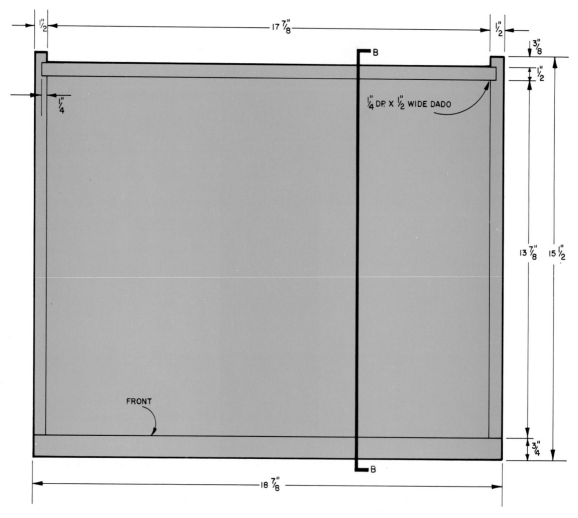

DRAWER LAYOUT/TOP VIEW

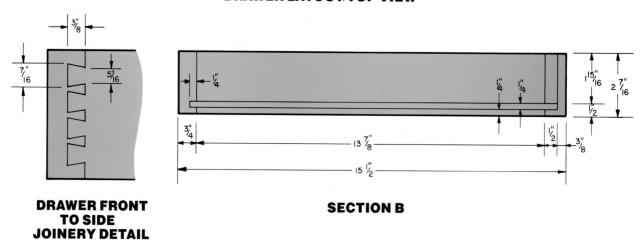

**DRAWER FRONT
TO SIDE
JOINERY DETAIL**

SECTION B

Final Assembly

drawings. These holes must match up with the holes in the legs and aprons.

Finally, glue up stock for the top. Shape the back and side edges, then glue a book ledge to the front edge of the top. Shape the ends of the book ledge to match the edge treatment on the top.

Now comes the hard part. At this point, you have to assemble the legs, aprons, drawer guides, and storage shelf *all at the same time*. This can be a family project, you know. Or an excuse to invite the neighbors for drinks and sawdust hors d'oeuvres. But if you have a small shop, there is a way to do this by yourself.

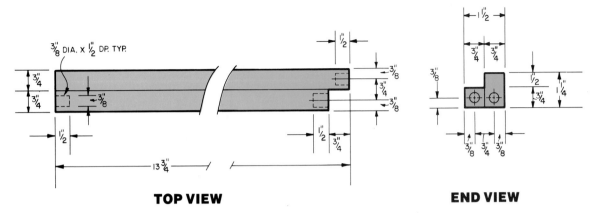

TOP VIEW

END VIEW

DRAWER GUIDE LAYOUT

First, make sure that all parts that can be sanded are sanded. Then, glue the legs to the front and back aprons and put a band clamp around each assembly. Tighten the clamp so that it's snug enough to keep the legs and aprons from coming apart, but not too tight. Put glue in the holes in the legs where you wish to mount the storage shelf and insert the 'floater' dowels in these holes. Slightly spread the two front legs and insert the floater dowels in the front of the storage shelf. Repeat this step for the back. Replace the band clamps with bar clamps. Tighten the clamps and check the assembly for squareness.

Next, glue the drawer guides, the side aprons, and the top support rail to the back leg assembly. Then glue these parts to the front leg assembly. By pivoting the shelf on the shelf supports, you can get enough play to do this. Put bar clamps across all joints and tighten the clamps. When you're finished, the assembly should look something like that shown in Figure 15.

> **Tip ◆** As you glue up the parts, keep a wet rag and a pail of water handy. As the glue squeezes out of the joints, wipe it off with the rag. This will raise the grain slightly, but sanding down the raised grain won't be near as much work as chiseling off all the glue beads.

Hinge the front top apron, using a piano hinge. Make sure that the pin of this hinge is far enough forward so that the top doesn't bind on the legs as it pivots. Install drawer pulls in the drawer, then insert the drawer in the table. Put the top support in place on the top support rail, and cut ¼″ thick panels to fit between the rail and the aprons.

In choosing drawer hardware, get something that goes with the legs. For example, cabriole legs call for a Chippendale pull with an elegant brass bail and escutcheon. If you made straight or tapered legs, you might try a flush 'campaign desk' pull for a modern appearance. Jim opted for simple brass bail pulls.

Finishing Up

When you're satisfied that all the parts work well and look good together, remove all hardware from the project. Finish sand any parts that still need it.

I try to keep my advice on finishes to a minimum. Most woodworkers have some favorite finish and/or finishing technique that works well for them. But I do have one small bit of advice on this particular project: Avoid 'building' finishes such as varnish or polyurethane. You'll find it a real bear to rub these glossy finishes out between the bookend spokes and the floater dowels.

Figure 15. Hold the assembly together with bar clamps while the glue dries. Wipe off any excess glue with a wet rag.

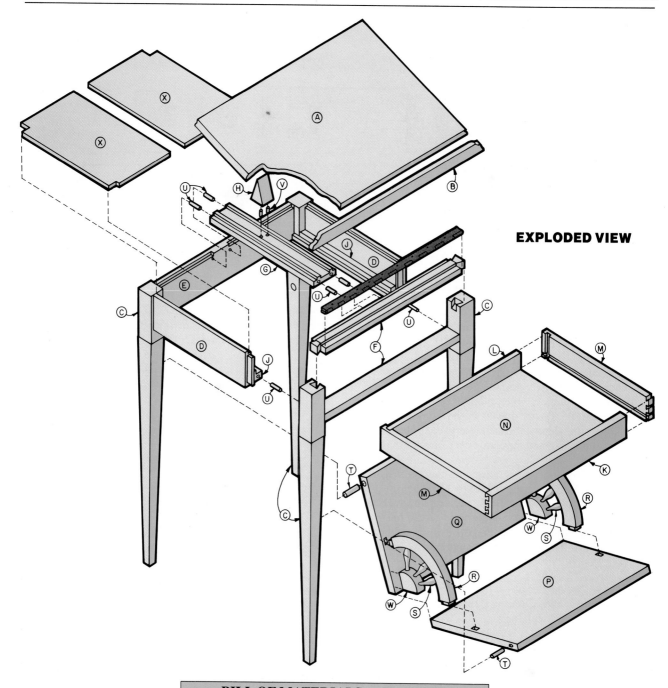

EXPLODED VIEW

BILL OF MATERIALS — Bookstand

Finished Dimensions in Inches

A.	Top	¾ x 17½ x 24
B.	Book Ledge	½ x 1½ x 24
C.	Legs (4)	1¾ x 1¾ x 32
D.	Side Aprons (2)	¾ x 4 x 14½
E.	Back Apron	¾ x 4 x 20½
F.	Upper/Lower Front Rails (2)	¾ x 1¾ x 20½
G.	Top Rail	¾ x 3 x 13¾
H.	Top Support	1½ x 1½ x 2¹³/₁₆
J.	Drawer Guides (2)	1¼ x 1½ x 13¾
K.	Drawer Front	¾ x 2⁷/₁₆ x 18⅞
L.	Drawer Back	½ x 1¹⁵/₁₆ x 18⅜
M.	Drawer Sides (2)	½ x 2⁷/₁₆ x 15⅛
N.	Drawer Bottom	¼ x 14⅝ x 18⅜

P.	Book Shelf	¾ x 10¾ x 18
Q.	Shelf Back	¾ x 13½ x 18
R.	Wheels (2)	¾ x 3 x 10½
S.	Spokes (6)	⅝ Dia. x 4¾
T.	Shelf Dowels (4)	½ Dia. x 2½
U.	Drawer Guide Dowels (6)	⅜ Dia. x 1
V.	Top Support Dowels (2)	¼ Dia. x ¾
W.	Hubs (2)	¾ x 2 x 2
X.	Dust Shields (2)	¼ x 9¼ x 14¼

Hardware

Drawer pulls (2)
¾" x 19" Piano hinge and mounting screws

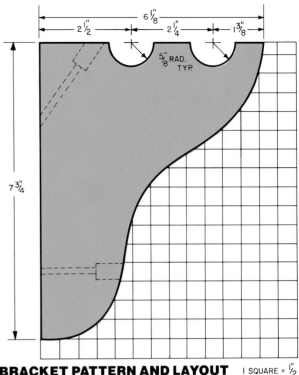

BRACKET PATTERN AND LAYOUT   I SQUARE = $\frac{1}{2}$"

Designed and Produced by Nick Engler

Double Curtain Brackets

Hang two curtain rods from one bracket.

Have you ever shopped for a simple wooden bracket that will hold *two* curtain rods? Chances are, you won't be able to find them. Yet, 'double curtain' brackets are used quite often — for hanging a curtain and a valance, a curtain and plants, two contrasting curtain panels, etc.

If you can't find what you need, don't waste your time chasing from store to store. You can make the brackets you need in just an hour or two.

Using the bandsaw, cut the brackets out of stock that's *at least* ¾" thick. Sand away any millmarks, then counterbore holes for the mounting screws. Drill the large hole for the screw head first, then the smaller hole for the screw shank. If you're making a lot of brackets, make a simple jig to hold the workpiece while you drill the angled holes. (See Figure 1.)

If you wish, shape the front edge of the brackets. Use a pin to help guide the work, and a push stick to help keep your fingers out of danger. (See Figure 2.)

To mount the brackets, first mark the hole positions on the wall or window molding, then drill pilot holes. If you're mounting the brackets to plaster or drywall, you'll have to sink molly anchors in the wall. Remember that the top mounting screw is angled at 45°. The top molly anchor will have to be angled to match it.

Finally, mount the brackets to the wall with #10 flathead wood screws, and cover the screw heads with wood plugs. The mounting screws should bite *at least* 1½" into the wall.

Figure 1. When drilling or boring the angled holes in the top edge of the brackets, use a simple jig to hold the workpiece.

Figure 2. Shape the front edge of the brackets. Use a pin to help guide the work, and a push stick to keep your fingers out of danger.

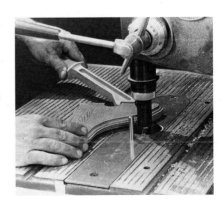

Designed and Built by Casey Chaffin

Wooden Icebox

Adjustable shelves give this age-old favorite a new twist.

Old iceboxes never die, they're reborn again and again in new roles. The time has long since passed when you would actually want to use them as an icebox; but they make marvelous linen closets, china cupboards, and entertainment centers.

Casey Chaffin, of Dayton, Ohio built this 'icebox' to house his stereo system. On the outside, it's a replica of the Grand Rapids style cabinet that houses so many turn-of-the-century iceboxes. But once you open the doors, the similarity ends. Gone are the metal racks, baked enamel lining, and drip pan. Instead, Casey has designed a system of adjustable shelves to hold the audio system he has now — and any components he may buy in the future. This shelving system lets you adapt his design to any use that you may have in mind for an old icebox.

Casey's icebox is all frame-and-panel construction. The frames are joined together with tongues and grooves to make the case. This construction makes the icebox much lighter than it looks to be, without sacrificing strength. It's a massive piece of furniture when you see it in Casey's living room, but it can be easily lifted by two people.

This type of construction adds to the total number of parts in the piece. However, despite the long Bill of Materials, the piece is relatively easy to build. Most of the parts are machined in the same manner — Casey used the same tongue-and-groove joint everywhere he could. If you plan ahead so that you machine all these joints at one time, your major problem won't be making the parts, but keeping them all straight.

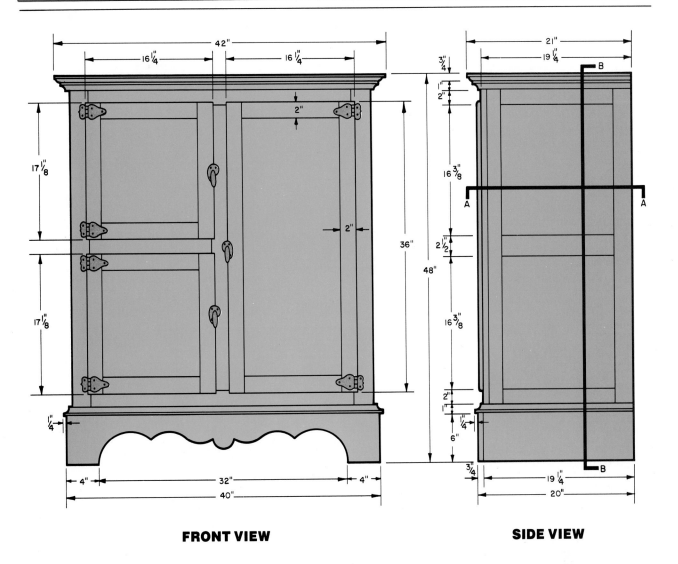

FRONT VIEW   **SIDE VIEW**

Making the Case

Cut all the pieces for the frames — front frame, side frames, back frame, and shelf frames. Also cut the ¾″ shelf panels. Note that many of the pieces in the various frames are the same dimensions. This is an old Grand Rapids production trick — standardized parts that will work in several different assemblies. You can use this trick here to your advantage by setting up to 'mass produce' those parts that are the same.

First, set up to rip all the stock of a certain width, then all the stock of another width, and so on until you have several different bundles of boards, each bundle cut to the same width. To cut parts to an exact, uniform length, use a 'stop block'. (See Figure 1.) Attach this stop block to the fence of your saw. Butt the wood up against it to gauge the length, then make the cut. All lengths will be exactly the same.

Next cut the grooves in those pieces that need them. All the grooves are exactly the same size — ¼″ wide x ⅜″ deep. (See Figure 2.) Use a dado blade on your table saw to cut these grooves, and a featherboard to keep the stock flat up against the rip fence. A push stick comes in handy to help guide the stock over the blade.

Figure 1. Attach a stop block to the fence of your radial arm saw, as shown. Use this block to 'mass produce' parts of the same length.

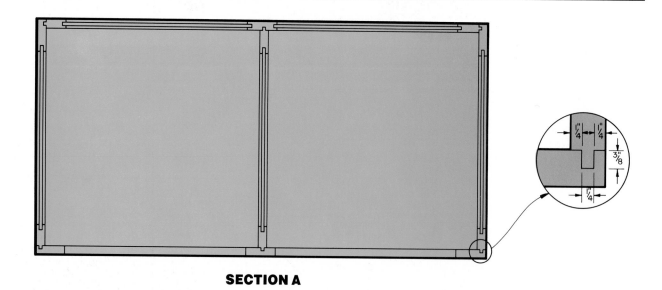

SECTION A

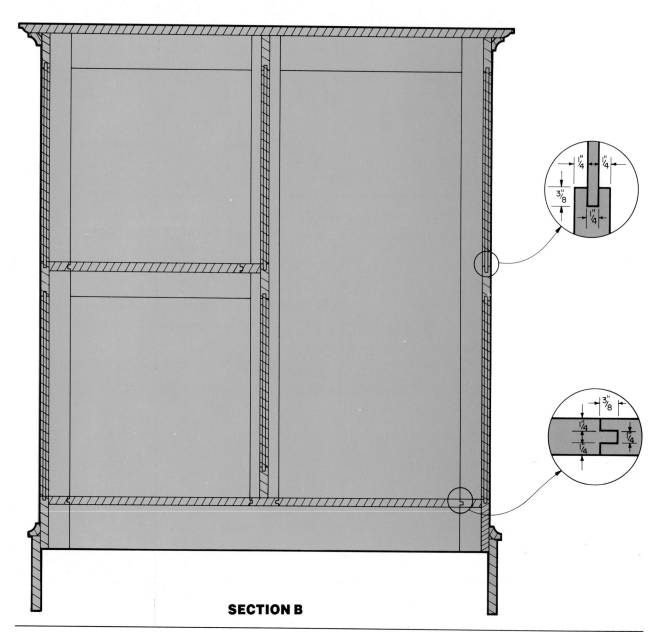

SECTION B

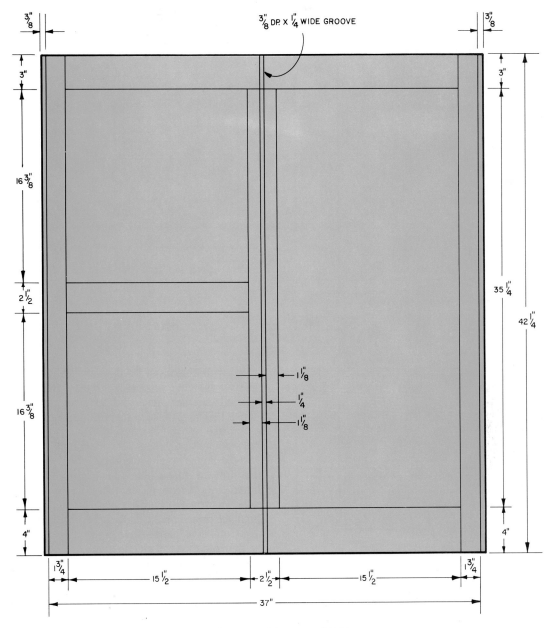

BACK FRAME LAYOUT

Without changing the blade or the blade height, set up to cut the tongues. When cutting the tongues in the ends of boards, use a tenoning jig to help keep the frame members square to the blade. (See Figure 3.) You won't need this jig when cutting the tongues in the shelf panels or the long sides of the frame members, but you will need to be careful to keep the stock flat against the rip fence.

Tip ◆ When cutting the tongues in the ends of the frame members, put a scrap at the back of the board to keep the wood from tearing out when you finish the cut. Replace this scrap with each cut.

There are several parts which get joinery other than grooves and tongues. The inside faces of the side frame members and both faces of the middle frame members are

Figure 2. Cut all the grooves in the frame members. Use a fingerboard and a push stick to help guide the stock.

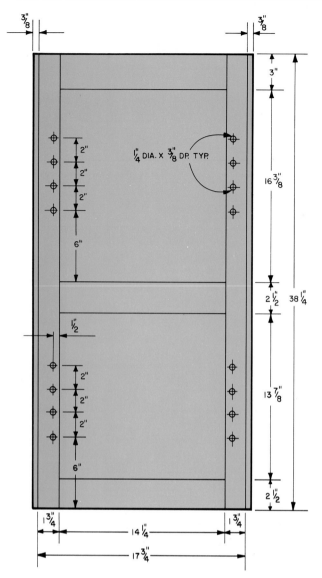

¼" DIA. X ⅜" DP. TYP.

MIDDLE FRAME LAYOUT

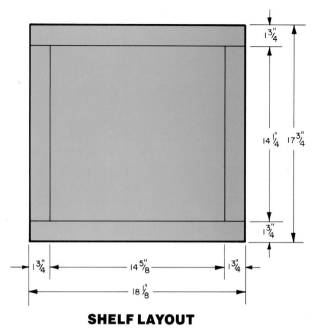

SHELF LAYOUT

drilled with a series of ¼″ diameter, ½″ deep holes to hold pin-style shelving supports. The front frame members are doweled together, since they have no panel grooves. (See Figure 4.) The stationary shelf frame members are attached in the case by wood screws in screw pockets. Make these screw pockets on your drill press with the table tilted at 15°. Drill the larger hole — the counterbore or 'pocket' — first, then drill the shank hole. (See Figure 5.) The shank hole should emerge from the center of the frame members edge, as shown in the working drawings. Remember, these pockets should be drilled on the *underside* of the shelf parts.

Cut the ¼″ panels, then dry assemble all parts to check the fit. Hold the case together with band clamps, and install the stationary shelves with wood screws. When you're satisfied that all the parts of the case fit properly, remove the wood screws and disassemble all parts.

Finish sand all the parts of the case, and apply a finish to

Figure 3. When cutting the tongues in the ends of the frame members, use a tenoning jig to help keep the stock square to the blade. A scrap of wood at the back of each piece helps prevent tear-out.

Figure 4. Use a doweling jig to help position the dowel holes in the front frame members.

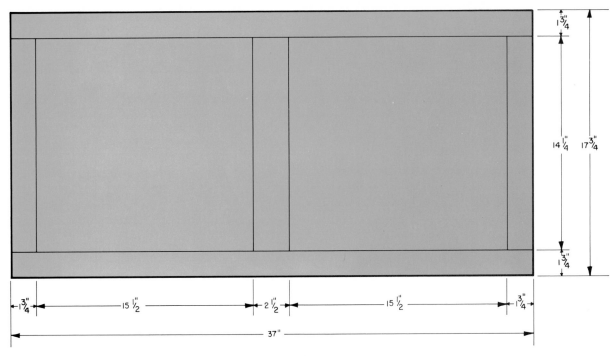

BOTTOM LAYOUT

the ¼″ panels. Casey used a medium walnut oil stain to finish his icebox. These panels must have at least one coat of finish *before* final assembly. This will prevent you from seeing thin lines of raw wood later on if the panels happen to shrink slightly. When the finish dries on the panels, assemble all frames with glue. Let the glue set up, then cut a ⅛″ kerf in the tops of the side frames and middle frame, where shown in the working drawings. You'll use these kerfs later on to attach the top.

Assemble the case with glue and wood screws. Check the assembly as you go to make sure all parts are square to each other. As you assemble the case, you can also assemble the floating shelves. Install them in the finished case with shelving supports to check the fit.

Figure 5. Drill screw pockets in the undersides of the stationary shelf frame members.

Making the Doors

The doors are assembled with tongues and grooves, like the other frames. However, to add strength to the doors, the frame joints are reinforced with dowels. Drill the holes for the dowels first, just as you did when you doweled the front frame members together. However, drill each dowel hole ⅜″ deeper than you ordinarily would. For example, if you're using 2″ dowels, drill each dowel hole 1⅜″ deep.

When you've finished drilling, make the tongues and grooves as you did before. If you wish, round the outside inner edge of the frame members, as shown in the working drawings. Use a ¼″ quarter-round shaper cutter or router bit. This will add a little decoration to the doors.

Dry assemble the doors and check the fit of the joints. With the dowels in place, the joints should look like the one shown in Figure 6. When you're satisfied that the door frame joints look right and fit properly, cut the door panels. Apply a coat of finish to the panels as you did before, then glue up the doors. Make sure that the doors are square in the clamps as the glue sets up.

Rabbet all the inside edges of the door frames to form a ⅜″ wide, ⅜″ deep door lip. Round over the outside edges with a ¼″ quarter-round cutter.

Note: Some icebox door hinges require a ½″ wide door lip. Check the instructions that come with the hardware.

Install the doors on the case with icebox hardware. There are several sources for this hardware:

Constantines
2050 Eastchester Road
Bronx, NY 10461

The Woodworkers Store
21801 Industrial Blvd.
Rogers, MN 55374

The Brass Tree
308 N. Main St.
St Charles, MO 63301

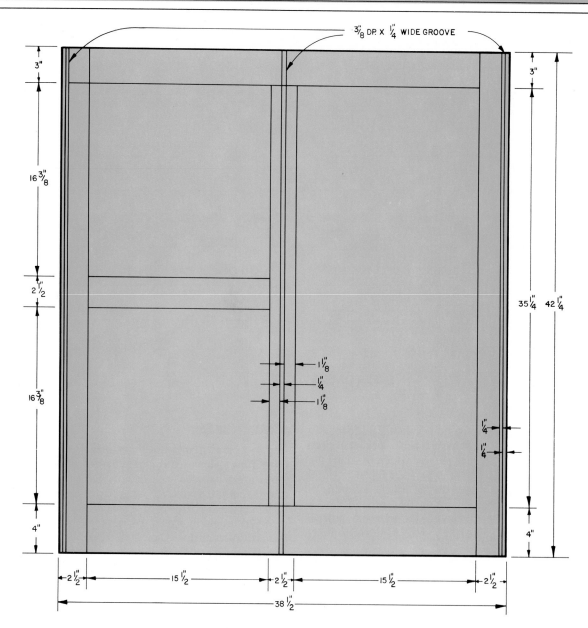

$\frac{3}{8}''$ DP. X $\frac{1}{4}''$ WIDE GROOVE

3"

3"

16 $\frac{3}{8}''$

2 $\frac{1}{2}''$

35 $\frac{1}{4}''$ 42 $\frac{1}{4}''$

16 $\frac{3}{8}''$

1 $\frac{1}{8}''$

$\frac{1}{4}''$

1 $\frac{1}{8}''$

$\frac{1}{4}''$

$\frac{1}{4}''$

4"

4"

2 $\frac{1}{2}''$ 15 $\frac{1}{2}''$ 2 $\frac{1}{2}''$ 15 $\frac{1}{2}''$ 2 $\frac{1}{2}''$

38 $\frac{1}{2}''$

FRONT PANEL LAYOUT

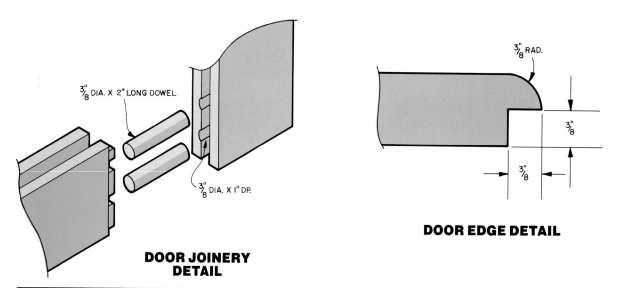

$\frac{3}{8}''$ DIA. X 2" LONG DOWEL

$\frac{3}{8}''$ DIA. X 1" DP.

$\frac{3}{8}''$ RAD.

$\frac{3}{8}''$

$\frac{3}{8}''$

DOOR JOINERY
DETAIL

DOOR EDGE DETAIL

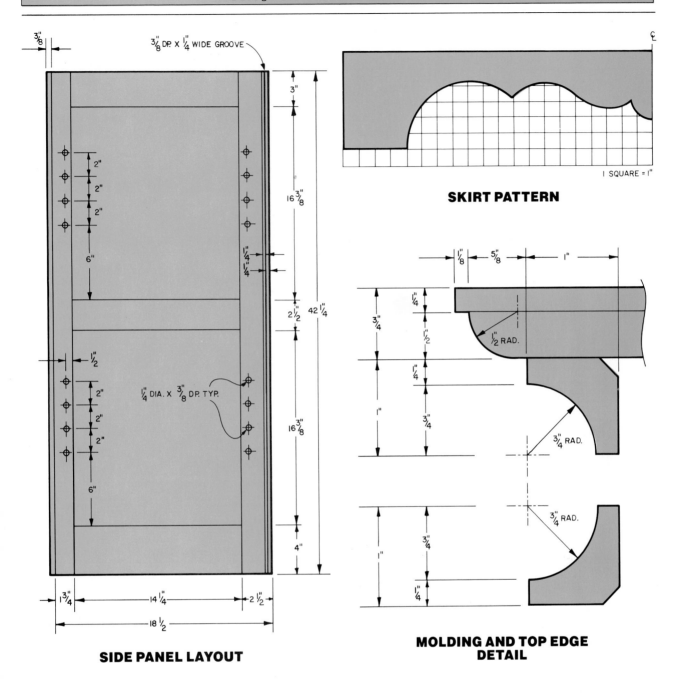

SKIRT PATTERN

I SQUARE = I"

SIDE PANEL LAYOUT

MOLDING AND TOP EDGE DETAIL

Try to get solid brass hardware. It will cost more, but it's worth it. Casey tried a set made from stamped metal and finally decided they weren't worth the bother. Cheap hardware just detracts from good woodworking.

Finishing Up

Glue up stock for the top, and shape the edge, as shown in the working drawings. Attach the top to the case with tabletop fasteners. These fasteners screw to the underside of the top, then hook in the kerfs that you cut in the middle and side frames. They are available from Constantines and The Woodworker's Store, mentioned previously.

Cut the skirt pieces to size, miter the ends, and cut a design with the front skirt on your bandsaw. Sand the skirt pieces, then attach the skirt to the case with glue and wood

Figure 6. When assembling the door frames, reinforce the tongue-and-groove joints with dowels. Do the doweling first, then cut the tongues and grooves.

screws. Pass the wood screws through from the *inside* of the frames, so that they don't show on the outside.

With a ½″ cove cutter on your shaper or molder, make enough cove molding for both the top and bottom of the icebox. To make the molding, *first* cut a cove in the edge of a board. *Then* rip the molding from the board. (See Figure 7.) Trying to shape or mold narrow stock is dangerous. Miter the molding, and attach it to the case with glue and brads. Countersink the head of the brads.

Finally, remove all hardware from the icebox, disassembling the doors and top. Also remove the floating shelves from the case. Finish sand any parts that still need sanding, then apply several coats of finish to the entire project. Be sure to finish both the inside *and* the outside of the icebox. When the finish is dry, reassemble the parts and fill the icebox with anything you want to — except frozen food.

Figure 7. Rip the cove molding from wider stock *after* you've cut the cove. Never try to shape narrow stock.

BILL OF MATERIALS — Wooden Icebox

Finished Dimensions in Inches

Front Frame

A.	Wide Corner Stiles (2)	¾ x 2½ x 42¼
B.	Front Middle Stile	¾ x 2½ x 35¼
C.	Front Upper Rail	¾ x 3 x 33½
D.	Front Middle Rail	¾ x 2½ x 15½
E.	Front Lower Rail	¾ x 4 x 33½

Side Frames

A.	Wide Corner Stiles (2)	¾ x 2½ x 42¼
F.	Narrow Corner Stiles (2)	¾ x 2⅛ x 42¼
G.	Upper Rails (2)	¾ x 3 x 15
H.	Middle Rails (2)	¾ x 2½ x 15
J.	Lower Side Rails (2)	¾ x 2½ x 15
K.	Panels (2)	¼ x 15 x 17⅛

Back Frame

F.	Narrow Corner Stiles (2)	¾ x 2⅛ x 42¼
L.	Back Middle Stile	¾ x 2½ x 36
M.	Back Upper Rail	¾ x 3 x 34¼
N.	Back Middle Rail	¾ x 2½ x 16¼
P.	Back Lower Rail	¾ x 4 x 34¼
Q.	Small Back Panels (2)	¼ x 16¼ x 17⅛
R.	Large Back Panel	¼ x 16¼ x 36

Middle Frame

G.	Upper Rail	¾ x 3 x 15
H.	Middle Rails (2)	¾ x 2½ x15
K.	Panel	¼ x 15 x 17⅛
S.	Short Stiles (2)	¾ x 2⅛ x 38¼
T.	Small Panel	¼ x 15 x 16⅝

Bottom Frame

V.	End Stiles	¾ x 1¾ x 15
W.	Bottom Middle Stile	¾ x 2½ x 15
X.	Bottom Rails	¾ x 1¾ x 37
Y.	Bottom Panels (2)	¾ x 15 x 16¼

Shelf Frames (Make 4)

V.	End Stiles (8)	¾ x 1¾ x 15
Z.	Shelf Rails (8)	¾ x 1¾ x 18⅛
AA.	Shelf Panels (4)	¾ x 15 x 15⅛

Small Doors (Make 2)

BB.	Small Door Stiles (4)	¾ x 2 x 17⅛
CC.	Door Rails (4)	¾ x 2 x 13
DD.	Small Door Panels (2)	¼ x 13 x 13⅞

Large Doors

CC.	Door Rails (2)	¾ x 2 x 13
EE.	Large Door Stiles (2)	¾ x 2 x 36
FF.	Large Door Panel	¼ x 13 x 32¾

Miscellaneous

GG.	Top	¾ x 21 x 42
HH.	Cove Molding (total)	¾ x 1⁷⁄₁₆ x 121½
JJ.	Side Skirts (2)	¾ x 6 x 19¼
KK.	Front Skirt	¾ x 6 x 40
LL.	Dowels (40)	⅜ Dia. x 2

Hardware

#8 x 1¼″ Flathead wood screws (2-3 dozen)
Tabletop fasteners and mounting screws (6)
2d finishing nails (¼ lb.)
Icebox hinges and mounting screws (3 pair)
Icebox latches and mounting screws (3)
Icebox medallion (optional)

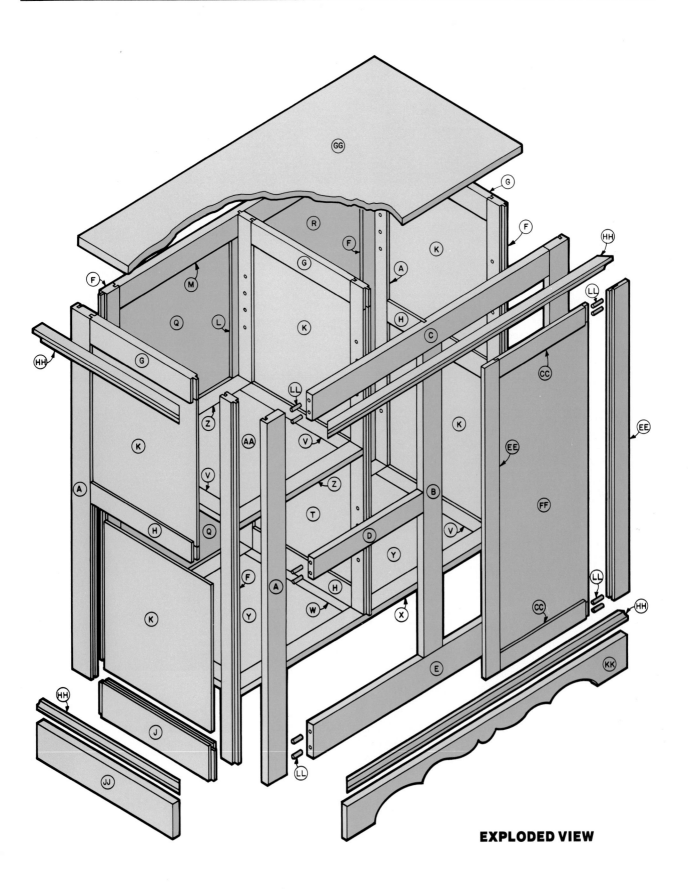

EXPLODED VIEW

Designed and Built by Nick Engler,
Painting by Alexandra Eldridge

Play Center

Child-size storage bench converts to a worktable and a drawing board.

It's hard to imagine that children would get excited over a piece of furniture, but when I showed this 'play center' to a young friend of mine, he told me, "Wow! It's just like a Transformer!"

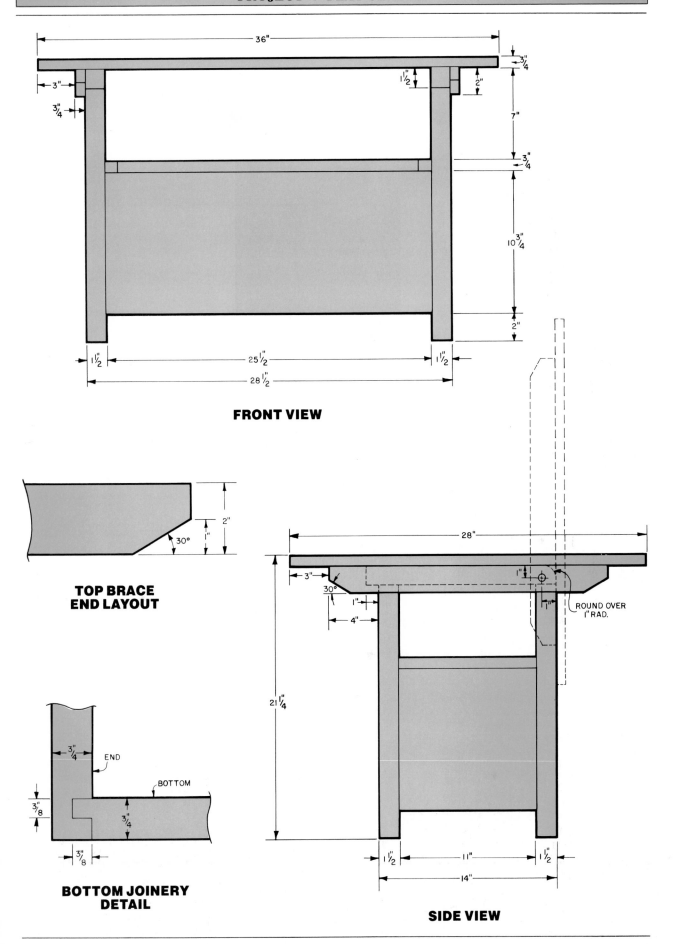

FRONT VIEW

TOP BRACE END LAYOUT

BOTTOM JOINERY DETAIL

SIDE VIEW

ROUND OVER 1" RAD.

END

BOTTOM

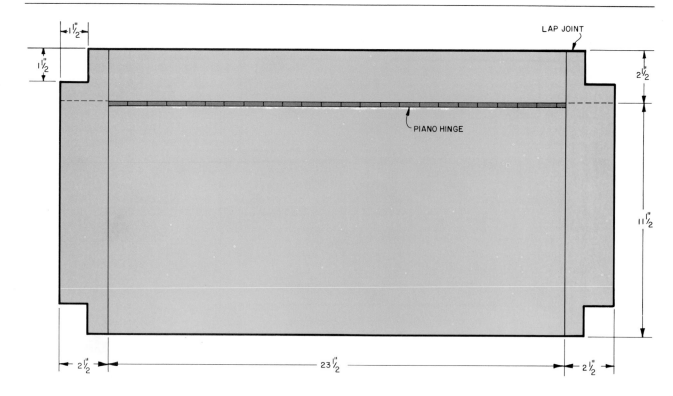

TOP LAYOUT

Those of you who have a lot to do with kids in this day and age will understand what Transformers® are. They're clever toy robots that fold up into dozens of different shapes — space ships, cars, animals, and so on. I suppose that, in a way, this piece of furniture could be called a Transformer®. Its design is based on the classic 'table/chair' concept — a table whose top flips up to make a chair. However, this particular piece serves not just two, but *four* functions. With the top up, it's a bench. The bench seat lifts up and the base can be used as a toy chest. With the top down, it's a play table that's just the right height for children 3-7 years old. (See Figure 1.) And

finally, the top can be braced at a slight angle to make an easel. (See Figure 2.)

Making the Base

The joinery in this project is very simple — rabbets and dadoes — but very strong. It has to be, to take the kind of abuse that kids dish out.

Begin by making the legs. These are perhaps the most complex parts in the project. They have a rabbet on one end that laps the arms, and a stop rabbet on the inside corner to accommodate the base. You can make a stop rabbet with a

Figure 1. The top of the play center tilts 90° so that your children can use it as a bench *or* a play table. The bench seat lifts up, as the base can be used as a toy chest.

Figure 2. Also, the top can be braced at an angle to make an art easel.

Designs by Alexandra Eldridge

POSSIBLE DESIGN PATTERNS

router, and then clean up the corners with a hand chisel. But that takes a lot of time to set up.

Instead, I elected to do it an easier way. Make each leg in *two* pieces. The outside piece is ¾″ x 1½″ x 20½″, and the inside piece is ¾″ x 1½″ x 19″. Using the bandsaw, cut a notch on the inside piece to form the stop rabbet. (See Figure 3.) Then glue the two pieces together. They will form a single leg with a lap joint on one end and a stop rabbet along the inside corner. (See Figure 4.)

Remember that the front and back legs must be mirror images of each other. The stop rabbet should be on the left

inside corner on two of the legs, and on the right on the other two.

While the glue on the legs is setting up, build the chest. This is just a simple box, joined at the corners with rabbets. Using a dado or router, cut rabbets in the ends and the bottom, as shown in the working drawings. Also cut a dado near the bottom edge of the end.

Assemble the chest with glue and wood screws. Counterbore and cover any screw heads that will show in the completed project, where the sides join the bottom. Use glue liberally where the sides join the ends and where the sides butt up to the bottom. However, *don't* put any glue in the dado or the rabbet where the bottom joins the ends. This joint must be free to expand and contract with the weather.

> **Tip** ◆ When you glue up the chest, be very careful that all the parts are square to one another. If any part is out of square, the rest of the project will be difficult to assemble.

When the glue has set up, finish sand the legs and the chest. Dry assemble them to check the fit. Make the arms and fit them to the legs, cutting the lap joints with a dado or bandsaw. Don't glue them in place yet; there is one more subassembly to make before you can assemble the base.

Cut the lap joints in the bench sides and bench back, using a dado or table saw. Glue these parts up, checking that they're square. After the glue is dry, cut the notches in the four corners to accommodate the legs. I suggest you cut the notches just a little small at first, then use a rasp to enlarge them until you get the fit you're after.

When you're satisfied that the legs, arms, chest, and benchtop assemblies all fit correctly, disassemble the base. Finish sand any parts that still need sanding, then reassemble the base with glue and wood screws. Once again, counterbore and cover the heads of any screws that will show in the completed project. *Don't* put screws in the lap joints where the arms join the legs.

Figure 3. Make the legs in two pieces, one a little shorter than the other. Cut a notch in the short piece to form the stop rabbet.

Figure 4. When you clamp the two pieces together, they'll form a leg with a lap joint on one end and a stop rabbet on the inside corner.

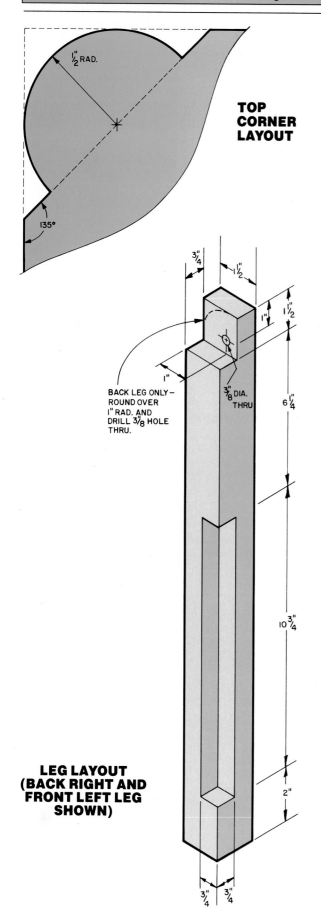

**TOP
CORNER
LAYOUT**

½" RAD.

135°

¾"

1½"

1"

1½"

1"

⅜" DIA.
THRU

6¼"

BACK LEG ONLY –
ROUND OVER
1" RAD. AND
DRILL ⅜ HOLE
THRU.

10¾"

2"

**LEG LAYOUT
(BACK RIGHT AND
FRONT LEFT LEG
SHOWN)**

¾"   ¾"

Making the Top

While the glue is drying on the base, glue up the stock for the top. Be careful that the end grains are all facing the same way and that they curve *up,* as shown in Figure 5. If the end grains are arranged randomly, the top may become wavy as time goes by. If the grains curve down, the edges may cup up. But if the end grains curve up, you can control the tendency of the top to cup with just a few screws.

Trim the top to size, and cut designs in the corners, if you wish. Finish sand the top and the braces, then carefully measure where you want to position the braces on the underside of the top. There should be about ¹⁄₁₆" gap between the braces and the arms when the top is centered on the base.

When you've got the braces properly positioned, attach them to the top with wood screws. *Do not* glue the braces to the top. If you do, the top will not be able to expand and contract properly with the weather, and it may warp. Instead, counterbore the screws so that the heads can be covered. Then slightly elongate the holes for the screw shafts. (See Figure 6.) This will allow for any movement of the wood.

Final Assembly

Fit the bench lid to the base and attach it with a piano hinge. Install a lid support so that the lid doesn't come banging down on little fingers. I chose to use a friction support, as shown in Figure 7. This support will hold the lid open at any angle.

Scribe a 1" radius arc on the back corners of the arms, as shown in the drawings, and round them over with a sabre saw and rasp. Carefully mark the center of the arc and drill a ⅜" hole for the pivot bolt.

Center the top assembly on the base and clamp it in place. Using the pivot holes in the arms as guides, drill through the top braces. Clamp a block of wood on the outside of the braces where the holes will come through to prevent tear-out.

> **Tip ◆** In order to drill these holes in the braces, you may have to use a right-angle adapter on your drill. (See Figure 8.) If you don't have an adapter, mark the position of the holes and remove the screws that hold the brace to the top. Once you've detached the braces, you can drill the holes in them with a drill press.

Attach the top to the base with ⅜" carriage bolts, flat washers, and stop nuts. The heads of the bolts should be on the inside of the arms, and the stop nuts on the outside of the braces. Place washers between the braces and the arms, as well as on the ends of the bolts, between the braces and the stop nuts. Tighten the stop nuts down until it takes a positive force to raise or lower the table. The friction generated by the stop nuts squeezing the washers and wooden parts together will keep the top from slamming down unexpectedly.

To help keep the top in the vertical position, you should also install bullet catches in the braces. Drill small stopped holes in the legs to fit these catches. (See Figure 9.)

Finally, drill ½" stopped holes in the top and one arm to accommodate the easel brace. If you wish, you can drill several sets of holes so that the 'easel' can be adjusted to different angles.

Finishing the Play Center

Finish sand any parts that still need it, then apply an oil finish to the project. I used Watco Danish Oil, since this finish becomes non-toxic after it's set up for several weeks.

If you wish, you can paint right on top of the oil finish and decorate the play center any way you wish. I've included several possible designs, in varying degrees of complexity, with the plans.

Figure 5. When gluing up the stock for the top, make sure that the end grains all curve *up*, towards the top surface. If they're arranged randomly, or if they curve down, the surface may become uneven.

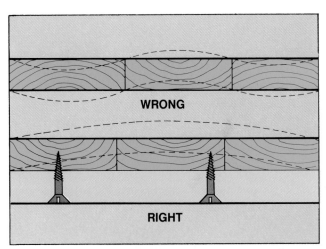

WRONG

RIGHT

Figure 6. When joining the top to the braces, slightly elongate the holes for the screw shanks. This will allow the top to expand and contract with the weather.

Figure 7. A friction lid support will hold the lid to the chest open at any angle — and keep it from slamming down on tiny fingers.

Figure 8. A right-angle adapter for your drill lets you drill corners in some tight places. You may have to use an adapter like this to drill the pivot holes in the braces.

Figure 9. Install bullet catches in the braces to help hold the top in the vertical position.

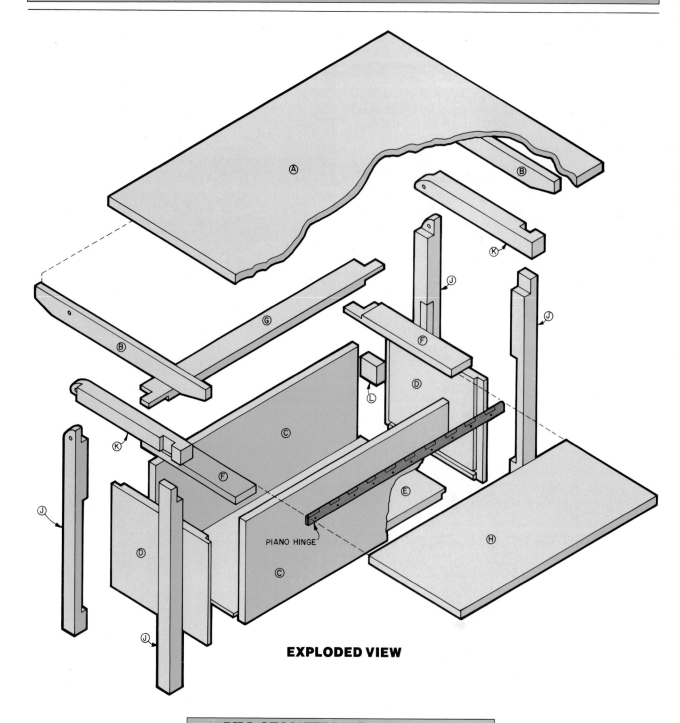

EXPLODED VIEW

PIANO HINGE

BILL OF MATERIALS — Play Center

Finished Dimensions in Inches

A.	Top	¾ x 28 x 36
B.	Top Braces (2)	¾ x 2 x 22
C.	Sides (2)	¾ x 10¾ x 26¼
D.	Ends (2)	¾ x 10¾ x 12½
E.	Bottom	¾ x 11 x 26¼
F.	Bench sides (2)	¾ x 2½ x 14
G.	Bench back	¾ x 2½ x 28½
H.	Bench lid	¾ x 11½ x 23½
J.	Legs (4)	1½ x 1½ x 20½
K.	Arms (2)	1½ x 1½ x 15
L.	Mounting block	1 x 2 x 2

Hardware

⅜" x 3" Carriage bolts (2)
⅜" Flat washers (4)
⅜" Stop nuts (2)
1½" (open) x 23½" Piano hinge and mounting screws
Friction lid support and mounting screws
Bullet catches (2)
#8 x 1¼" Flathead wood screws (2-3 dozen)
#8 x 1¼" Roundhead wood screws and flat washers (6)

Designed and Built by Nick Engler

Fence-Sittin' Bird Feeder

Mount this bird feeder right to your fence.

You've probably seen bird feeders similar to this before. But I doubt that you've seen any quite so easy to mount in your backyard. There are no poles to plant, or hooks to install. All you do is set it atop a fence or privacy screen.

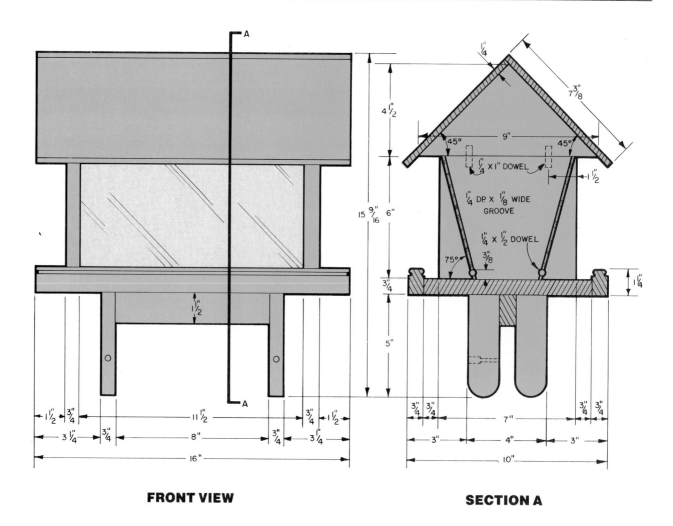

FRONT VIEW

SECTION A

Making the Feeder

To make the feeder, first measure the thickness of the boards in the fence where you want to place the feeder. This will determine the width of the slots in the fence mounts. You should make the slots 1/16"–1/8" wider than the fence boards to allow for expansion and contraction of the wood.

Next, choose the wood you'll use to make this project. Since the feeder will sit outside, redwood or cedar are your best choices. Avoid pressure-treated lumber. The chemicals used in some pressure treatments may be hazardous to wildlife, particularly if these chemicals should leech out into the feed.

Cut all the parts to size, and cut the shape of the mounts on a bandsaw. Use a taper jig to saw the kerfs in the ends that will hold the glass. (See Figure 1.) Drill 1/4" holes near the bottom of each kerf, and insert dowels in the holes. These dowels will keep the bottom edge of the glass slightly above the base.

Cut the bead on the lip with a molder or a shaper. This bead serves as a toehold for the birds, so that they get a good grip when they land on the feeder.

Figure 1. Use a taper jig to cut the 1/8" kerfs in the sides.

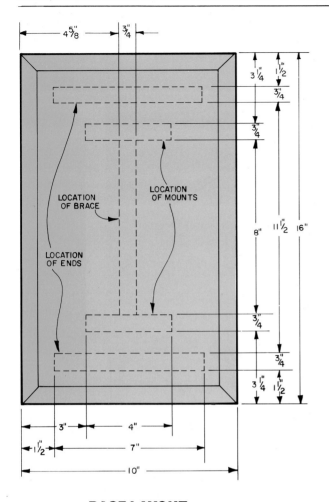

BASE LAYOUT

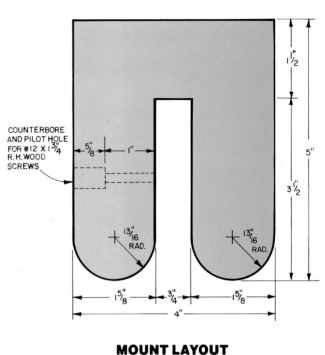

MOUNT LAYOUT

Figure 2. Dowel the gable ends to the ends of the feeder. That way, you can remove the roof when you need to fill the feeder.

Assemble all parts with galvanized nails and resorcinol glue. Reinforce the butt joints between the mounts and the base with brass wood screws. The galvanized nails and brass screws won't rust and stain the wood. The resorcinol glue is waterproof, and is especially made for use outdoors. *Don't glue the gable ends to the ends. Instead, dowel these parts together.* (See Figure 2.) That way, you'll be able to easily remove the roof and refill the feeder with seeds.

Tip ◆ The dowel should be snug; you don't want the roof blowing off in a wind storm.

Fill the finished feeder with seeds and set it along your fence wherever you can easily watch the birds come and go. If you want to attach it to the fence more permanently, sink brass screws through the mounts into the fence.

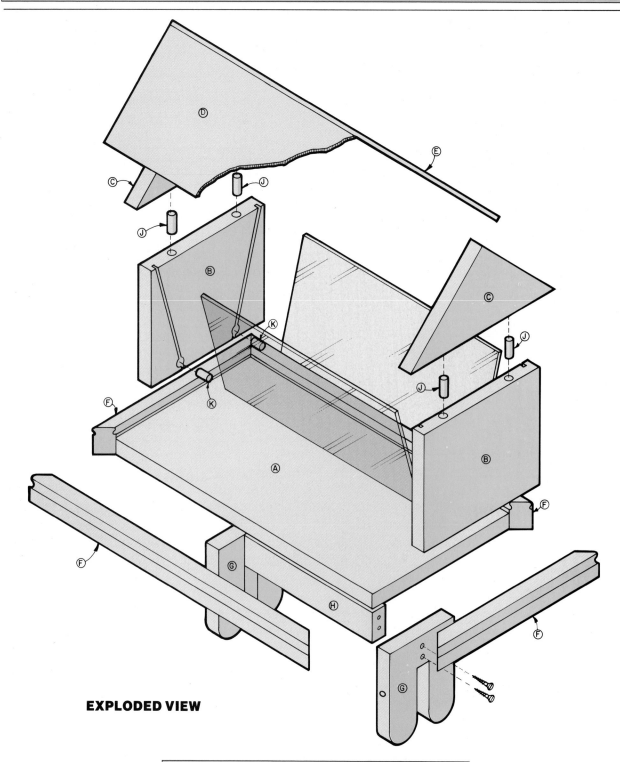

EXPLODED VIEW

BILL OF MATERIALS — Bird Feeder

Finished Dimensions in Inches

A.	Base	¾ x 8½ x 14½	**J.**	Dowels (4)	¼ dia. x 1
B.	Ends (2)	¾ x 6 x 7	**K.**	Glass stops (4)	¼ dia. x ½
C.	Gable ends (2)	¾ x 4½ x 9			
D.	Short roof	¼ x 7⅛ x 16			
E.	Long roof	¼ x 7⅜ x 16			
F.	Lip (total)	¾ x 1¼ x 53½			
G.	Mounts (2)	¾ x 4 x 5			
H.	Brace	¾ x 1½ x 8			

Hardware

#12 x 1¾" Roundhead wood screws (2)
#8 x 1½" Brass flathead wood screws (4)
6d Galvanized finishing nails (8-12)
⅛" x 5¾" x 12" Glass (2)

Designed and Built by Nick Engler

Video Tower

This roll-about television stand also stores a VCR and tapes.

I t's hardly tall enough to be a tower, I know. But it does store all your video equipment and accessories on one handy vertical cart.

As shown, the television sits atop the cart. Below it, there is a shelf for a VCR. And below that are two drawers to store video cassette tapes and other accessories. (See Figure 1.) It may not take any prizes as far as towers go, but it's pretty handy for its size.

Making the Cart

To build this tiny 'tower', start with the basic cart. Glue up the stock for the sides and shelves. Cut the stock to size, then cut the dadoes in the sides. Since these are 'stopped' dadoes —

they're closed at one end — the easiest tool to use to make them is a router.

Measure the distance from the edge of your router's base plate to the center of the chuck. This is the *radius* of your router. On the sides, mark the centerlines of the dadoes you want to cut. Clamp a *straight* scrap of wood to a side, parallel to the first dado and exactly the same distance away from the centerline as the radius of your router. Adjust the router to cut

Figure 1. The bottom of this 'video tower' sports two drawers. Each drawer will store dozens of video cassette tapes, plus other video accessories.

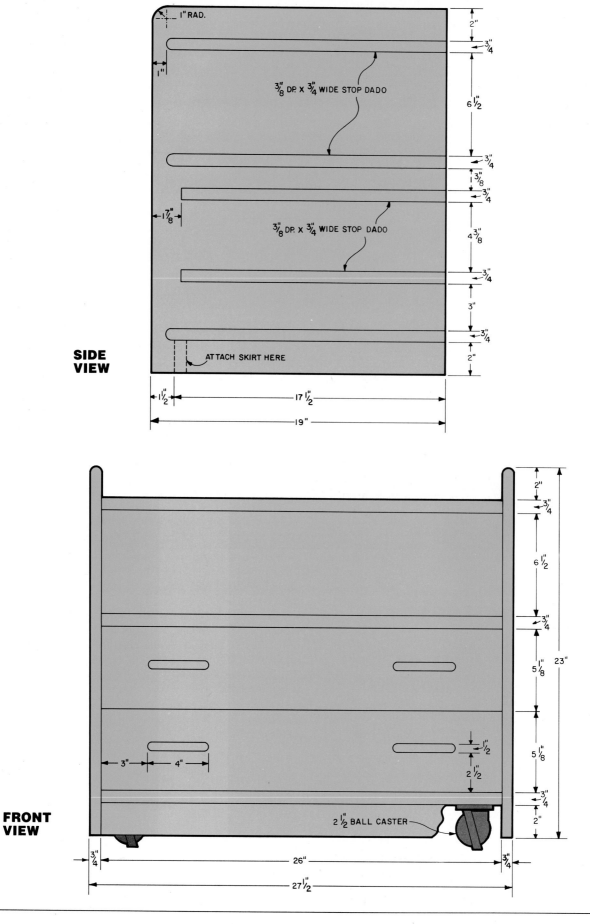

SIDE VIEW

1" RAD.

2"
3/4"
1"
6 1/2"
3/8" DP. X 3/4" WIDE STOP DADO
3/4"
1 3/8"
3/4"
1 7/8"
3/8" DP. X 3/4" WIDE STOP DADO
4 3/8"
3/4"
3"
3/4"
ATTACH SKIRT HERE
2"

1 1/2"
17 1/2"
19"

FRONT VIEW

2"
3/4"
6 1/2"
3/4"
5 1/8"
23"
1/2"
5 1/8"
2 1/2"
3/4"
2"
3"
4"
2 1/2" BALL CASTER

3/4"
26"
3/4"
27 1/2"

132

no more than ⅛″ deep and make the first pass, keeping the router pressed firmly against the makeshift fence. (See Figure 2.) Stop the cut as you reach the point where you want to 'stop' the dado. Turn the router off, adjust it to cut another ⅛″ deeper, and make another pass. Repeat this process until you have cut the dado as deep as specified on the working drawings. Then move the fence and rout another dado.

You can also use a router arm to cut the dadoes, if the throat of the tool is deep enough to cut the dadoes in the middle of the sides. To use the router arm, simply set the fence the proper distance away from the bit and make your cut. (See Figure 3.) Once again, rout each dado in several passes, cutting no more than ⅛″ deeper with each pass.

> **Tip** ◆ Whether you use a hand-held router or a router arm, feed the bit into the wood (or the wood into the bit) so that the rotation of the bit helps hold the power tool (or the workpiece) against the fence. (See Figure 4.)

With a bandsaw or a sabre saw, round off the front top corners of the sides. Then round over the front and top edges of the sides, and the front edges of the shelves and front stretcher. Use a ⅜″ quarter-round bit in your router or shaper to round these edges. (See Figure 5.)

Make the drawer guides and round the front ends to fit the dadoes. You can do this last bit of rounding with a rasp or a sander.

Dry assemble all the parts of the cart to check their fit. When you're convinced that they fit correctly, disassemble the parts and finish sand all surfaces. Reassemble the parts with glue and wood screws. Countersink and counterbore all screws, and cover the heads with wooden plugs.

Making the Drawers

The drawers are simple boxes, with a ⅜″ face mounted to the front. The back, front, and sides are assembled with lock joints. To make a lock joint, first cut dadoes in the drawer sides. (See Figure 6.) Then cut a groove in the ends of the drawer backs and fronts, creating two tenons in each end. (See Figure 7.) A tenoning jig helps to keep the workpiece square to the blade. Finally, cut all the *inside* tenons on each end of each part to the proper length to fit the grooves in the sides. (See Figure 8.) Cut narrow grooves on the inside surfaces of all drawer parts to hold the drawer bottoms.

Dry assemble the drawers and check their fit in the cart. When you're satisfied, glue them up. When the glue is dry, cut the grooves on the outside surfaces of the drawer sides to fit the drawer guides. These grooves should be $1/32″$-$1/16″$ wider than the drawer guides. Finish off the drawers by gluing the drawer faces to the drawer front. Place the drawer faces carefully; they must not rub when the drawers are pulled in and out.

Figure 2. To cut the dadoes with a hand-held router, clamp a straight scrap of wood to the work-piece to serve as a fence.

Figure 3. If you have a router arm, use the fence as a guide to cut the dadoes. Cut each dado in several passes, cutting a little deeper with each pass.

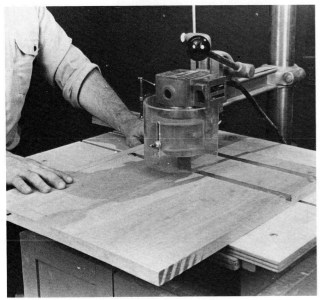

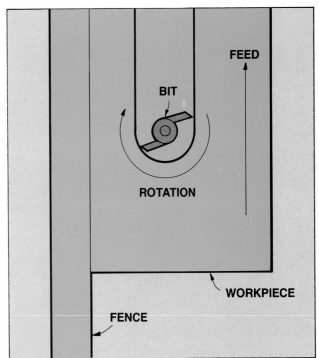

Figure 4. Pay attention to how you feed the bit into the wood (or the wood into the bit). Use the rotation of the bit to help hold the power tool (or the workpiece) against the fence.

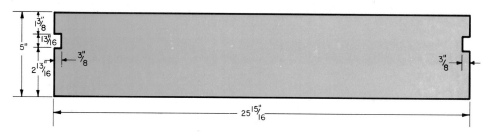

DRAWER/BACK VIEW

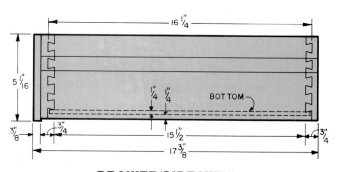

DRAWER/SIDE VIEW

Finishing Up

Finish sand any parts that still need it, and attach the drawer pulls to the drawer faces. The type of pulls used here are called 'wire pulls'. These are made from wood, but you can also get them in metal. They're available from:

The Woodworker's Store
21801 Industrial Blvd.
Rogers, MN 55374

Finally, apply a finish to the drawer faces and the cart. Be careful to finish the inside of the cart as well as the outside. This will keep the wood from warping. After the finish dries, attach casters to the stretchers, if you so desire, and apply a little paraffin wax to the drawer guides to help the drawers slide smoothly.

Figure 7. Cut a groove in the ends of the drawer fronts and backs, making two tenons in each end. The depth of this groove should be equal to the thickness of the sides. A tenoning jig helps keep the workpiece square to the blade.

Figure 8. Finally, cut the *inside* tenons on the drawer backs and front to the proper length to fit the dadoes in the sides.

Figure 5. Use a ⅜″ quarter-round bit in your router or shaper to round over the various edges of the parts of the cart.

Figure 6. To make a lock joint, first cut dadoes on the inside surfaces of the sides.

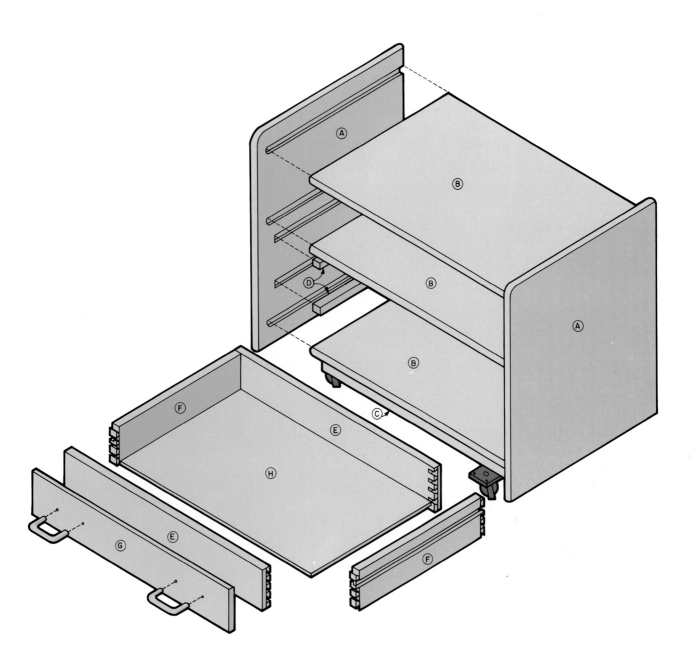

EXPLODED VIEW

BILL OF MATERIALS — Video Tower

Finished Dimensions in Inches

A.	Sides (2)	¾ x 19 x 23
B.	Shelves (3)	¾ x 18 x 26¾
C.	Skirt	¾ x 2 x 26
D.	Drawer Guides (4)	¾ x ¾ x 17⅛
E.	Drawer Ends (4)	¾ x 5 x 25¹⁵⁄₁₆
F.	Drawer Sides (4)	¾ x 5 x 16¼
G.	Drawer Fronts (2)	⅜ x 5¹⁄₁₆ x 25¹⁵⁄₁₆
H.	Drawer Bottoms (2)	¼ x 16 x 24¹⁵⁄₁₆

Hardware

2½″ Ball casters and mounting screws (4)
Rope drawer pulls (4)
#8 x 1¼″ Flathead wood screws (12-18)

Designed and Built by Ethan Perry

Windsor Dining Chair

This elegant chair is simpler to make than it looks.

Have you ever heard how the Windsor chair was 'discovered'? I can't vouch that this is plain, unvarnished history, but this is how I heard the story:

It used to be that the best wooden chairs had solid seats and backs. These parts were either all wood, or they were frames that were 'woven in', such as a cane chair. The next best chair design used horizontal wooden slats for the back. Anything else was thought of as uncomfortable.

Then, one day in the early part of the seventeenth century, the Duke of Windsor was out riding around his countryside. He came upon a chairmaker who was making chairs with backs composed of thin, vertical spindles. This was normally considered to be a peasant's design — inexpensive, rough, and uncomfortable. Nonetheless, the Duke was

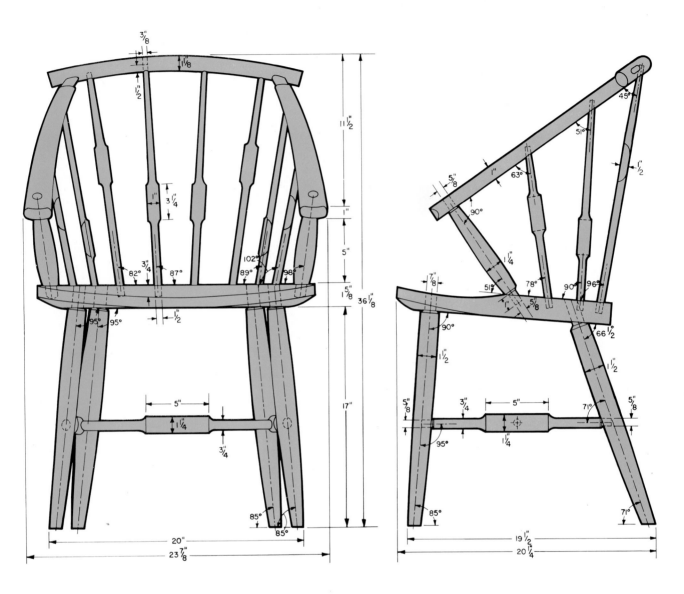

FRONT VIEW

SIDE VIEW

intrigued by the quality of this particular craftsman's work. The spindles were delicate and well-turned, and the overall design was appealing. When he sat in one of the chairs, he got a pleasant surprise. The chair was as comfortable as anything he presently owned.

The Duke ordered a set for his dining room, and began using them when he entertained. The upper class who visited Windsor Castle admired the Duke's chairs, and soon began to ask their cabinetmakers for 'Windsor chairs'. The design — and the name — caught on quickly, and its popularity hasn't abated to this day.

Throughout the following centuries, there have been many different variations on the Windsor theme. The elegant arm chair you see here is one of the most recent. It was

crafted by Ethan Perry, a professional cabinetmaker in Frenchtown, New York. The chair looks difficult to make, but Ethan designed this chair so that he could make four of them rather quickly. Despite its appearance, there is no wood to be bent and no tricky spindle-turning in this project. Ethan's chair is yet another example of what the Duke of Windsor discovered so long ago: Fine woodworking doesn't depend on fancy, complicated woodworking. All it takes is a good design and careful work.

Making the Parts

The techniques used to make the individual parts of this chair are rather common. It's Ethan's application that's ingenious.

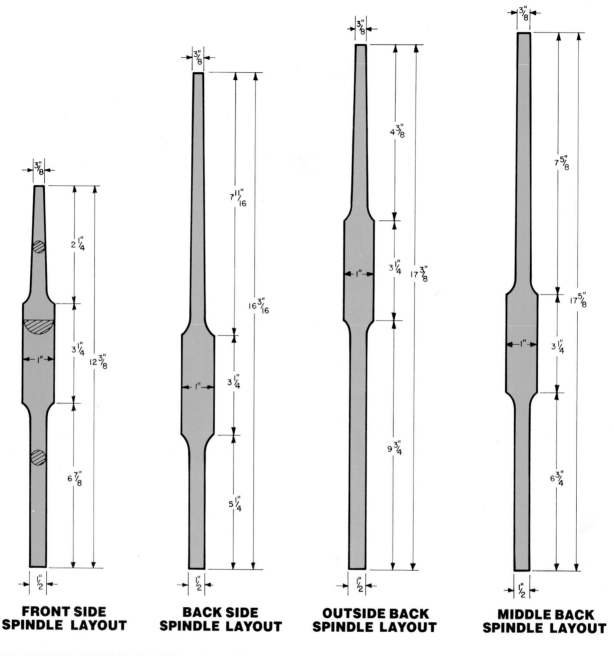

**FRONT SIDE
SPINDLE LAYOUT**

**BACK SIDE
SPINDLE LAYOUT**

**OUTSIDE BACK
SPINDLE LAYOUT**

**MIDDLE BACK
SPINDLE LAYOUT**

Figure 1. Cut the rough shape of the spindles on a band-saw. Leave a wide, flat area in the middle of each spindle.

The side and back spindles look as if they were turned on two different centers. Actually, they aren't turned at all. Ethan contoured these parts with a bandsaw and a shaper!

To make the spindles, first select straight-grained stock, 1⅛″ wide and ⅝″ thick. (The finished spindles will be 1″ x ½″, as shown in the Bill of Materials. You'll need the extra stock so that you have 'room to work'.) Avoid any figuring. This will not only make the spindles difficult to shape; it may weaken them.

Draw the spindle pattern on the face of the stock, and cut it out on a bandsaw. (See Figure 1.) Each spindle should have a 1″ 'flat', 3¼″ long in the middle. Note that position of these flats changes with each spindle — some up, some down, depending on the spindle's position in the chair. This flat should taper quickly to ½″ at both ends. The lower part of the

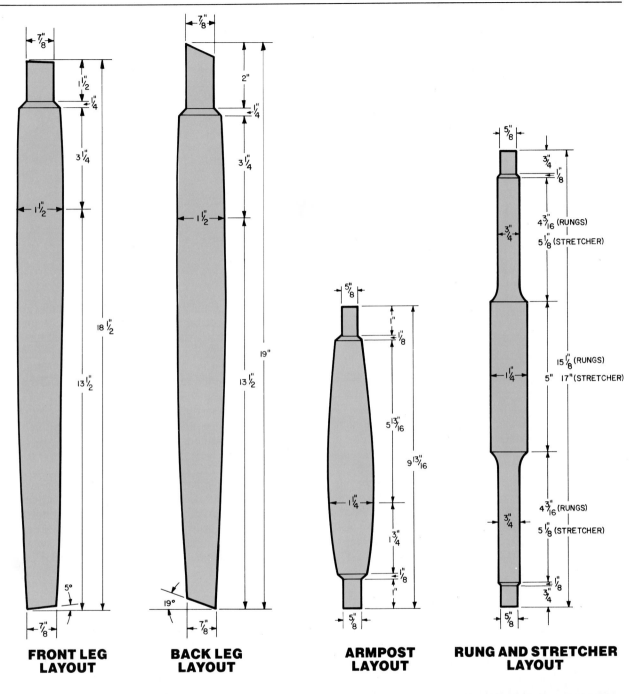

FRONT LEG LAYOUT

BACK LEG LAYOUT

ARMPOST LAYOUT

RUNG AND STRETCHER LAYOUT

spindle remains a constant ½″ wide to the end, but the upper parts taper down to ⅜″. Cut a little wide of these dimensions, so that you have room to scrape and sand.

Round over the back edges of the flats with a ½″ quarter-round cutter on your shaper. (See Figure 2.) Then round over all edges of the narrow parts with a ¼″ quarter-round cutter. (See Figure 3.) This will give you the rough shape of the spindle. Finally, scrape each spindle down with a spokeshave, rasp, and sandpaper, until you have removed all the millmarks and the transition from the narrows to the flats is smooth and flowing.

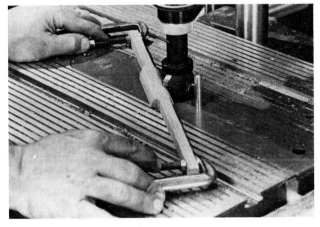

Figure 2. Shape the back side of the flats with a ½″ quarter-round cutter.

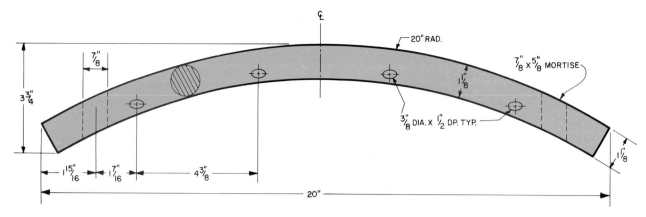

HEADPIECE LAYOUT

The headpiece and the arms are made in the same fashion. The exception here is that the joinery must be cut before you contour the parts. Trace the shape of the headpiece on 1¼″ thick stock, and the arms on 1″ thick stock. Carefully mark the position of the mortises in the headpiece, then make these mortises on your drill press. (See Figure 4.) Drill a series of holes, then clean up the sides of the mortise with a chisel. Cut the curves of the headpiece with a bandsaw, then round over all edges with a ⅝″ quarter-round shaper cutter. A rule-joint cutter will cut a ⅝″ round. If you don't have one of these, you can always cut a ½″ round, then work the piece down by hand.

Cut the tenons in the arm stock with a dado cutter. If you wish, you can angle the miter gauge at 25° to cut the long shoulders of the tenon, then cut the edges by hand. This will give you a closer fit when you slip the arms into the headpiece. However, Ethan cut square tenons, and they look just

fine. Round over the edges of each tenon to fit the mortises. (See Figure 5.) Then cut two long notches in each tenon, each notch approximately ⅛″ wide. These notches will accommodate wedges when you assemble the chair. (See Figure 6.)

Round over the edges of the arms with a ½″ quarter-round shaper cutter. Scrape and sand the arms and the headpiece to remove all millmarks.

The armpost, rungs, stretcher, and legs are all turned on a lathe. There is nothing special about the way that they're turned; just remember to score the rungs and the legs so that you can properly position the holes afterwards. Or, if you prefer, you can drill these holes *before* you do the turning. However, if you drill the holes first, you must be very careful that you turn the contours so that the holes end up in the proper position. After you turn the legs, cut a long notch in the tenons. Like the arms, these pieces will be wedged in place.

Finally, cut the shape of the seat on a bandsaw, and drill the holes for the spindles and the armposts. But don't scoop it out or drill the leg holes just yet.

Assembly

When you have a project with this many angles, assembly can be difficult. Add to this the fact that many of these angles

Figure 3. Shape the narrow parts of the spindles with a ¼″ quarter-round shaper cutter, then clean up the spindles with a spokeshave.

Figure 4. Drill the mortises in the headpiece before you cut the curves on the bandsaw.

are *compound*. For example, the back middle spindles lean at 93° to each side, and 96° to the back. If it was necessary to be absolutely accurate, assembly would be a nightmare. However, one of the best features about Windsor design is that there's a lot of leeway in the angles. The thin spindles will flex a great deal. You can 'eyeball' the holes, and if you've got a good eye and a steady hand with the drill, you should get good results.

Dry assemble the legs, rungs, and stretcher; and set them all to their proper angles. Mark the seat for the leg holes, but *don't* drill them yet. Set the seat atop the legs, then walk around the assembly and eyeball the parts. Will the holes work if you drill them as marked? Should you move them slightly? Change the angles slightly? Adjust the position and angles of the leg holes as you think necessary, then drill them.

If you're a little skittish about doing this for the first time, make a 'practice seat' out of construction lumber. Drill four practice holes and see how the legs fit. Once you've got your confidence up, do it for real.

Dry assemble the legs to the seat, then insert the spindles and the armposts in the seat. Mark headpiece and arms where the joinery holes should be drilled, according to the working drawings. Dry assemble the arms and headpiece, then set them atop the spindles. Once again, eyeball the parts.

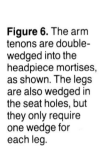

Figure 5. Round the edges of the tenons in the arms to fit the mortises in the headpiece.

Figure 6. The arm tenons are double-wedged into the headpiece mortises, as shown. The legs are also wedged in the seat holes, but they only require one wedge for each leg.

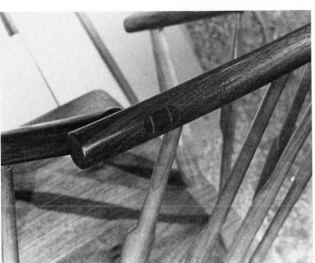

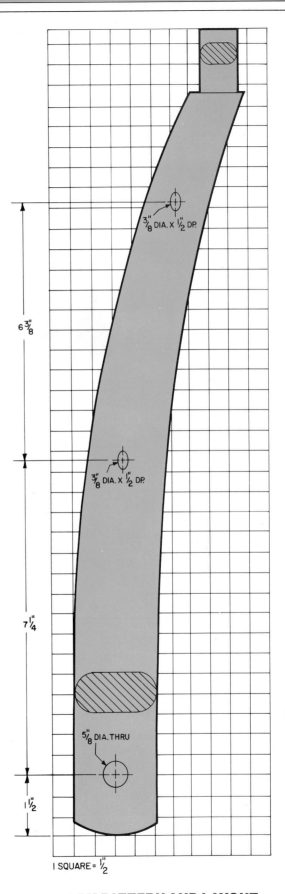

$6\frac{3}{8}$

$7\frac{1}{4}$

$1\frac{1}{2}$

$\frac{3}{8}"$ DIA. X $\frac{1}{2}"$ DP.

$\frac{3}{8}"$ DIA. X $\frac{1}{2}"$ DP.

$\frac{5}{8}"$ DIA. THRU

I SQUARE = $\frac{1}{2}$

ARM PATTERN AND LAYOUT

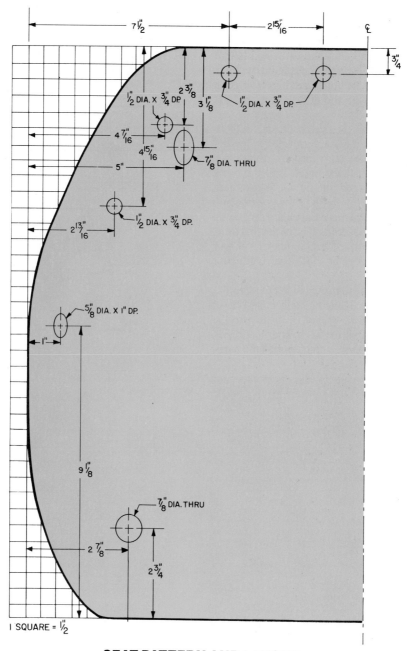

SEAT PATTERN AND LAYOUT

Decide if you want to move the position or adjust the angle of any holes, then drill them. Dry assemble the arms and headpiece to the chair to check the fit of all the parts.

When you're satisfied that all parts fit together reasonably well, disassemble the chair. Scoop out the seat according to the working drawings. There are many tools you can use for scooping, besides the obvious 'chair scoop'. Different chair designers have used gouges, ball mills mounted in routers, even the nose of a chainsaw. Ethan used a core-box bit in a router to cut the deepest parts of the seat, then finished up with a round-bottomed spokeshave.

Finish sand any parts that still need it, then reassemble the chair parts with glue and wedges. Keep a bucket of water and a wet rag handy, and wipe off any glue that squeezes out of the joints before it dries. This will raise the grain slightly, but it won't be as much work to sand the grain down again as it is to sand off glue beads from between the spindles. Wrap the entire assembly with band clamps, and let the glue cure.

Sand the wedges and the tenons flush with the surface of the chair, and give the chair a final sanding with very fine sandpaper. Also, cut the ends of the legs at an angle so they sit flush with the surface. Once again, this is an operation that you have to eyeball. Apply a good, hard finish that will show off the wood grain. When the finish is dry, rub it down with paste wax and 0000 steel wool. Then take a breather — sit down in the chair and relax.

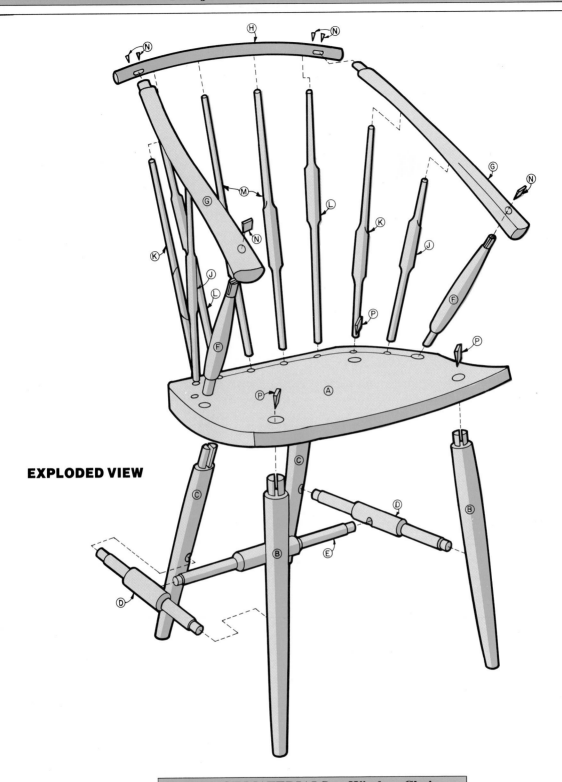

EXPLODED VIEW

BILL OF MATERIALS — Windsor Chair

Finished Dimensions in Inches

A.	Seat	1⅝ x 17 x 21⅞	**H.**	Headpiece	1⅛ x 3¾ x 20
B.	Front legs (2)	1½ dia. x 18½	**J.**	Front side spindles (2)	½ x 1 x 12⅜
C.	Back legs (2)	1½ dia. x 19	**K.**	Back side spindles (2)	½ x 1 x 16³⁄₁₆
D.	Rungs (2)	1¼ dia. x 15⅛	**L.**	Outside back spindles (2)	½ x 1 x 17⅜
E.	Stretcher	1¼ dia. x 17	**M.**	Middle back spindles (2)	½ x 1 x 17⅝
F.	Armposts (2)	1¼ dia. x 9¹³⁄₁₆	**N.**	Arm wedges (6)	⅛ x ⅝ x 1
G.	Arms (2)	1 x 4½ x 19⅞	**P.**	Leg wedges (4)	⅛ x 1¼ x 1½

TECHNIQUES

Text by Nick Engler and Jim McCann

The Dovetail Joint

Whether you make it by hand or machine, the dovetail is one classy joint.

The dovetail joint is perhaps the most beautiful and the most intriguing joint in all of woodworking. A well-made dovetail has an aesthetic quality that enhances any piece of furniture. And part of this appeal is its mystery: How do those odd-shaped tails and pins fit together? And how does a craftsman cut so many different angles and get them all to fit together so well?

Cutting a dovetail joint is a lesson in patience, but it isn't as hard as it looks. The precision you need to make a good-looking dovetail is more a matter of time than skill. You simply need to understand the steps involved, then take the time to perform each step carefully.

A Little History

Believe it or not, the dovetail joint started out as housebuilding joint. That's right — the primary purpose of this delicate bit of woodworking was to hold huge timbers together in timberframe houses and buildings.

In medieval times, there was no real distinction between carpenters and cabinetmakers. Anyone who worked wood was a joiner — you joined pieces of wood. During the spring, summer, and fall, when the weather was good, you built houses and barns. During the winter, or when the weather turned sour, you built things that went in houses — furniture. There's a good reason that so many of the pieces of medieval furniture that survive today are massive. They were built by woodworkers whose tools and skills were oriented towards joining huge timbers and planks. Try to cut a ¼″ wide tenon in a ½″ thick board with a bowsaw and an axe.

The most common joint in medieval housebuilding was the mortise-and-tenon. Nails and other hardware were scarce, so joiners cut timbers to lock together without metal fasteners. The tenon was usually pinned in the mortise with a peg, until some nameless joiner had the bright idea of widening the end of the tenon and narrowing the beginning of the mortise. The result was a mortise-and-tenon that pinned itself together. Since the tenon now splayed out like a dove's tail, that's what the joiners named the joint — the dovetail.

The dovetail didn't completely replace the mortise-and-tenon, of course. But joiners did find many uses for it. The joint could only be pulled apart from one direction, and so they used it to hold together timbers that were being pulled or pushed apart from another direction. For instance, dovetails were used to join floor and ceiling joists to sills and plates. Not only did the dovetail hold the joists in place, they kept the walls from splaying out.

In making furniture, joiners began to find other uses for dovetails. Sometimes the front rails or 'bearing' rails of a chest were dovetailed into the side panels. This kept the sides from splaying out. However, some of the other common uses that we associate with dovetails — such as joining the parts of a drawer together — didn't come until much later, with the advent of more precise woodworking tools and methods.

During the Renaissance, some joiners began to specialize in building furniture. The occupation of cabinetmaker was born. With this new occupation came new tools. Saws and planes evolved that could pare wood down to smaller and smaller dimensions. With smaller boards, cabinetmakers began to build delicate furniture. This furniture, of course, was put together with delicate joints. Among them was the cabinetmaker's dovetail.

Types of Dovetails

There are several types of dovetail joints. First of all, there is a distinction between the 'joiner's dovetail' and the 'cabinetmaker's dovetail', as you might have guessed from the history lesson you just read. The major differences are the size of the 'pins', and the splay of the 'tail'. In a joiner's dovetail, the tail is wide and the pins are massive. They have to be, in order to support and hold the weight of house timbers. The cabinetmaker's tails are much more subtle, and the pins are tiny. Sometimes, the pins are barely there. (See Figure 1.)

Among cabinetmaker's dovetails, there are three types that are used commonly — the 'full' dovetail, the 'half-blind' dovetail, and the 'french' dovetail. On a full dovetail, you can see both the tails and the pins at the corner of the joint. On a half-blind dovetail, the pins aren't cut all the way through the board so that all you see are the tails. A french dovetail is really a long dovetail tenon that fits in a slot whose sides are angled to match the tenon. (See Figure 2.)

Making a Full Dovetail

The hardest part in making a dovetail is deciding where to start. Some woodworkers prefer starting with the pins, some prefer making the tail first. For this operation we'll make the tails first.

Mark out the tails on the end of a board. You can use any angle that suits you, but the most common angles are between 10° and 12°. Use a sliding T-bevel to mark the splay of the tails, or make a marking jig. There are also

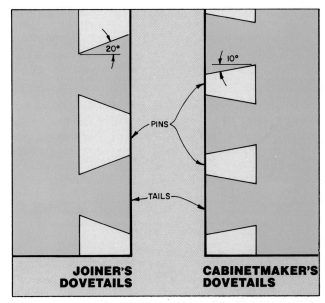

Figure 1. The tails of the cabinetmaker's dovetail joint are less splayed, and the pins are smaller than those of the joiner's dovetail.

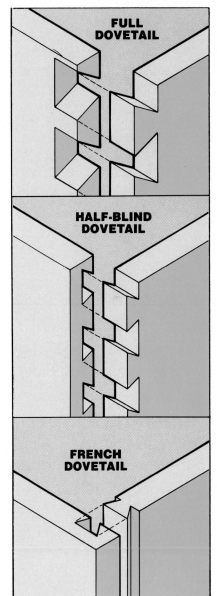

Figure 2. Three of the most common dovetail joints are the full dovetail, the half-blind dovetail, and the french dovetail.

several commercial dovetail marking jigs on the market. (See Figure 3.)

> **Tip** ◆ Use a very sharp pencil or an awl to mark your dovetails. The finer the liner, the easier it will be to be accurate.

Cut the tails on your bandsaw. Cut wide of the marks, then carefully 'nibble' away the waste at the base of the gullets between each tail. Use the moving blade as a rasp to scrape away stock on the sides of the tails until you have scraped right up to the line. (See Figure 4.) If you wish, you can smooth the inside faces of the tails even further with a small bench chisel.

Use the tails as a marking gauge for the pins. There are several ways to cut these pins. The most common way is to saw them with a small backsaw, often called a 'dovetail' saw. (See Figure 5.) You can also use your bandsaw, tilting the table to the left, and then to the right. If the table won't tilt far enough in one direction, shim it up on its mount with several washers. You can also use a sabre saw, a jigsaw, or a scroll saw in the same manner.

Drill out most of the waste with a bit that is slightly smaller than the narrowest distance between the pins. (See Figure 6.) Then clean out any waste that's left with a small hand chisel. This chisel must be *very* sharp.

Test the fit of the pins and tails. If they're too tight, pare away some more stock with a chisel.

Figure 3. Mark the splay of the tails with a sliding T-bevel or a marking jig. Use a very sharp pencil or awl.

Figure 4. Cut the waste from between the tails on a bandsaw. Cut wide of the line, then use the moving blade as a rasp to carefully scrape away stock until you've scraped right up to the line.

Figure 5. Make the cuts between the pins with a small back saw or 'dovetail' saw. You can also use a bandsaw, sabre saw, jigsaw, or any power saw with a small blade and a table that will tilt both right *and* left.

Figure 6. Drill out what waste you can from between the pins. Remove the rest with a sharp chisel.

Figure 7. Mark the pins for a half-blind dovetail, keeping in mind that the pins don't go all the way through the board. Shown here is a commercial dovetail marking jig.

Making a Half-Blind Dovetail

If you want, you can make this joint in much the same fashion as you made the full dovetail. Start by marking the tails or the pins — let's start with the pins this time. Keep in mind that the pins don't go all the way through the board. (See Figure 7.) In a ¾″ board, they're usually no more than ½″ long.

Saw the pins with a dovetail saw. Keep the saw at an angle, sawing up to the base lines on both the edge and the face of the board. Be careful not to saw any further. (See Figure 8.) Drill out as much of the waste as you can, stopping the bit at the proper depth. (See Figure 9.) Then clean out the rest of the waste with a chisel, taking care not to cut the pins any deeper than they should be. (See Figure 10.)

Use the pins as a marking gauge for the tails, then cut the tails on the bandsaw in exactly the same manner as you would for a full dovetail. Only the slots between the pins are blind, not the tails.

If you have a router, by far the easiest way to make half-blind dovetails is with a dovetail jig. The specific techniques involved in using one of these jigs may differ from manufacturer to manufacturer, but there are some things they all have in common.

First of all, they all cut the pins and tails at the same time. This is not only done to save time; it ensures that both parts match exactly. The dovetail bit is always guided in a jig. This means that you not only have to purchase a jig; you'll have to get a set of guide bushings. (See Figure 11.)

Place the board in the jig and adjust the depth of cut of the router bit, according to the instructions that came with the jig. Then make a shallow pass from right to left to score the 'tail' board. (See Figure 12.) This will keep the wood from tearing out when you cut deeper. Finally cut the dovetail,

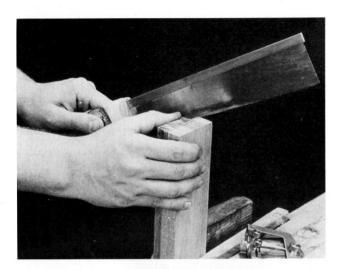

Figure 8. Hold the dovetail saw at an angle, and cut up to the base lines on the face and on the edge of the board.

Figure 9. Drill out as much of the waste as you can, stopping the bit at the same depth as the base line.

Figure 10. Clean out the rest of the waste with a chisel. Be careful not to make the slots between the pins any deeper than they should be.

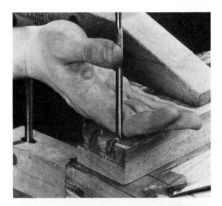

Figure 11. To use a dovetail routing jig, you'll have to attach a guide bushing to the base of your router.

Figure 12. Pass the router from right to left, scoring the 'tail' board lightly before you begin to cut the tails and pins. This will help prevent the wood from chipping.

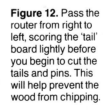

pushing the router in and out of the jig. Repeat this again to make sure you've routed all the parts completely. (See Figure 13.) When you remove the wood from the jig, you should have two boards that mate precisely. (See Figure 14.)

Making a French Dovetail

Like the half-blind dovetail, the french dovetail is best made with a router or a router attachment for your drill press.

Start by cutting the dovetail slot. Feed the wood into the router bit slowly, giving the tool plenty of time to clear the chips. Usually, you can make a routed joint in several passes, cutting a little deeper with each pass. That way, you don't 'hog' the bit and burn the wood. But when you're routing a dovetail slot, you have to make it in one pass. So take it slow and easy. Use a fence to help guide the work. (See Figure 15.)

Make the tenon to match the slot. Use the same dovetail bit that you used to rout the slot to cut both faces of the 'tail' board. This will form a dovetail tenon that splays at exactly the same angle as the slot. (See Figure 16.) To adjust the width of the tenon, move the wood closer or further away from the bit.

Figure 13. Cut the tails and pins, letting the router follow the jig. Make two passes to be sure you've routed all the areas that need routing.

Figure 14. When you remove the boards from the jig, the tails and pins should mate precisely, forming a half-blind dovetail.

Figure 15. Rout the dovetail slot first, feeding the board into the router bit. Use a fence as a guide.

Figure 16. Rout both faces of the tail board to make the tenon. Move the guide fence closer to the bit to make a narrower tenon, and further away to make a fatter tenon.

Text by Nick Engler and Jim McCann

Lathe Duplication

One good turning deserves another... and another... and another...

Turned legs and spindles add a touch of class to almost any woodworking project. The problem is that the project plans always specify two or more identical spindles, or four identical legs. Turning a single leg is fairly easy, but turning three more just like the first can tax your lathe skills.

Lathe chisels are somewhat capricious. Without guidelines, they will seem to work differently from one piece of wood to the next. The coves and beads you cut in one turning will turn out a little deeper or a little higher in the next, even though you used the same techniques. It could be that the angle you held the chisels at was just a little different, or that you fed the chisels with a little more pressure than before. Tiny differences in the way you hold and move the chisels will show up as big differences between turnings.

Fortunately, there are simple ways to compensate for these differences. If you carefully measure and mark your stock, then stay within your own guidelines, you can make one identical turning after the next. Here's how:

Using a Storystick

The first trick to making duplicate lathe turnings, is to make up a good pattern that you can constantly refer to as you turn. Don't just draw up a paper pattern and hang it on the wall. Trace your pattern on a thin scrap of wood or hardboard that you can hold right up to the turning as you work. This is often called a *storystick*.

Put all the major and minor dimensions of the turnings right on this storystick. The major dimensions are the 'high spots' in your turnings — the crests of beads, the largest diameter of tapers. The minor dimensions are the 'low spots' — the bottoms of coves and the least diameter of tapers. You'll also need the diameter of any 'flats' in the turnings — areas where the diameter remains constant. If you're turning a long taper, mark the diameter of the taper every 3"-4".

Once you've written all the contours and dimensions of the turning on your storystick, use the storystick to mark the positions of the coves, beads, flats, and tapers on your turning stock. Begin by marking those areas where the turning breaks from square stock to round — this is called a shoulder. Mark the major *and* minor dimensions of each shoulder — where the shoulders begin and end. (See Figure 1.)

> **Tip ◆** Each time you use the storystick to mark the stock, always line it up with the same reference point. In the photos, we're lining up the end of our stick so that it's always flush with the drive center end of the spindle.

Using your skew chisel, score the minor dimensions of the shoulders. (See Figure 2.) This will help keep the wood from splintering on the shoulders as you work it. Round the stock just below the shoulders, then cut the shoulders with a skew. (See Figure 3.) Always work from the major to minor diameter. Check the minor diameter with calipers to make sure that you've made the shoulder deep enough.

> **Tip ◆** To duplicate exact spindles you must control each tool and each cut. The best way to assure this exact control is to use *only* razor-sharp tools. As tools dull you must work harder to force the tool to cut. Forcing the tool causes fatigue and mistakes.

Round the rest of the stock, then use the storystick to mark the flats, beads, coves, and tapers. (See Figure 4.) Turn on the lathe and darken the marks so that they stand out. High spots of beads are marked as a broken or partial line. This will appear as a lite line while turning. 'Code' the coves by moving the pencil back and forth between the major diameters and darkening the area between the marks. (See Figure 5.) Since you turn the coves last, you'll be able to use these darkened areas as reference points for most of the time that you're working on the spindle. It will also help you mentally envision the contours before you actually turn them.

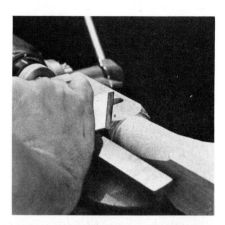

Figure 3. Round the spindle just below the shoulder. Then turn cut the shoulder with a skew chisel. Always cut from the major to the minor diameter.

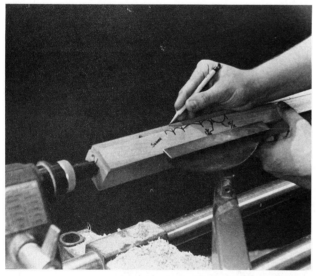

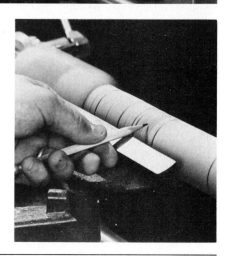

Figure 1. Before you start turning, trace the spindle pattern on a scrap board to make a 'storystick'. Use this storystick to mark the pattern on the spindle. First, mark the major and minor dimensions of the shoulders.

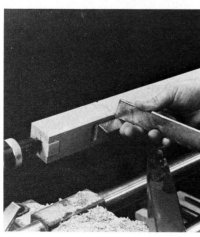

Figure 2. Score the minor dimension of a shoulder with a skew chisel.

Figure 4. After you've cut the shoulders, mark the position of the beads, coves, flats, and tapers on the spindle using the storystick.

Figure 5. Code the coves by darkening the area in between the major diameters with a pencil.

Turning the Beads and Coves

Once you have the spindle marked and coded, turn the major and minor diameters of the various contours. Start with the beads and the flats. You don't want to turn the coves first because the coves are usually the narrowest part of a turning. As soon as you turn the coves, the spindle is slightly weaker at the narrow points, and this increases the chances that the stock will 'whip' on the lathe. For this reason, leave the coves till last.

To turn to exact diameters, use a parting tool and calipers. Set the calipers to the diameters that you want to turn.

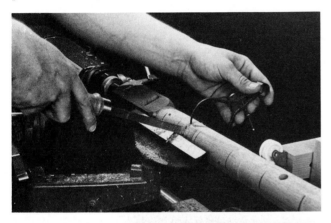

Hold the calipers in one hand and the parting tool securely in the other. Slowly feed the parting tool into the wood while holding the calipers in the groove created by the parting tool. (See Figure 6.) As soon as the calipers slip over the diameter, stop cutting.

> **Tip ◆** If you're making a series of beads that aren't separated by flats, turn just the major diameter of each bead. The valley between each bead is V-shaped. If you try to turn the minor dimension of this valley with a parting tool, you'll leave a flat between beads.

Cut the beads with a skew chisel. Once again work from the major to the minor diameters. (See Figure 7.) Make the flats with a parting tool then complete them with a skew or a parting tool. Work your way down the spindle, switching back and forth between the parting tool and the skew as you go. (See Figures 8 and 9.) Don't make all the parting tool cuts, then all the beads. Once again, this weakens the spindle before it's necessary.

> **Tip ◆** In the turnings that we made, the wood was already beginning to whip as we turned the beads in the lower part of the legs. So we used a steadyrest to help keep the wood under control.

Once you've cut the beads, go back and make the shallow coves in a similar manner. Turn the minor diameters with a parting tool, then hollow out the cove with a gouge. (See Figure 10.) Once again, work from the major to minor diameters.

Figure 6. Using a parting tool and calipers, turn to the diameters of the beads and the flats.

Figure 7. Turn the beads with a skew chisel, working from the major to the minor diameters.

Figure 8. Work your way along the spindle, switching back and forth between the parting tool and the skew chisel. First cut the diameters with the parting tool.

Figure 9. Then cut the beads and flats with the skew.

Figure 10. After you've cut the beads and flats, turn the coves with a gouge.

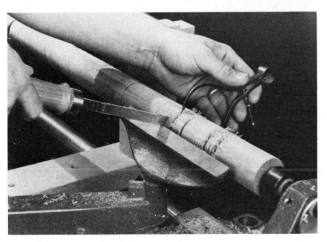

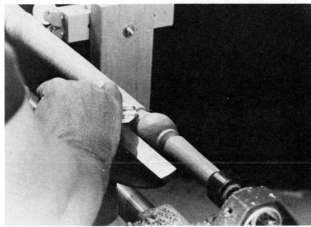

Tip ◆ We elected to leave the large cove at the top of the leg until the very last. It was turned *after* we made the taper, because it weakened the spindle so. This only goes to show that the instructions here are just guidelines, not rules. Use your horse sense when deciding what part of a spindle to turn next.

Turning the Tapers

Using the parting tool and the calipers, turn to the diameters of the tapers that you marked every 3″-4″. Then rough out the tapers with a gouge. (See Figure 11.) Turn the spindle down to within 1/16″ of the diameters, but don't turn it all the way down to the diameters. The tapers should still be broken by some shallow grooves.

Switch to the skew and turn the tapers down to the diameters, *but no farther.* (See Figure 12.) Carefully shear away stock until the grooves disappear. When you're finished, you should have a long, even taper. If not, the dimensions on your storystick are probably off slightly, and you need to adjust them.

Finish sand the spindle on the lathe. Start with 100# sandpaper, and work your way up to 180#. *Don't* sand the spindle with coarser grits if you can possibly help it. 50# and 80# sandpapers remove stock quickly, and there's a chance that you could alter the contours of a spindle so that it wouldn't match the others.

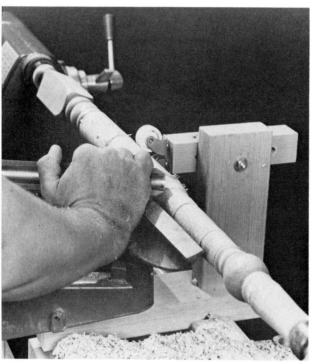

Figure 11. Rough out the taper with a gouge. Turn the spindle down to within 1/16″ of the diameters that you've marked with a parting tool.

Figure 12. Switch to a skew chisel and finish the taper. Turn down to the diameters until the groove disappears.

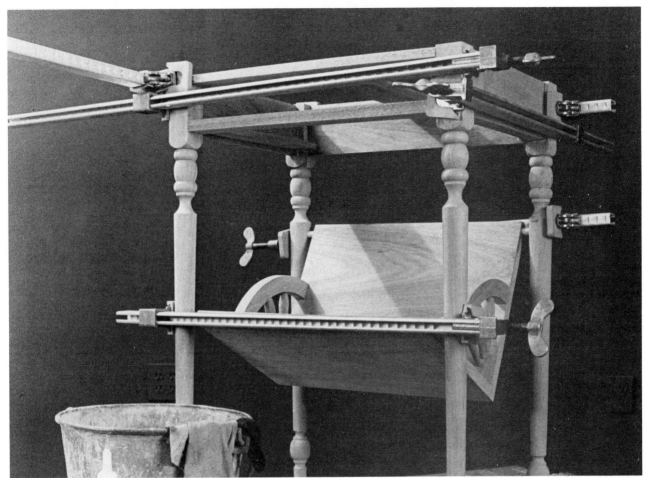

Text by Nick Engler

Table Construction

You can't tell a table by its top.

Tables are all constructed so that they have one thing in common — a table top. The whole purpose of a table is to give you a place to set things, such as your dinner. This requires a broad surface that is somehow supported at a comfortable height. The breadth of this surface is usually determined by the size of your dinner, or whatever you have to put on it.

The breadth of a table top has very little to do with the way tables are constructed, however. Table construction differs widely according to the way table tops are supported. There are three basic types of supports, or table bases: leg-and-rail, trestle, and pedestal.

Leg-and-Rail Table Bases

There are several good examples of leg-and-rail construction in this edition of the *Woodworking Projects Yearbook* — the "Gateleg Table", the "Reference Book Stand", and the "Writing Table". (See Figures 1 and 2.) In these tables, the legs are joined to connecting rails, or 'aprons'. The table top is attached to the rails.

Figure 1. The gateleg table uses typical leg-and-rail construction. The legs are joined to the rail by mortise-and-tenon joints.

Figure 2. The writing table is an example of modern leg-and-rail construction. In this table, the legs are held to the rails by hanger blocks and hanger bolts. The legs can be simply removed by loosening the nuts on the hanger bolts.

The legs of the first two, the gateleg table and the book stand, are attached to the aprons by a mortise-and-tenon joint. (See Figure 3.) This is the 'traditional' way to join legs and aprons. Mortise-and-tenon joints, if made properly, are extremely strong. Even though the legs are not braced, they will not wobble. On large tables, such as the gateleg table, it's advisable to pin the tenons in the mortises with dowels.

The legs of the writing table are attached to the aprons with hanger bolts and blocks. (See Figure 4.) The legs aren't attached permanently, as they are with mortises and tenons. Instead, they are easily removed by loosening the nuts on the hanger bolts. This 'knock-down' system is a fairly recent invention. It was developed around the turn of the century, so

that manufacturers could ship their tables more easily. It is surprisingly strong. If the leg wobbles, simply tighten the nuts on the bolts.

Trestle Table Bases

The "Play Center" is a good example of a trestle table, although it does not use what you would commonly think of as a trestle. (See Figure 5.) The dictionary defines a "trestle" as a "horizontal beam fastened to spreading legs". The first 'trestle' was what we call a sawhorse today. Planks were laid across the sawhorses to make a temporary table. Later, as trestle tables evolved, the definition of a trestle expanded. In the play center, the trestles are the arms of a bench. In a picnic table, the trestles are X-shaped frames.

The classic trestle table uses two broad pieces of wood, almost as wide as the table top, for the trestles. (See Figure 6.) These trestle pieces are usually braced by a stretcher that runs between them. The stretcher has tenons on either end which fit in 'through-mortises' in the trestles. These tenons are pinned in the mortises by a wedge, as shown in Figure 6. To tighten the trestles and keep them from wobbling, tap the wedge into its slot a little further.

Pedestal Table Bases

The pedestal table employs a single, central post to support the table top. This post, in turn, is supported by legs. In the "Shaker Sewing Stand", the legs hold the pedestal off the ground. (See Figure 7.) In some heavier tables, the pedestal sits on the ground and the legs merely keep it from tipping over.

The legs of the sewing stand are tenoned, and fit in mortises in the pedestal. This is a fairly common construction, but it may not be the best possible construction. On many of the better pedestal tables, the legs are joined to the pedestal by French dovetails. (See Figure 8.) The dovetail tenons fit in long dovetail slots, where they keep the legs from splaying out.

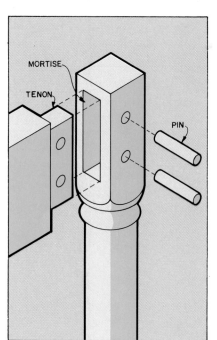

Figure 3. The mortise-and-tenon joint is considered the 'traditional' way to join legs to rails. On large tables, the tenons should be pinned in the mortises.

Figure 4. In the hanger system, legs can be easily removed by loosening the nuts on the bolts. This is often called a 'knock-down' system.

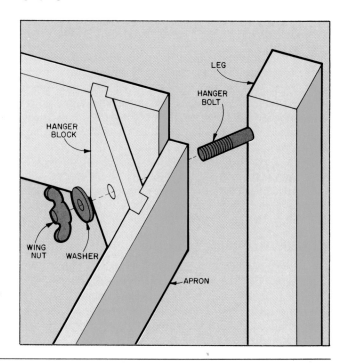

Table Tops

While the bases are all different, the tops are all similar — and they all share similar problems. What sort of a glue joint do you make between the edges of boards to make wide stock? How do you glue up stock wide enough to make a table top, but keep it from cupping with changes in the weather? How do you attach it to the base and allow for the expansion and contraction of the wood?

Joining stock edge to edge — Many woodworkers use dowel joints to strengthen edge-to-edge seams. However, it's doubtful that the dowels add much extra strength. They may, in some cases, *weaken* the joint. Because the dowel grain is perpendicular to the stock, the dowels will not expand and contract with the table top. For this reason, use *short* dowels, if you use any at all. They are helpful in one respect: They align the edges for you.

Spline joints are similar to dowel joints. They align the edges, but they don't add strength unless the grain of the spline is perpendicular to the grain of the stock. And if the grains are perpendicular...well, you know the song from this point on. We just sang it for you in the last paragraph.

Figure 5. The top of the play center lays across the arms of the bench, making them a 'trestle' of sorts.

Figure 6. In a classic trestle table, the trestles are broad pieces of wood, with a stretcher in between. This stretcher has tenons on either end, which fit through the stretchers.

Figure 7. The "Shaker Sewing Stand" is an example of a pedestal table. In this case, the pedestal is held off the ground by three 'spider' legs.

Figure 8. In many pedestal tables, the legs are attached to the tables by French dovetails.

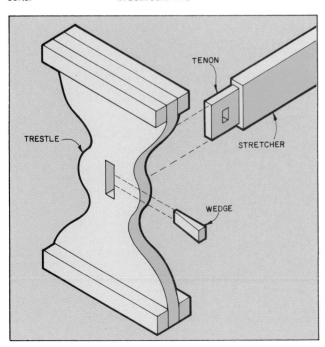

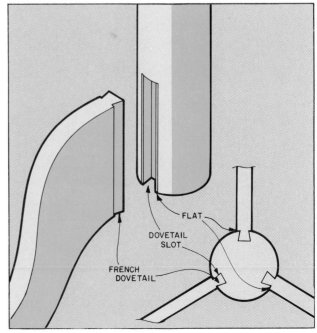

Perhaps the best joint for wide stock is called a 'glue joint'. This joint is made with a shaper cutter or molder knives, creating fingers that interlock. (See Figure 9.) This joint adds strength because it increases the gluing surface. *And* it aligns the boards.

However, for all but the largest tables, jointed boards butted edge to edge will hold just fine. Craftsmen from the eighteenth century joined boards in this manner, and many of their tables have survived in good shape.

Controlling cupping — When gluing stock edge to edge, the traditional wisdom says to alternate the direction of the annual rings — one up, one down, one up, etc. Then, if the wood cups, the top may become 'wavy', but it will stay relatively level.

This is a good theory, but in only works in practice on leaves or other kinds of table tops that aren't braced. If you're going to attach the top to aprons, trestles, or some other sort of brace, it's best to arrange the boards so that the annual rings all curve in the same direction. (See Figure 10.) Attach the top to the base with the rings curving up, as shown. If the wood cups, the table top will want to bow in the middle. The brace will stop this from happening.

You can also use wood that resists cupping, and avoid this problem altogether. 'Quarter-sawn' and 'rift-sawn' lumber is sliced so that the wide face of the wood is perpendicular to the annual rings. The curve of the rings through the wood is reduced considerably, and so is the tendency to cup. (See Figure 11.) However, this wood is very expensive and sometimes hard to come by.

Allowing for wood movement — It stands to reason that the top must be attached to the table base. However, it must not be *too* attached. The joint must allow for the expansion and contraction of the wood.

Wood 'moves' with changes in humidity and temperature. Also, it moves ten times more across the grain than with the grain. This can sometimes be as much as ¼" for every 12" of width. If you fasten the table top down too tightly, or glue it in place, the movement of the wood will distort the table, splitting the joints in the table base or the top.

There are several ways that you can compensate for the movement of the wood and still attach the top firmly to the base. If you plan to screw the top to the base, drill two pilot holes for the screws oversize. You may even want to enlarge them into slots. As the top expands and contracts, the screws will move back and forth in the slots.

Another way to allow for movement is to use tabletop clips. (See Figure 12.) This hardware screws to the underside of the table. The clip end fits in a ⅛" kerf in the apron or the trestle. As the top moves with the weather, the clips slide back and forth in the kerfs.

Summing Up

There are, of course, many more ways to build a table than what we have room to discuss. However, they are all variations on the basics that were presented here. At its heart, a table is a simple construction. Make a sturdy base, attach a level top, and you've got a table.

Figure 9. When gluing stock edge to edge, glue joints increase the gluing surface *and* align the edges of the boards. These joints are made with a shaper cutter or molder knives.

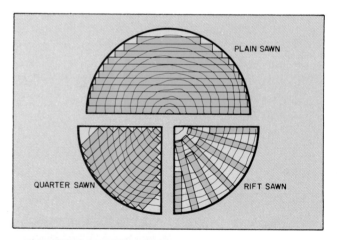

Figure 11. 'Quarter-sawn' and 'rift-sawn' lumber is cut so that the annual rings are perpendicular to the face of the wood. This greatly reduces the tendency to cup.

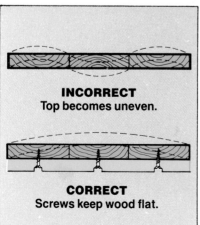

INCORRECT
Top becomes uneven.

CORRECT
Screws keep wood flat.

Figure 10. To control cupping, arrange the annual rings so that they all curve in the same direction. The wood will want to bow in the middle, but the apron, trestle, or brace will prevent this.

Figure 12. Tabletop clips compensate for the expansion and contraction of the top. They fit in kerfs on the inside face of the aprons or trestles.

THE
WORKSHOP

Text by Nick Engler and Wayne Howe

Setting Up Shop

With a little bit of forethought, you can make your shop work better for you.

Just recently, I moved my shop for the fifth and final time — I hope.

Each time I set up my shop anew, I think to myself, "This time I'm going to build the perfect shop." As I begin to fill the empty space with tools and workbenches, I have the highest of hopes. And each time, the new shop has fallen short of my expectations. But I've always learned something about setting up shop, something I file away in the back of my mind and tell myself, "If I ever do this again…"

This time, when I set up shop, I started with a more realistic premise. I didn't start out to build the perfect shop. Instead, I hoped to build the perfect shop *for me*. Planning a shop should focus on the tasks that you hope to accomplish in it, the tools you have (or hope to acquire), and the projects you want to build. Woodworking is a personal thing, and every woodworker does it a little differently. We all don't have the same tools or build the same projects. So the perfect shop for one woodworker may be a nightmare for another.

Set up a work triangle.

That's perhaps the most important thing I've learned about setting up a shop. In order to get the best of all possible shops, you need to customize your workspace. Take the space that's available and make it work for *you*. Don't try to copy those glitzy shops in the power tool advertisements. Nine times out of ten, those aren't shops, anyway — they're just photo sets.

First, start by deciding just how much space you can devote to a shop. You may not be able to devote all the space

160

you'd *like* for your shop, but chances are with a little ingenuity you can make the space you have work for you. Claustrophobia is the mother of invention.

My first shop occupied a space 8' x 7'. Into that tiny shop, I managed to fit a radial arm saw, a benchtop bandsaw and belt sander, a jointer, and an assortment of hand tools. By making some tools roll away under the workbench and others to hang from the rafters, I made the space work for me. In many ways, that shop worked better than a few others I set up afterwards. At least all the tools were within a few steps of each other.

That brings me to our next concern. Once you've decided how much space you have for a shop, how do you arrange your tools? Most woodworkers strive to set up a classic "work triangle". Decide on three basic work stations that you visit most frequently, and arrange your tools so that the work flows easily from station to station. For most woodworkers, these stations are the stationary power tools, workbench, and shelved hand tools and supplies. Arrange these work stations or areas in a triangle so that you take as few steps as possible when moving from one spot to the next. (See Figure 1.)

> **Tip** ◆ Rectangular spaces are best for shops, I've found from experience. It's hard to set up a good work triangle in an odd shape. One shop I had was L-shaped. One arm of the 'L' went virtually unused and tended to fill up with junk.

After I set up my fourth shop, I learned that sometimes the major work stations shift, depending on the project or the type of woodworking you're doing. Sometimes my shop arrangement worked; other times it left a little to be desired. In my latest shop, I decided to mount all the tools *and* the workbenches on casters. That way, I can rearrange them whenever it suits me. Sometimes I'll make a work triangle out of the planer, table saw, and jointer. Other times, I use the stationary sander, hand tools, and gluing bench. With 'floating' tools and benches, I'm not limited by my arrangement.

To work up your own work triangle (or floating system), start by graphing out the space you've set aside for your shop. (Remember to allow for that space which you may add later.) Use scaled cutouts of your stationary tools and benches, arranging them in various ways to create work triangles that seem to fit the type of work you do. (See Figure 2.) Keep the sides of the triangle as short as possible, but still allow enough space between tools so that you don't feel cramped.

Arrange your tools around structures that can't be moved: Doors, windows, water heaters, and duct work. Or, if your shop is in a garage and you share the space with a car, design an arrangement that can be set up quickly after you pull the car out. For stationary tools that require lots of clearance (jointers, table saws, radial arm saws), make use of open doors and windows for the extra space you need.

> **Tip** ◆ Whatever arrangement you come up with, don't cast it in concrete. Don't go out to your shop and immediately anchor the tools to the floor and build in the benches. Set up the shop *temporarily* and work with the arrangement for a few months. There's nothing like experience to help you fine-tune your plans.

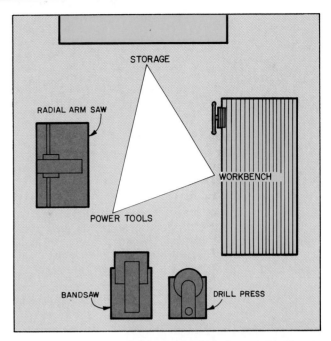

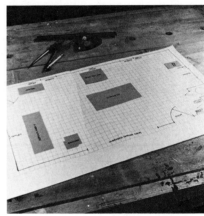

Figure 1. Arrange the major work stations in your shop in a 'work triangle'. This will save you steps and help the work flow easily.

Figure 2. Graph out your shop space, then make scaled cutouts of your tools and benches. Arrange these in different ways until you come up with an arrangement that appeals to you.

Comfort is important.

As you plan, remember that a shop is more than a workplace. You'll be doing a lot of thinking and planning in your shop. Of the total time that it takes you to make a project, as much as 80% of that time is spent *thinking* about it — drawing the plans and deciding what to do next.

You'll need a comfortable place to sit and draw as you plan out each project. My shop includes a drawing board. If you don't have room, your workbench will serve you just as well — but you'll need a comfortable stool to match it. And the bench should be designed with a 'knee hole' so that you don't bump your legs.

Include a shelf somewhere near your planning area for your how-to books. They shouldn't remain clean and untouched in your living room or den — get them out where they can earn their keep. I keep mine in a little cabinet with doors. That keeps most of the dust and dirt off of them.

In northern latitudes, keep your shop warm enough for comfort but cool enough for clear thinking. If you use a space heater, avoid exposed heating elements and open flames. The safest type of heater that I've found is the oil-filled portable baseboard heaters.

Figure 3. A foam rubber 'anti-fatigue' mat helps to keep your feet from getting tired. It has a smooth surface so that it can be easily cleaned.

My present shop has wood heat. There are pros and cons to this. The pro is that the heat is cheap, and you have a convenient use for all your wood scraps. The con is that the wood stove may ignite sawdust or scraps if you don't clean it properly. Not only must the pipes be kept free of creosote; you have to make sure that sawdust doesn't settle on the outside of the stove. I sweep mine off several times each evening when I'm working.

And when you're finishing, you can't fire up the stove. First of all, the fumes from many types of finishes are flammable. And second, the stove kicks up a lot of ash and soot that will ruin a fine finish. I end up hauling most of my projects into the house to finish them. In the final analysis, I find that wood heat is economical and comfortable, but you must take some precautions in order to use it safely. And there are times that you just can't use it at all.

Spare your feet.

While we're on the subject of comfort, think about that part of your body that takes the most abuse while you're woodworking: your feet. By carefully placing your tools, you can eliminate some steps and help save those tired dogs. But there is something more you can do.

What tools do you use the most? Table saw? Radial arm saw? Sander? Keep the tool where it's convenient and leave enough space around it so that you're not continually banging your shins or stubbing your toe on other tools and benches.

Also, install a resilient mat or carpet under your feet when you're standing at that tool. Most woodworkers have their shops in basements and garages — on concrete floors. Concrete is brutal on your feet. A foam rubber 'anti-fatigue' mat will do wonders for your arches. (See Figure 3.) These lie flat on the floor so that you can easily sweep the scraps and sawdust off of them. If you can't afford mats, use scraps of carpet that you can pick up periodically and shake out.

Keep accessories near the tools.

Another trick that will help you save steps is to keep accessories for your tools stored near the tools themselves. For instance, bandsaw blades should be stored near the bandsaw, not in a cabinet marked "Assorted Blades".

Setting up some tools involves a screwdriver or a wrench. These are relatively inexpensive tools, and you should buy extras and keep them with the tool. To change the blades in my jigsaw, I need to use a screwdriver. So I bought an extra screwdriver and hung it on the jigsaw stand. It cost

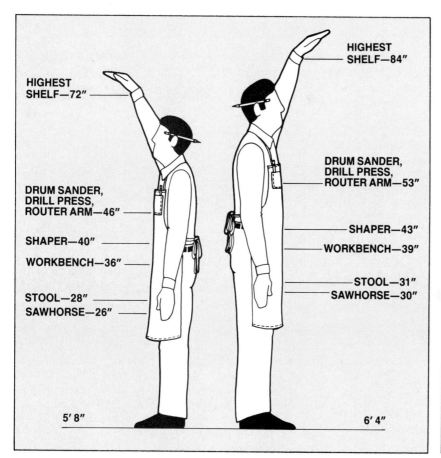

HIGHEST SHELF—72″

HIGHEST SHELF—84″

DRUM SANDER, DRILL PRESS, ROUTER ARM—46″

DRUM SANDER, DRILL PRESS, ROUTER ARM—53″

SHAPER—40″

SHAPER—43″

WORKBENCH—36″

WORKBENCH—39″

STOOL—28″

STOOL—31″

SAWHORSE—26″

SAWHORSE—30″

5′ 8″

6′ 4″

Figure 4. When designing a shop, arrange the work surface to fit *you* —don't use some standardized measurement. As shown, the optimum height for tools, shelves, and benches will change depending on your height.

Tool or Work Surface	Usually Placed
Highest shelf	12″ below peak reach
Drum sander	Mid-chest
Drill press	Mid-chest
Belt sander	Waist
Shaper	Waist
Radial arm saw	Waist
Table saw	4″ below waist
Jointer	4″ below waist
Workbench	4″ below waist
Stool	8″ clearance under bench
Sawhorses	Mid-thigh

me $.59, but it saves me the aggravation of rummaging through the hand tool chest every time a jigsaw blade breaks.

For the same reasons, I keep all my lathe tools and accessories with the lathe — chisels, calipers, and faceplates. The clamps lie on a shelf under the clamping bench. I've made safety devices for each tool and I hang them where I can reach them quickly. There's a push stick hanging on the front of the bandsaw, table saw, radial arm saw, and jointer. And I'm about to make another one for the shaper.

Other safety devices, such as hearing protectors, face shield, and dust masks are hanging right by the door. They are the first thing I reach for when I walk in the shop. I flick on the light switch and reach for the safety glasses. It becomes a habit after a while, just like putting on your seat belt when you first get into your car.

Make the work surfaces fit you.

Not only should a workshop be comfortable and handy, it should fit you like an old pair of shoes. As a refuge from the standardized world out there, this should be the one place that is customized to *your* own physical needs and no one else's. It should be an extension of yourself.

Carve out a 'personal zone' for yourself when you build the benches, cabinets, and tool stands in your shop. You don't have to accept someone else's idea of how high a sawhorse or a workbench should be. Adjust each work surface to a height that fits you according to your maximum reach, the height of your waist (which helps determine the best height for work surfaces), the height of your shoulders, your overall height, or any other physical characteristics that affect the way you work. Here are a few suggestions to help you. (See Figure 4 and chart below.) Use these as *guidelines* only. You may want to adjust these figures an inch or two either way, depending on your own preferences. Remember, *your* comfort is paramount.

Keep things in plain sight.

If you can't see it, you can't use it. Screws, nails, and small hardware should be easy to see, easy to get, and easy to sort through. Keep small items stored on shallow shelves in small jars, or in small plastic bins on a rack.

Thin, narrow strips of lumber and dowels can be stored overhead or in a bin that lets you see what you've got and pull out what you need. Plywood should rest on edge between two stable objects, such as a wall and a workbench. That way, you can sort through your selection as you would the pages of a book. You don't have to struggle with holding all the pieces up at one time so that you can retrieve the plywood on the bottom.

Two small boxes for scraps — one for softwood, the other for hardwood — are better than one large box. You can find the piece you want easier.

Get as much daylight as possible into your shop. Keep the walls light and arrange the artificial lighting so that you have as few shadows as possible. When I installed the overhead fluorescent lights in my shop, I put some of them in the middle of the ceiling, and others around the edges. That way, I'm never standing in my own light.

Make things accessible.

Keep the heavy tools on the lower shelves. Lighter accessories and supplies can go on higher shelves. Use pull-out shelves rather than fixed shelves, if you can; and lazy susans rather than deep, dark cabinets with blind corners.

Keep the most-used items in the most convenient locations. For instance, all my hand sanders, scrapers, and rasps are stored on a shelf under the workbench where I do most of my sanding and smoothing. There is one exception to this rule: I keep the fire extinguisher on a shelf out in plain sight with *nothing* around it so that it can be reached at a moment's notice from any corner of my shop. It's not the most used item in my shop; in fact, it's never been used at all. But I still keep it handy.

Install enough power.

In the first three shops that I worked in, there was never enough power. I was always unplugging one tool so that I could plug in another. Sometimes, when I was working with someone and we would run two tools at the same time, we'd blow the breaker.

As soon as I could afford it, I installed lots of outlets and plenty of power. My present shop is on a sub-box all its own with 50 amps available. There are seven different circuits and lots of outlets so that I can run several tools at once without fear. You may think you can't afford this luxury, but my own experience tells me that you can't afford not to have it. Adequate electrical power isn't just a convenience; *your shop isn't safe without it.*

> **Tip ◆** Have a licensed, qualified electrician check your shop and install additional wiring, if it's needed. You'll be surprised at the difference just one or two more circuits can make.

Having outlets near your tools is a must, too. An extension cord is an accident waiting to happen. If you don't trip over it, then you'll saw through it or wear off the insulation by rolling tools over it. But what about those tools that you use in the middle of your shop and *require* extension cords? I recently installed an electrical reel on the ceiling of my shop. (See Figure 5.) This is the greatest invention since the hammer. The reel keeps the cord up off the floor and away from the work. I honestly don't know how I did without one. They're available through many tool stores and mail-order houses.

Figure 5. An electrical reel on your ceiling will keep you from tripping over extension cords.

Make your shop easy to enter, easy to exit.

Doors to your shop should be wide and unobstructed. Once inside, you shouldn't have to spend a lot of time rearranging tools and supplies just so that you can begin work. Even 'fold-up' shops that have to be set up can be designed so that they will fold up and fold down with a minimum of effort.

As you're working, don't put things near the doors. You never know when an emergency will arise and you'll need to make a quick exit. You don't want to have to climb over a half-finished project just to get a bandage.

When you're finished, you should be able to clean up and go quickly without spending a lot of time "tucking the shop up". Design your shop so that it's easy to clean, and clean it as you work. That way, when it's time to go, you can go.

Set it up for safety.

Woodworking equipment is dangerous; there's no getting around that. But you can help to make your shop a safer place with a little bit of forethought when you set it up. Here are a few things to consider:

Allow for ventilation of dust and vapors. Clean air not only makes your woodworking safer; it makes it more comfortable.

Install the necessary emergency equipment and keep it where you can get at it. I've already mentioned a fire extinguisher. You should also have a small first-aid kit, complete with tweezers and eye wash. If your shop is damp, consider installing ground fault interrupters on all your electrical circuits. This will eliminate the chance of an electrical shock.

Make sure your shop can be locked. Your shop should be safe enough for children to enjoy, but only when you're there with them.

Finally, the most basic rule that I've stumbled across in my five shops is that you should design and build your shop in a way that fits *you*. If it fits you, it will be probably be a safe *and* comfortable place to work. In the end, *you* are the center of your shop. Set up your shop with that in mind.

Portions of this chapter first appeared in the May/June '82 edition of HANDS ON! Magazine, in an article by Wayne Howe. Our thanks to Mr. Howe for allowing us to publish his material here.

TIPS
SETTING UP SHOP

Quick-change Chocks for Casters

Mounting your tools on casters so that they 'float' around your shop gives you a lot of flexibility. You can change your shop setup every time you start a new project. Unfortunately, though casters are a boon, they create another headache. Your tools want to 'creep' when you use them.

I've tried casters with brakes, thinking this would keep the tools from creeping, but they don't. It's hard to know when the brakes are tight enough to keep the casters from rolling. And even when they are tight, the caster may

pivot, letting the tool or the workbench change positions suddenly.

◆ The best solution, I've found, is to 'chock' the casters. (See Figure A.) The circular chocks you see here keep the casters from rolling *and* pivoting. A crowbar-like 'jack' lets you put the chocks in place or take them out quickly and easily. (See Figure B.)

Figure A. A scrap of plywood with a circle cut in it will 'chock' a caster to keep it from rolling and turning.

Figure B. You can make this simple 'jack' to help set the chocks and remove them.

Designed and Built by Nick Engler

Wood Storage Rack

This simple rack stores all different types and sizes of lumber.

For years, I got away with storing my lumber in a corner of the shop, leaning against the wall. And every year, it got harder and harder to sort through my stack and find the boards I needed. It also seemed like my corner was getting further and further away from the front of the stack.

Part of this problem is that woodworkers also tend to be wood collectors. Whenever I find a really nice board, I put it in the stack and tell myself, "I'm not going to use that until I

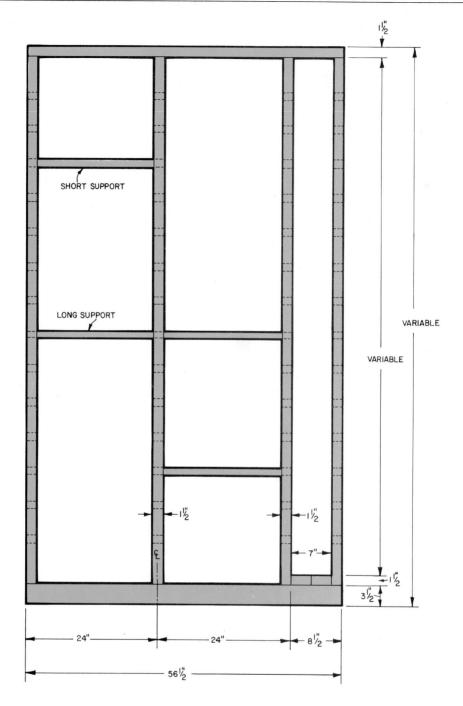

FRONT VIEW

have something really special to build." Of course, those special projects don't come around as often as the special boards, so the wood tends to accumulate. Don't laugh; I know this happens to you, too.

Anyway, I finally broke down and built myself a wood rack. It's a simple project; it only takes an evening to make; but it does everything a wood rack should do. You can sort your lumber and store it in small compartments, so that you can find and retrieve the wood you're after with a minimum of fuss. You can adjust the size of these compartments to fit your changing needs for lumber storage. And there's a special rack for storing sheet materials (such as plywood and paneling) on edge.

Making the Rack

The first step in making the rack is deciding where you're going to attach it to your shop building. This isn't a freestanding project; it has to be attached securely to the wall and ceiling. If your garage or basement has open studs and joists, that makes the first chore a lot easier.

166

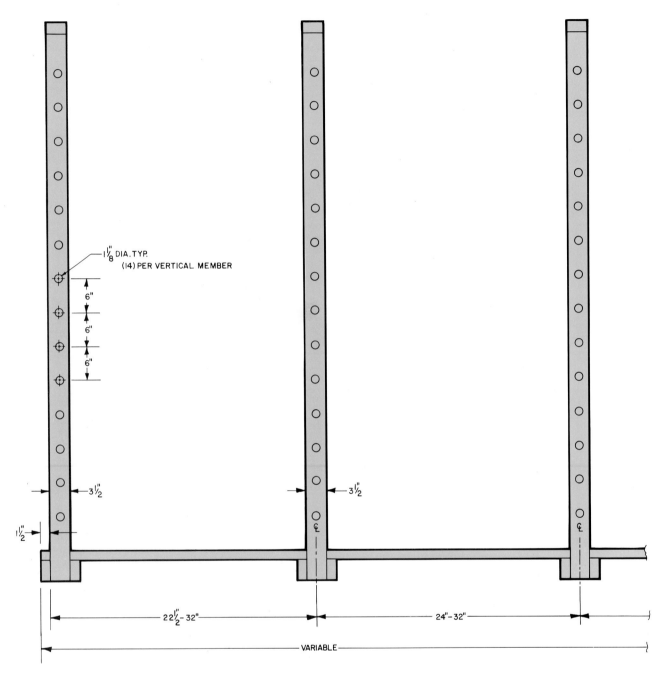

$1\frac{1}{8}$" DIA. TYP.
(14) PER VERTICAL MEMBER

6"

6"

6"

$3\frac{1}{2}$

$3\frac{1}{2}$

$1\frac{1}{2}$

$22\frac{1}{2}$"-32"

24"-32"

VARIABLE

SIDE VIEW

If the framework is covered, you're going to have to locate the frame members. I've used a 'stud finder' before, but I much prefer the 'knock and hope' method. Tap on the wall with a hammer until it sounds like you're over something solid, then drive a nail through the drywall to see if you're right. You end up with a few unnecessary holes in the wall, but these can be patched easily.

Tip ◆ Use long, slender finishing nails to hunt for the studs and joists. These leave smaller holes.

Once you've located the studs and joists and you know where you are going to attach the rack to the building, make several rack frames as shown in the working drawings. You should place one rack frame every 24"-32" to properly support your lumber. An 8' long rack will require four to five rack frames. The height of these frames should be equal to the height from your shop floor to the ceiling *plus* ¹⁄₁₆". This extra height will ensure a snug fit, and help keep the rack in place.

Drill 1⅛" holes, 6" on center, in the vertical members of the rack frames *before* you assemble the frames. These holes will hold lengths of 1" hardwood dowel which, in turn, support the lumber. The ⅛" 'slop' — the difference between the hole diameter and the dowel diameter — makes it easier to get the dowel in and out of the holes so that you can change the position of the wood supports.

Glue and screw the frames together. Lay a bead of construction adhesive down on the floor where the lower horizontal members will rest, then stand the frames up in place. (See Figure 1.) With a level, check that vertical members are straight up and down, then attach the vertical members and upper horizontal members to the wall and ceiling with lag bolts.

Tip ◆ If your shop has open ceiling joists, as mine does, you can dispense with the upper horizontal members of the rack. Just bolt the vertical pieces directly to the joists. (See Figure 2.)

Figure 1. Use industrial adhesive to attach the lower horizontal members to the floor, and keep them from sliding around.

Figure 2. If your shop has open ceiling joists, you can attach the vertical members directly to these joists.

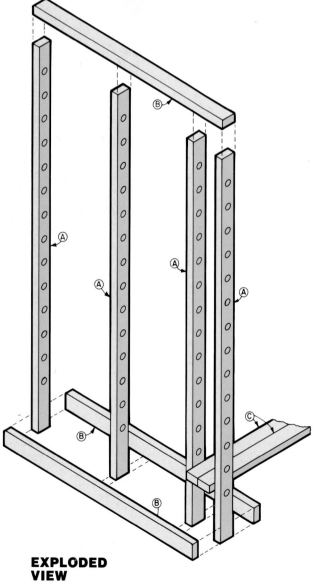

EXPLODED VIEW

Cut as many lengths of dowel as you think you'll need to organize and store your lumber. I'd suggest you make quite a few. The more supports you have, the smaller the individual piles of lumber will be in the rack. You don't want any one pile to be any thicker than 12" — it's too hard to get the board off the bottom of the pile. And you know from experience that the board you want is *always* on the bottom of the pile.

BILL OF MATERIALS — Wood Storage Rack

Finished Dimensions in Inches

A.	Vertical members (24)	1½ x 3½ x (Variable)
B.	Horizontal members (18)	1½ x 3½ x 56½
C.	Stretchers (2)	1½ x 3½ x 120
D.	Long lumber supports (as required)	1 dia x 48
E.	Short lumber supports (as required)	1 dia x 24¾

Hardware

16d Common nails (2-3 lbs.)
⁵⁄₁₆" x 4" Lag bolts and washers (25)

*The materials listed here will build a wood rack 10' long, with the individual frames on 24" centers. If you have different requirements, adjust the materials and the dimensions accordingly.

Designed and Built by Nick Engler

Shop Highboy

This 'highboy' offers lots of storage space — and takes up very little floor space.

I f you have a shop, you're short of storage space. That's a given; it comes with the territory. I've never been in a shop that doesn't need more storage space; I've never heard of a shop that doesn't need more storage space; if someone were to write me and say that he or she has a shop that doesn't need more storage space, then that woodworker would be a liar, or crazy, or very, very rich.

If you've read this far, you're probably honest, sane, and have to balance your own checkbook. You also need storage space. Here's one possible solution to your problem — a shop 'highboy'.

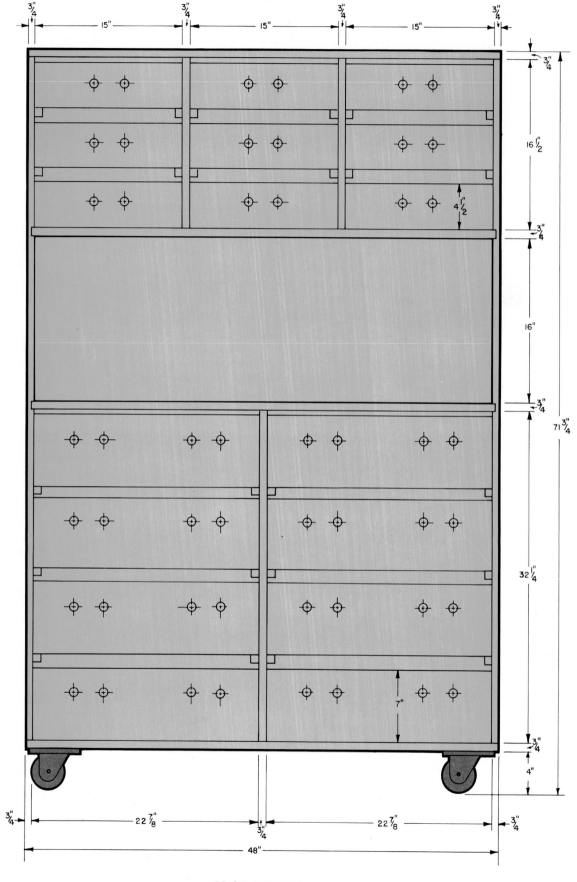

FRONT VIEW

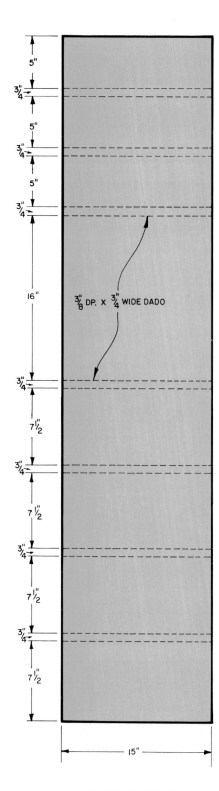

5"

3/4"

5"

3/4"

5"

3/4"

16" $\frac{3}{8}''$ DP. X $\frac{3}{4}''$ WIDE DADO

3/4"

7$\frac{1}{2}$"

3/4"

7 1/2"

3/4"

7$\frac{1}{2}''$

3/4"

7$\frac{1}{2}''$

15"

SIDE LAYOUT

Boxes in a Box

This highboy is actually a lot of small boxes that fit inside a much larger box. The large box is divided into two sections — one for medium-size boxes, and one for small boxes. There is an open area in between the sections where you can put the boxes and sort through them. Except for this open area, the arrangement is very much like a classic American highboy — though not as classy, or hard to build.

The joinery in this project is extremely simple. The large box has a few dadoes, all the rest of the boxes are put together with butt joints. If you set up to mass produce all the medium-size and small box pieces, you can knock this project out in an evening or two.

Building the Large Box

Start by building the large box. Cut the plywood pieces, then cut the dadoes in the sides. There are two ways to make these dadoes. If your table saw has enough 'throw' between the rip fence and the blade, you can cut them on the saw with a dado blade. (See Figure 1.) If not, make them with a router and a ¾" straight bit. Clamp a long, straight board to the workpiece to act as a guide fence. (See Figure 2.)

Nail and glue the support strips to the sides and partitions, then assemble the box with glue and drywall screws. Attach the ¼" thick plywood back with glue and finish nails. This back is important to the project — it keeps the large box square.

Building the Rest of the Boxes

While the glue on the large box is setting up, make the medium-sized and small boxes. As I mentioned before, you can set up to mass produce the parts for these boxes. Look

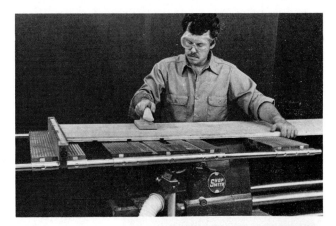

Figure 1. If your table saw has the capacity, cut the dadoes on the saw with a dado blade.

Figure 2. You can also use a router and a guide fence to make the dadoes.

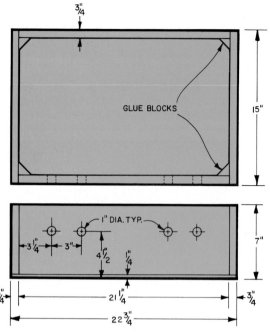

GLUE BLOCKS

15"

I" DIA. TYP.

7"

4½"
¼"

3¾" 3"

¾" 21¼ ¾"

22¾"

LARGE DRAWER LAYOUT

3/4"

15"

I" DIA. TYP.

4½"

¼" 2½" 3" 5³⁄₁₆

¾" 13⅜" ¾"

14⅞"

SMALL DRAWER LAYOUT

over the Bill of Materials; figure out how many *linear feet* you need of each width of stock involved. Rip all the stock on your table saw, then cut them all to the proper length. Use a stop block clamped to your rip fence to gauge the lengths, so that you don't have to measure each and every part. (See Figure 3.)

> **Tip ◆** Clamp the stop block to the fence, as close to the front of the table as possible. If the block is opposite the blade, the stock may bind and kick back when you cut it.

Drill finger holes in the front *and* backs of the boxes. This makes the boxes easier to handle when you take them out of the highboy. To save time, you can 'pad' drill these holes. (See Figure 4.) Then assemble the boxes with drywall screws and glue. If you're going to be storing heavy items in any of the boxes, you may want to reinforce the corners with glue blocks. (See Figure 5.) Otherwise, you shouldn't need to reinforce any of the butt joints, or cut any fancy joints.

When you've finished assembling all the boxes, attach casters to the large box. I recommend heavy-duty 4″ casters. When you load all the boxes up, there's going to be a lot of weight riding on those wheels. Paint all the boxes, if you want, and place the smaller boxes in the large box.

That's all there is to it. With all those boxes, this project must offer all the storage support you need, right? Don't fool yourself.

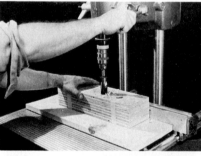

Figure 4. Pad drill the finger holes in the box fronts and backs.

Figure 3. Use a stop block clamped to your rip fence to help cut the box parts. The stop block 'automatically' measures the proper length, and helps you cut each part exactly the same. However, make sure that you set the stop block well *in front* of the blade, as shown here, so that the stock doesn't bind as you feed it into the blade.

Figure 5. If you're going to store something extremely heavy in a box, you may want to reinforce the corners with glue blocks.

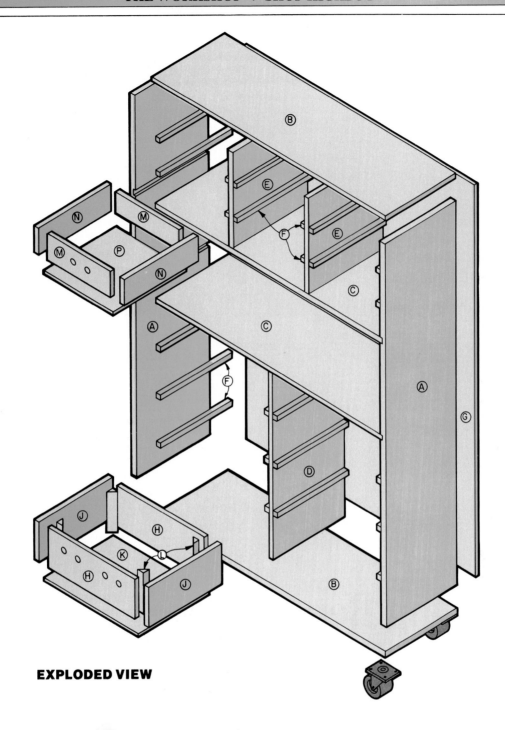

EXPLODED VIEW

BILL OF MATERIALS — Shop Highboy

Finished Dimensions in Inches

A.	Sides (2)	¾ x 15 x 66¼
B.	Top/Bottom (2)	¾ x 15 x 48
C.	Shelves (2)	¾ x 15 x 47½
D.	Lower Partition	¾ x 15 x 32¼
E.	Upper Partitions (2)	¾ x 15 x 16½
F.	Drawer Supports (24)	¾ x ¾ x 15
G.	Back	¼ x 48 x 67¾
H.	Lower Drawer Front/Back (16)	¾ x 6¾ x 21¼
J.	Lower Drawer Sides (16)	¾ x 6¾ x 15
K.	Lower Drawer Bottoms (8)	¼ x 15 x 22¾

L.	Corner Blocks (32)	1 x 1 x 6¾
M.	Upper Drawer Front/Back (18)	¾ x 4¼ x 13⅜
N.	Upper Drawer Sides (18)	¾ x 4¼ x 15
P.	Upper Drawer Bottoms (9)	¼ x 14⅞ x 15

Hardware

4″ Casters and mounting screws (4)
1⅝″ Drywall screws (2-3 lbs.)
4d Finishing nails (1-2 lbs.)

173

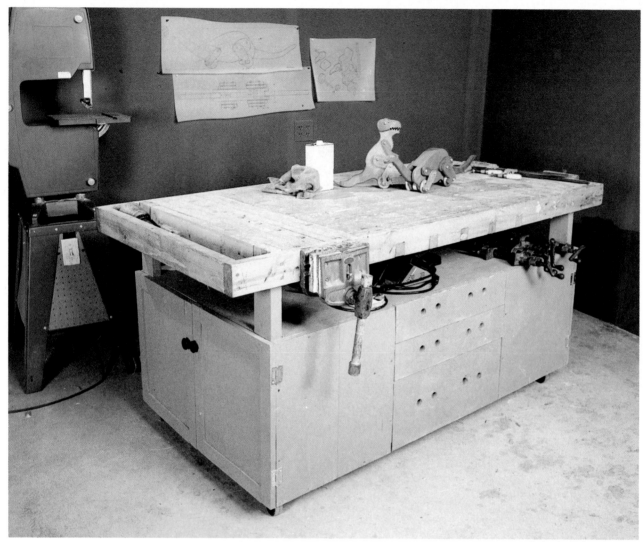

Designed and Built by Nick Engler

Clamping Bench

This workbench has several ingenious features to help you assemble projects of all sizes and shapes.

What's the most important tool in your workshop? If you're like most woodworkers, it's probably your workbench. Think about it: You use it to lay out your work; it holds workpieces while you cut, shape, and carve; you assemble projects on its work surface; you use it while you sand and finish them.

Since you use it for so much, shouldn't you have something more than just a work surface and a vise? The workbench you see here is commonly called a 'clamping bench'. It does the same things that most workbenches do, but it does them a lot better. It incorporates an ingenious system of vises, dogs, and work surfaces to hold almost any type of workpiece. In addition, there's plenty of storage under the work surface for clamps and other hand tools.

What makes this bench so special? Let's start with its work surface: It's made from softwood, not hardwood. Many woodworkers prefer softwood because, even though it wears out sooner, it won't damage your projects. The middle of the bench lifts out to reveal a 'clamping grid'. This grid is useful in holding odd-shaped pieces together while they're being glued up. (See Figure 1.) There are three vises on the edges of the bench, each with a pop-up 'dog'. The top of the bench is covered with dozens of holes for 'bench dogs'. By using these dogs, you can clamp up assemblies up to six feet long. (See Figure 2.)

There are other features, too. For instance, a small tool tray at one end holds finishes so you won't accidentally knock them off the bench. The bottom of this tray is removable so that you can clean it easily. There is a shelf immediately beneath the work surface to hold clamps and other tools at ready. And the entire base is a huge storage cabinet, with plenty of drawer and storage space.

TOP VIEW

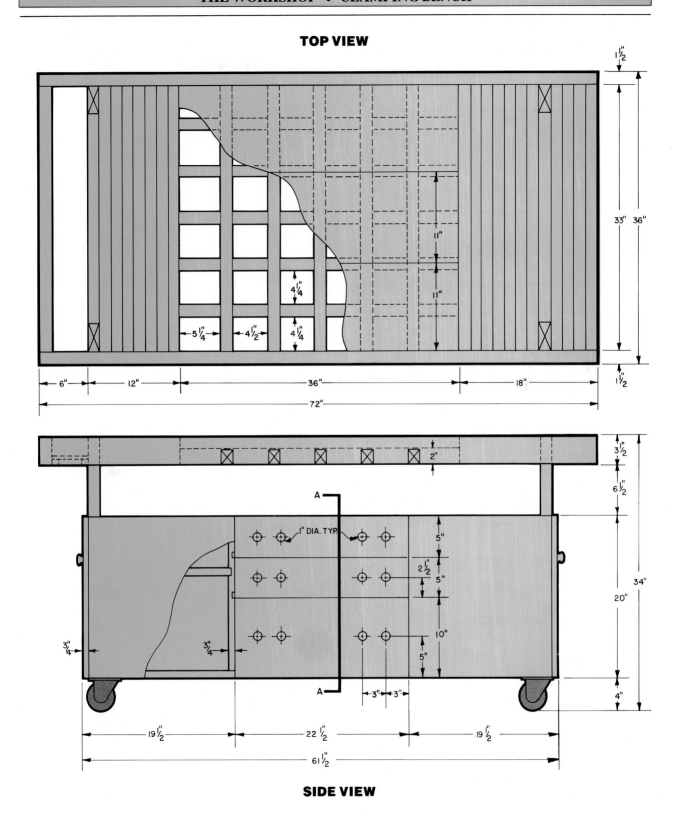

SIDE VIEW

Making the Base

To make a clamping bench, begin with the base. Cut the parts to size, and cut the dadoes in the partitions and the 2x4 uprights. Then glue and screw together the top, bottom, and the partitions.

Tip ◆ Use drywall screws to assemble this project. (See Figure 3.) They don't require any pilot holes, and they can be easily installed with a drill or power screwdriver.

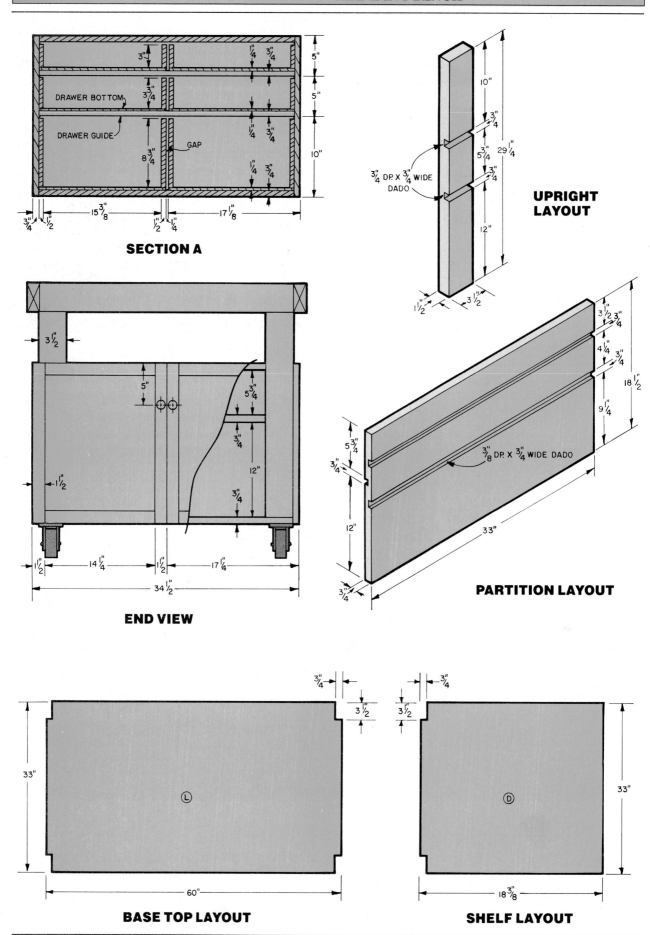

SECTION A

3"

DRAWER BOTTOM

DRAWER GUIDE

GAP

1/4   3/4

5"

3/4

5"

3/4

8 3/4"

1/4   3/4

10"

3/4 1/2   15 3/8"   1/2 1/4   17 1/8"

UPRIGHT LAYOUT

10"

3/4

5 3/4"   29 1/4"

3/4

3/4" DP. X 3/4" WIDE DADO

12"

1 1/2"   3 1/2"

END VIEW

3 1/2"

5"

5 3/4"

3/4"

12"

3/4"

1 1/2"

1 1/2"   14 1/4"   1 1/2"   17 1/4"

34 1/2"

PARTITION LAYOUT

3 1/2" 3/4"

4 1/4"   3/4"

18 1/2"

9 1/4"

5 3/4"

3/4"

3/8" DP. X 3/4" WIDE DADO

12"

3/4"

33"

BASE TOP LAYOUT

3/4"

3 1/2"

33"

Ⓛ

60"

SHELF LAYOUT

3/4"

3 1/2"

33"

Ⓓ

18 3/8"

176

With the base assembly lying on its side, put the shelves and the uprights in position, and attach them with glue and screws. Attach the side panels to the side that's facing up; turn the base over on its other side, and attach the other side panels.

Making and Attaching the Top

Put the base aside for a moment and get to work on the bench top. Start by making the clamping grid. Mark and cut the dadoes in the 2x2's that form the lap joints. You can make these dadoes with a dado cutter, or with a saw and chisel.

To make dadoes with a saw and chisel, first cut the sides of the dadoes on your table saw. (See Figure 4.) Then split out the waste with a hand chisel. (See Figure 5.) If you use this method, select stock with fairly straight grain. It's difficult to chisel out a good dado from stock that's full of knots. You want to use straight-grained stock for another reason, too. Knots will weaken the grid.

Next, cut the benchtop sides and fillers. Cut the sides 2"-3" longer than you need — you'll cut them off later. Cut dadoes in the sides and the two 'inside' fillers. When you

Figure 1. One of the most useful features of this bench is the clamping grid. You can use it to hold almost any size or shape.

Figure 4. To cut a dado with a saw and chisel, first cut the sides of the dado on your table saw.

Figure 5. Then knock out the waste with a hand chisel.

Figure 2. The system of vises and bench dogs will help you to clamp up small, medium, or large projects quickly and easily.

Figure 3. Use drywall screws to assemble the parts of this project. They can be installed quickly, without drilling pilot holes.

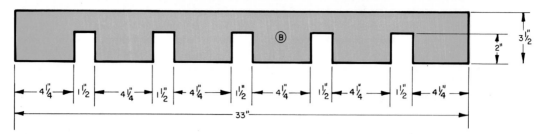

INSIDE FILLER LAYOUT

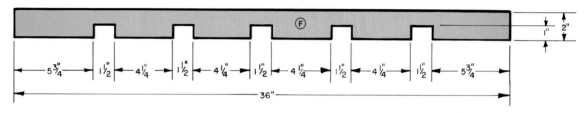

SHORT GRID MEMBER LAYOUT

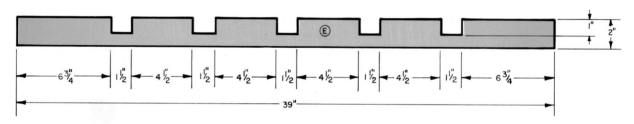

LONG GRID MEMBER LAYOUT

measure the sides to mark the dadoes, make sure the boards are 'long on both ends'. In other words, the lines of dadoes should be centered in the boards, so that there is 1″-1½″ of extra stock on either side of the dadoes.

Put the clamping grid, sides, and inside fillers together with glue and screws, then turn the benchtop assembly upside down on the floor of your shop. Add six fillers to both ends of the bench top — twelve in all — nailing them in place as you go. Nail a filler to the filler that preceded it, then put two more nails through the sides, into the ends of the fillers. Remember that you're going to drill dog holes in the bench top later. Position the nails so that they won't interfere with the holes.

Do not nail the twelfth filler in place. Leave it loose between the sides. You may need to remove it during the next step.

When you've added six fillers to either side, turn the base upside down over the bench top. Position the uprights between the benchtop sides, as shown on the working drawings. The uprights should be flush up against the fillers. If they are loose, you may have to cut a thin filler to take up the slack. If they are tight, you may have to remove the filler that you didn't nail in place and plane it down. When the uprights and fillers all fit like you want them to fit, nail the sides to the uprights. Then nail all the remaining fillers in place.

Finishing Up

While the bench is upside down, attach the casters to the bottom. Also, mortise out the underside of the bench top to install your vises. Then turn the assembly right side up.

Make six drawers, as shown in the working drawings. These drawers are just simple boxes, all butt-jointed together. If you want to reinforce the drawer joints, make glue blocks for the corners. Drill holes in the drawer fronts for pulls.

Tip ◆ *Don't* install drawer pulls on the drawers, unless the pulls lie flush with the drawer fronts. Otherwise, you'll find that you constantly bang your shins on the hardware.

Screw and glue the drawer guide to the dadoes in the partitions, then slide the drawers in place. Make sure that each drawer can be pulled in and out easily, without the drawer front hitting another drawer. If the drawer fronts do rub or hit each other, sand a little stock off the edges until you get the fit you're after.

If you want, make doors for the cabinet ends of the workbench. The doors you see here are frame-and-panel construction. The door stiles have slot mortises to hold the tenons on the door rails, and the panels ride in a groove on the

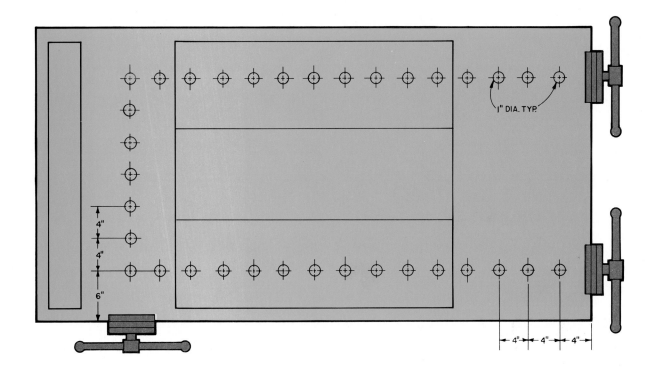

1" DIA. TYP.

4"

4"

6"

4" 4" 4"

SUGGESTED VISE AND DOG LAYOUT

inside edges of the frame parts. If you don't want to make anything that fancy, just four simple sheets of plywood will do for doors. Hinge these doors to the side panels, and use magnetic latches to hold them closed.

Install the removable benchtop pieces in place over the clamping grid. These are just pieces of 2x12, laid over the grid. When installed, the removable work surface shop should be flush with the stationary work surface. If not, plane one surface down to the level of the other.

Finish off the bench by installing your vises and drilling 1″ dog holes according to the pattern in the working drawings. You can use short lengths of dowels for the dogs, or make some with fancy heads to hold workpieces of various shapes. (See Figure 6.)

Paint the base of the bench, if you want, but *do not* paint the top. If you paint the top, it will wear off and discolor your projects. Leave the wood raw, and coat it with several heavy coats of paste wax. This will help prevent glue from sticking to the surface when you're clamping up your projects.

Figure 6. Here are several types of bench dogs you can make. Each will hold a different shape of workpiece.

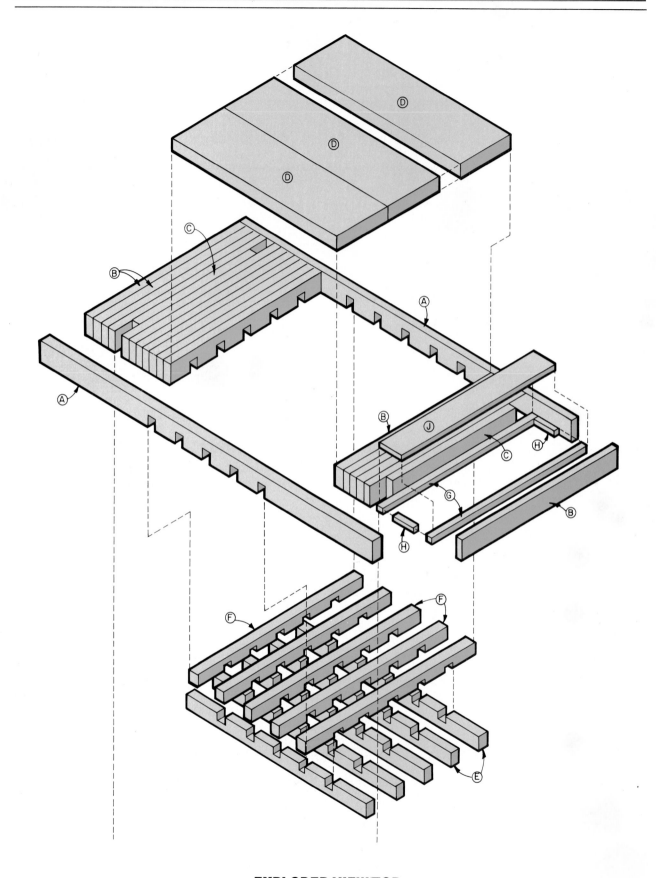

EXPLODED VIEW/TOP

EXPLODED VIEW/BASE

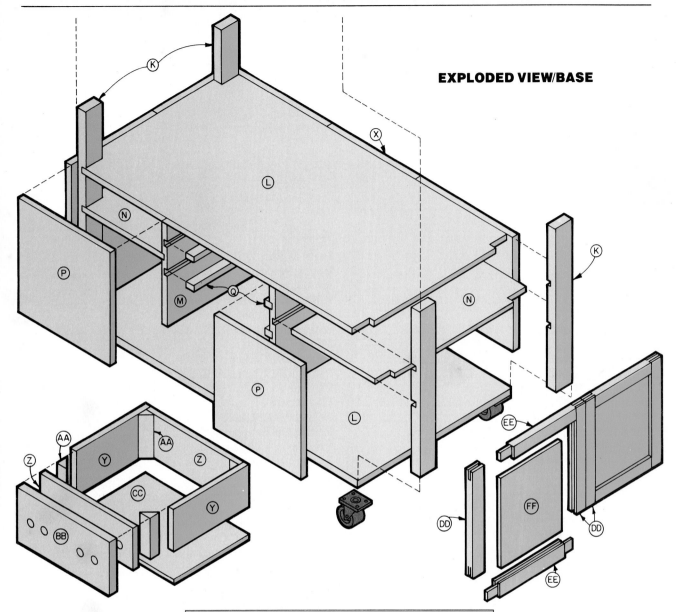

BILL OF MATERIALS — Clamping Bench

Finished Dimensions in Inches

A.	Top Sides (2)	1½ x 3½ x 72	**U.**	Middle Drawer Sides	½ x 3¾ x 16⅜
B.	Long Fillers (19)	1½ x 3½ x 33	**V.**	Middle Drawer Ends	½ x 3¾ x 21⅜
C.	Short Fillers (2)	1½ x 3½ x 26	**W.**	Middle Drawer Corner Blocks	1 x 1 x 3¾
D.	Removable Tops (3)	1½ x 11 x 36	**X.**	Upper/Middle Fronts (4)	¾ x 4¹⁵⁄₁₆ x 22⅜
E.	Long Grid Members (5)	1½ x 2 x 39	**Y.**	Lower Drawer Sides	½ x 8¾ x 16⅜
F.	Short Grid Members (5)	1½ x 2 x 36	**Z.**	Lower Drawer Ends	½ x 8¾ x 21⅜
G.	Long Cleats (2)	¾ x ¾ x 33	**AA.**	Lower Drawer Corner Blocks	1 x 1 x 8¾
H.	Short Cleats (2)	¾ x ¾ x 3	**BB.**	Lower Drawer Fronts	¾ x 9¹⁵⁄₁₆ x 22⅜
J.	Tool Tray	¼ x 4½ x 33	**CC.**	Drawer Bottoms (6)	¼ x 16⅜ x 22⅜
K.	Uprights	1½ x 3½ x 29¼	**DD.**	Door Stiles (8)	¾ x 1½ x 20
L.	Base Top/Bottom	¾ x 33 x 60	**EE.**	Door Rails (8)	¾ x 1½ x 17¼
M.	Partitions (2)	¾ x 18½ x 33	**FF.**	Door Panels (4)	¼ x 14¾ x 17½
N.	Shelves (2)	¾ x 18⅜ x 33			
P.	Base Sides (4)	¾ x 18¾ x 20			
Q.	Drawer Guides (4)	¾ x 1⅛ x 33			
R.	Upper Drawer Sides	½ x 3 x 16⅜			
S.	Upper Drawer Ends	½ x 3 x 21⅜			
T.	Upper Drawer Corner Blocks	1 x 1 x 3¾			

Hardware

4″ Casters and mounting screws (4)
3″ Butt hinges and mounting screws (4 pair)
Door pulls (4)
1⅝″ Drywall screws (2-3 lbs.)

Index